A

Philip E. Lilienthal

■   ■   ■

B O O K

The Philip E. Lilienthal imprint
honors special books
in commemoration of a man whose work
at University of California Press from 1954 to 1979
was marked by dedication to young authors
and to high standards in the field of Asian Studies.
Friends, family, authors, and foundations have together
endowed the Lilienthal Fund, which enables UC Press
to publish under this imprint selected books
in a way that reflects the taste and judgment
of a great and beloved editor.

The publisher and the University of California Press Foundation gratefully acknowledge the generous support of the Philip E. Lilienthal Imprint in Asian Studies, established by a major gift from Sally Lilienthal.

The Koreas

The Koreas

THE BIRTH OF TWO NATIONS DIVIDED

Theodore Jun Yoo

UNIVERSITY OF CALIFORNIA PRESS

University of California Press
Oakland, California

© 2020 by Theodore Jun Yoo

Library of Congress Cataloging-in-Publication Data

Names: Yoo, Theodore Jun, author.
Title: The Koreas : the birth of two nations divided / Theodore Jun Yoo
Description: Oakland, California : University of California Press, [2020] |
    Includes bibliographical references and index.
Identifiers: LCCN 2019057901 (print) | LCCN 2019057902 (ebook) |
    ISBN 9780520292338 (cloth) | ISBN 9780520965898 (ebook)
Subjects: LCSH: Korean diaspora—20th century. | Korea—History—20th century.
Classification: LCC DS916 .Y66 2020 (print) | LCC DS916 (ebook) |
    DDC 951.904—dc23
LC record available at https://lccn.loc.gov/2019057901
LC ebook record available at https://lccn.loc.gov/2019057902

Manufactured in the United States of America

25 24 23 22 21 20 19 18
10 9 8 7 6 5 4 3 2 1

To Yeonjun Isaac Yoo

Contents

Illustrations

Acknowledgments

In writing this book, I am indebted to many people. A special thanks goes to my editor, Reed Malcolm, whose initial encouragement led me to embark on the project. I am especially indebted to all the authors cited in the bibliography for advancing my work. I thank the BK21 Plus Program in the Department of Korean Language and Literature and the Future-Leading Research Initiative Grant at the Office of Research Affairs at Yonsei University for their generous support of this project.

The opportunity to discuss and debate various historical and cultural issues with colleagues had a significant influence on the framing of this book. I would especially like to thank John Lie, Jeong Myeong Kyo, Kim Hyunjoo, Kim Hyunmee, Kwon Bodurae, Shin Hyung Ki, Andre Schmid, and Theodore Hughes. I would also like to express my gratitude to all my colleagues in the Department of Korean Language and Literature at Yonsei University for sharing their ideas with me. My students have been a great resource, and I am grateful for the many opportunities to learn from Gia Kim, Hyewon Kim, Jihoon Chung, Hyejin Jeong, Junho Lee, Jonghyeok Yoo, and Nayoung Yoon.

Many more colleagues in the United States and Korea gave me inspiration and deserve special thanks here: Juhn Ahn, Jinsoo An, Bruce Cumings, Jonathan Glade, Jaeeun Kim, Kim Yerim, Laura Nelson, Park Aekyung, Rachel Park, Eilin Perez, Kathryn Ragsdale, Jooyeon Rhee, Woo Miseong, and Yoo Hyunkyung.

Invitations to speak at workshops, conferences, and seminars have been wonderful opportunities to gain critical feedback and refine my arguments. I would like to thank the Center for East Asian Studies at the University of Chicago, the Truman Institute at Hebrew University in Jerusalem, the Center for Korean Studies at the University of California, Berkeley, and the New Professors in the Humanities Lecture Series at Yonsei University.

It has been a pleasure to work with the University of California Press for many years. I thank three anonymous reviewers, whose thoughtful and insightful comments significantly improved the quality of the manuscript; UC Press staff Archna Patel and Cindy Fulton; and Jeff Wyneken for sharp and thoughtful copyediting.

Finally, I thank my sister, ChaeRan Freeze, for always supporting me and kindly offering many suggestions to improve this manuscript; my parents in Hawai'i for their daily calls; my partner, Juyeon, for having to deal with my crazy schedule; and our son, Yeonjun, who has been my best critic. This book is dedicated to him.

I would like to thank the University of Hawai'i Press for granting me permission to draw on previous publications: chapter 1 has a section drawn from "Shaken or Stirred: Recreating 'Makgeolli for the Twenty-First Century,'" in *Encounters Old and New in World History*, edited by Alan Karras and Laura J. Mitchell, 107–18 (Honolulu: University of Hawai'i Press, 2017); and chapter 5 has a section drawn from "Muhammad Kkansu and the Diasporic Other in the Two Koreas," *Korean Studies* 43 (2019): 145–68.

Korean names and terms have been transliterated according to the Revised Romanization of Korean system, except for words with commonly accepted alternative spellings (e.g., Park Chung Hee, Seoul, Kim). I have kept the last name first in referring to Koreans, unless they have their own romanized names. All translations are mine unless otherwise indicated. As always, any errors or shortcomings in this study are entirely my own.

Chronology

August 15, 1945	Korea is liberated from thirty-five years of Japanese colonial rule.
August 15, 1948	The Republic of Korea is established with Syngman Rhee installed as president.
September 9, 1948	The DPRK (Democratic People's Republic of Korea) is established with Kim Il-sung installed as leader
June 25, 1950	After roughly a year of military skirmishes along the thirty-eighth parallel by both sides, North Korea launches a surprise invasion of South Korea, triggering the Korean War.
July 27, 1953	The United Nations Command and North Korea sign the Armistice Agreement at Truce Village in Panmunjeom, which temporarily halts the fighting. Today a peace treaty has yet to be signed to formally end the conflict, and the two Koreas are technically still at war with each other.

December 1956	Kim Il-sung introduces the Cheollima movement to boost production shortly before the start of the first Five-Year Plan of 1957–61.
April 1960–May 1961	Syngman Rhee's regime is toppled and the Second Republic established.
May 16, 1961	A group of military officers engineer a coup d'état and the founding of the Third Republic, which lasts from 1963 to 1972 under President Park Chung-hee.
December 21, 1963	A first group of 123 South Korean miners depart for West Germany. Roughly 8,300 Korean miners, in addition to 13,000 nurses, would work in Germany between 1966 and 1976.
February 25, 1965	South Korea dispatches Task Force Dove, the first combat unit to Vietnam, in response to America's More Flags campaign. The combat units totaled more than 300,000 troops by 1973.
April 14, 1965	Kim Il-sung lays out the basic principles of *juche*, which includes political independence, economic self-sufficiency, and self-reliance in defense.
June 22, 1965	South Korea signs the Korea-Japan Basic Treaty, establishing diplomatic relations with its former colonial rulers. This includes a financial package of $200 million in public loans, $300 million in

	grants, and an additional $300 million in commercial credits.
July 19, 1966	The North Korean men's soccer team defeats the favorite Italian squad at Ayresome Park in the 1966 FIFA World Cup.
January 28, 1968	An unsuccessful raid of the Blue House by North Korean commandos is executed to assassinate Park Chung-hee.
July 4, 1972	North and South Korea issue a joint statement on peaceful reunification.
October 17, 1972	Park Chung-hee declares martial law and amends the Constitution, allowing him to become permanent head.
December 28, 1972	Kim Il-sung becomes president of North Korea.
October 26, 1979	Park Chung-hee is assassinated by his own intelligence chief. Chun Doo-hwan seizes power.
May 18–27, 1980	Citizens in Gwangju clash with government forces, resulting in the deaths of six hundred to one thousand persons.
December 12, 1985	The DPRK joins the International Nuclear Non-Proliferation Treaty.
June 10–29, 1987	Chun Doo-hwan is pushed out after nationwide mass protests in June, and Roh Tae-woo is elected president.
September 17– October 2, 1988	The Twenty-Fourth Summer Olympic games are held in Seoul.

August 8, 1991	North and South Korea join the United Nations.
February 25, 1993	Kim Young-sam is elected as the first civilian president in more than three decades, formally marking the end of military rule.
July 8, 1994	Kim Il-sung dies. Kim Jong-il succeeds his father.
October 25, 1996	South Korea is accepted into the OECD.
January 1996 to 1999	Severe famine is triggered by widespread floods between July 30 and August 18, 1995, resulting in the deaths of three million North Koreans from starvation.
December 3, 1997	South Korea agrees to terms for a $55 billion loan package, which includes $21 billion from the International Monetary Fund.
February 25, 1998	President Kim Dae-jung launches his Sunshine Policy, culminating in a summit with Kim Jong-il in Pyeongyang in June 2000, and a Nobel Peace Prize that same year.
April 15, 2002	North Korea stages its first Arirang Festival, or mass games, in Rungrado May Day Stadium in Pyeongyang over two months.
May 21–June 30, 2002	South Korea cohosts the FIFA World Cup with Japan.
January 10, 2003	North Korea withdraws form the Nuclear Non-Proliferation Treaty and

	the 1992 agreement with South Korea to keep the peninsula free from nuclear weapons.
February 25, 2003	As the new president of South Korea, Roh Moo-hyun promises to continue Kim's Sunshine Policy of engagement with North Korea.
December 1, 2005	South Korea's Truth and Reconciliation Commission is established to investigate historical incidents, from the Japanese colonial period in 1910 to 1993 when South Korea elected its first civilian president.
October 9, 2006	Pyeongyang announces its first nuclear explosion in a remote mountainous site, Punggye-ri.
February 25, 2008	Lee Myung-bak, a conservative politician and businessman, wins a landside victory to serve as president of South Korea.
	Skirmishes between the North and South Korean navies near the Northern Limit Line. Tensions escalate into the sinking of the *Cheonan,* a South Korean corvette, on March 26, 2010, allegedly by a North Korean torpedo.
December 17, 2011	Kim Jong-il dies. Kim Jong-un is lined up as successor and is officially elected leader of the Workers' Party in 2016.

July 15, 2012	Psy's "Gangnam Style" goes viral, reaching over one billion viewers on YouTube by December.
February 7, 2014	Amnesty International publishes a scathing critique of human and labor rights in the South, ranging from contractual deception to trafficking and unpaid overtime.
October 20, 2014	The United Nations Commission of Inquiry on human rights charges the DPRK of grave, systematic, and widespread human rights violations in its 372-page report.
January 6, 2016	North Korea announces its first successful hydrogen bomb test.
December 9, 2016	President Park Geun-hye is impeached.
May 10, 2017	Moon Jae-in is inaugurated as president of South Korea after a landslide victory.
February 9–25, 2018	North and South Korea march together under the same flag at the Twenty-Third Winter Olympic Games in Pyeongchang, South Korea.
April 27, 2018	Chairman Kim Jong-un becomes the first head of state from North Korea to enter the South, for talks with President Moon Jae-in in Panmunjeom.
June 12, 2018	US president Donald Trump meets Chairman Kim Jong-un in Singapore for the first summit between leaders of the United States and North Korea.

September 18–20, 2018	President Moon Jae-in meets Chairman Kim Jong-un in Pyeongyang and signs the Pyeongyang Joint Declaration.
February 27–28, 2019	The second summit between President Donald Trump and Chairman Kim Jong-un takes place, in Hanoi, Vietnam.
June 30, 2019	President Moon Jae-in, Chairman Kim Jong-un, and President Donald Trump meet at the Demilitarized Zone.

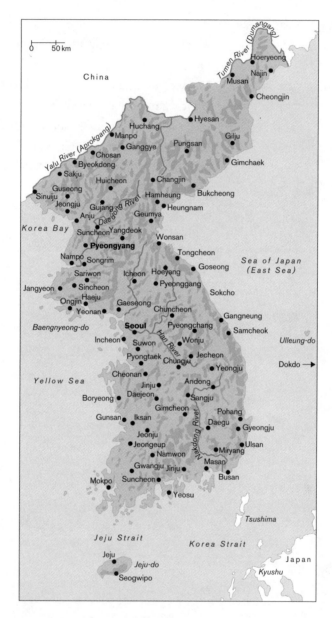

MAP 1. Map of Korean peninsula.

Introduction

Land of Exile

On February 9, 2018, Kim Yuna, a former figure-skating champion and final torchbearer, lit the cauldron, officially kicking off the much-anticipated twenty-third Olympic Winter Games in the sleepy mountain town of Hoenggye, roughly eighty kilometers south of the heavily fortified Demilitarized Zone dividing North and South Korea. For most South Koreans, the countdown to the opening ceremony was less about Olympic fatigue than wariness over months of vitriolic posturing between US president Donald Trump, who frequently took to Twitter to taunt his North Korean nemesis, and Kim Jong-un, who matched him tit-for-tat with fiery threats of his own about nuclear annihilation, conducting more ballistic missile tests in a year than had his father and grandfather. Amid the sky-high tensions, a hard-won Olympic détente with the North negotiated by South Korean president Moon Jae-in in the final days ahead of the games led to a few memorable moments at the Winter Games: musical performances by the North's most renowned Samjiyeon Orchestra, a special dinner reception for the North Korean delegation and foreign dignitaries, and a joint march by the North and South Korean athletes at the opening ceremony under a unified flag. The cameras captured US vice president Mike

Pence's unforgettable belligerent stare-down and deliberate refusal to stand during the unified march, while curious eyes fixed on Kim Yojong, the first female member of the North's ruling family to set foot in South Korea, and a squad of 229 enthralling North Korean female cheerleaders clad in matching red wool coats, urging on both teams with their synchronized dances and chants.

The opening ceremony differed remarkably from the elaborate coming-out party during Seoul's Summer Olympics in 1988. South Korea in 2018 was no longer a dictatorship and developing nation but the world's seventh-largest exporter with the eleventh-largest economy, an OECD (Organisation for Co-operation and Development) member nation, and an aid-donor country. While the high-tech pyrotechnics and twelve hundred drones lighting the skies with Olympic rings signaled progress and power, the opening ceremony did not deliver the same emotional punch that many Koreans had felt during the Sydney Olympics in 2000 when the two countries marched together for the first time, setting the mood for a thaw in cross-border relations under the so-called Sunshine Policy of President Kim Daejung. Instead, there was a distinct new raw energy as athletes challenged gender boundaries and defied national stereotypes—athletes like Chloe Kim, the first Korean American snowboarding teenage phenom who dominated the women's halfpipe, or Yun Sungbin whose dominant gold medal performance in the skeleton made him the first Asian to medal in the event. Five women nicknamed the Garlic Girls from the small town of Uiseong known for this pungent root plant sparked a curling fever in Korea when they made an unlikely run to the finals. The much-beloved team's skip and lead, Kim Eunjeong and the bespectacled Kim Yeongmi, flanked by three sweepers, garnered the catchy English nicknames Yogurt, Pancake, Steak, Sunny, and Chocho. While the chants "We are one" for the first unified Korean women's hockey team may have felt contrived for some, it was an epoch-making moment when twelve North Koreans and twenty-three South Koreans skated out on the ice together. Among the players were four North Americans of Korean heritage, including Marissa Brandt, an adoptee from Minnesota, and Randi Heesoo Griffin, a biracial athlete from North Carolina.

Witnessing the initial discomfort and tensions among the players and coaches evolve into familiarity and camaraderie on the humble skating rink made me ponder deeply about the past century. This team represented a snapshot of the two Koreas today, symbolizing the tragedy of national division and its diasporic population (including more than 160,000 children sent to adoptive homes in the West since the Korean War), as well as a hopeful vision of a unified future. No one could have predicted that a small step at rapprochement through a game of hockey would pave the road for the first meeting of Korean leaders in over a decade, followed by the unexpected summit in Singapore in June between Kim Jong-un and the unconventional Donald Trump, whose erratic showmanship would turn many heads in Washington and Seoul.

The drama of the two Koreas performed on the stage of the 2018 Olympics resonated with my own personal history in a profound way. I was born in Seoul in 1972, the year President Park Chung-hee declared the so-called Yushin Constitution (Revitalizing Reforms), which granted him full dictatorial powers, placing no limits on re-election, dissolving the National Assembly, and suspending the Constitution. At the same time, his adversary in the north, Kim Il-sung, proclaimed a revised constitution of his own where *juche* (self-reliance) replaced Marxism-Leninism as the official state ideology. My family were *wolnammin* (those who crossed to the south during the Korean War) from Sinuiju, a gateway city neighboring

Dandong, China, across the Aprok (Yalu) River. My grandparents on both sides hailed from the landed class, were Christians, and were products of the Japanese colonial education system. To avoid military conscription in 1944, my paternal grandfather gave up his dream of studying economics and enrolled in the Army Veterinarian School in Ōsaki, Miyagi Prefecture, which was part of the Army Horse Corps. My grandmother was a *sin yeoseong* (new woman), who crossed the straits with my grandfather during the height of the wartime period and intermittently studied nursing in Tokyo while raising my father. The unexpected surrender of Japan compelled many from the Korean landed class in the north to flee to the south in fear of retribution and targeted killings by aggrieved peasants and Communists, and temporarily find safe haven in Busan, the provisional wartime capital. Despite her privileged upbringing, my maternal grandmother (who also fled during this time) never hid the fact that she was one of the best traders of *meriyasu* (undergarments) at Busan's Gukje sijang (International Market), the neighborhood for war refugees, and one of many mothers who evaded the military police and peddled goods stolen from the military PX (post exchange) to feed their families during the war. As exiles, permanently separated from their families in the north, dislocation meant forging a completely new identity as "South Koreans," creating a new *hojeok* (family register) that identified Seoul as their place of birth and residence. And if that were not hard enough, it also meant extricating themselves completely from all things Japan, which included "unlearning" Japanese and exclusively using Korean—a very difficult thing for my grandmother, who until her death voraciously read Japanese novels and magazines and watched endless NHK dramas.

My wife's parents also hail from the north, and like many displaced elderly North Koreans in Seoul, they frequently dine at

Uraeok (Woo Lae Oak), a family-operated establishment. Tucked away in the back alleys of Seoul's old industrial district, surrounded by light fixture businesses and sewing machine parts stores, it offers the finest original Pyeongyang-style cold buckwheat noodles served in an icy beef broth. There is good reason why they are ardent supporters of the hard right and frequently hurl epithets like *ppalgaeng-i* (commie) at the current president, Moon Jae-in, or the late Kim Dae-jung. Emotionally scarred from displacement and a bloody civil war, their generation experienced extreme poverty and major postwar reconstruction efforts that required as much sacrifice as the war itself, first under Syngman Rhee and then Park Chung-hee. The latter's draconian policies pushed South Korea's economy to grow at an unprecedented rate—often referred to as the Miracle on the Han River. The acrimony between my parents' generation and mine is common as the former still revere Park Chung-hee as an anti-Communist hero who set South Korea on the right path to become an economic powerhouse.

Our parents' generation still remember the 1960s when South Korea was one of the poorest countries in the world, with only $79 per capita income compared to North Korea's $120, about 1.5 times higher than its southern counterpart. As a migrant-source country, Park Chung-hee's government sent thousands of Koreans abroad as farmers, miners, medical professionals, and construction workers to select countries in Africa, Latin America, Europe, and the Middle East during the 1960s and 1970s to earn foreign currency. One such person who took up the call was my father, Min Chul Yoo, who applied for a position as a government dispatch doctor to Ethiopia. Despite his being in the first group of students to learn the blepharoplasty (double-eyelid surgery) technique at Yonsei Severance Hospital, a procedure introduced to Koreans by

Dr. Ralph Millard (a surgeon who was stationed in Seoul during the Korean War to do reconstructive surgery for the wounded) and now a popular birthday or coming-of-age gift, the temptation to go abroad was strong at the time. The government promised doctors a diplomatic passport and the ability to earn up to three times more than what they could at home in US dollars. But above all, my father was young, oblivious to the dangers of civil war in Africa, and intrigued about traveling to different countries and working on two-year contracts. As members of the first group of South Korean aid workers to Africa, volunteers like my father would pave the road for future aid programs like KOICA (Korean International Cooperation Agency, established in 1991), which would transform South Korea from a recipient country to the fifteenth-largest donor country, spending more than $2.2 billion on official development assistance.

My family arrived in Addis Ababa, Ethiopia, in the fall of 1975 during the middle of a bloody revolution after a Communist military junta overthrew Emperor Haile Selassie's monarchy a year earlier. Mengistu Haile Mariam would emerge as the leader of the Derg (Communist junta) after a major shootout in 1977 when he consolidated his power base through the Red Terror campaigns against his rivals, whom he branded counterrevolutionaries. While many leaders of newly independent countries in Africa during the 1960s and the 1970s embraced Marxist-Leninist ideals, Mengistu was one of the few to express interest in North Korean *juche* ideology. In 1984 he created the Workers' Party of Ethiopia after meeting Kim Il-sung a year earlier, impressed with his cordial reception and the *juche* ideology. The North Korean Propaganda and Agitation Department, which coordinated the ideological education and campaigns as well as party and state propaganda, appealed to Mengistu who sought support to build a cult of personality through the construction of monuments, media, and mass games. With the help of North Korean cultural advisers, Mengistu adopted Kim's "on the spot guidance" trips around the country, plastering his photograph in villages, state-owned cooperatives, government offices, and other public spaces. No longer wearing his military uniform, Mengistu now donned a North Korean-made vinalon outfit, forcing party members to wear Communist lapels. He also commissioned Pyeongyang's Mansudae Overseas Art Studio to design and construct the Tiglachin [our struggle] Monument in Addis Ababa, a fifty-meter-tall obelisk (similar to the famous 1,700-year-old obelisk in Axum, which Mussolini had stolen) topped by a red star, with two wall reliefs flanking it on both sides, commemorating the fallen Ethiopian and Cuban soldiers who had fought over the Ogaden region between Ethiopia and Somalia between 1977 and 1978. The huge monument stood boldly in front of the Black Lion Hospital, where my father worked for thirty years. The monument is now a tourist site. North Korea enthusiastically sought to promote these kinds of cultural projects as part of their Third World solidarity movement initiatives and even donated hundreds of copies of Kim Il-sung's biographies, which certainly outnumbered *Das Kapital* and could be found on ministerial bookshelves and local libraries all over Addis Ababa. Yet despite all the promotion and investment to export *juche* ideology to developing countries, there were very few takers, making Mengistu an exception rather than the norm.

South Korea's humanitarian mission to Ethiopia was not simply a reciprocal gesture for the participation of the twelve hundred soldiers from Emperor Haile Selassie's Kagnew Battalion during the Korean War. My father discovered quickly that being a government dispatch doctor required other obligations beyond upholding Dr. Albert Schweitzer's ideal of reverence for life. A Korean CIA field agent attached to the embassy monitored the three doctors in Ethiopia, regularly requiring them to compile detailed reports of their activities, including interactions with medical personnel from China, Cuba, and the Soviet Union. Such reports became increasingly important as a venue for monitoring North Korean activities in Addis Ababa, especially during the height of the Cold War during the 1970s and 1980s as the North and South strove to gain support from countries in Africa, both with the aim of joining the United Nations. By the 1970s, the South Korean government had dispatched doctors to countries such as Botswana, Ethiopia, Gabon, Gambia, Kenya, Lesotho, Malawi, Niger, Swaziland, Uganda, and Upper Volta (now Burkina Faso). I left Ethiopia to attend college (and later graduate school at the University of Chicago) in the United States in 1987 after the devastating famine that killed tens of thousands and the escalation of Ethiopia's bloody civil war with Eritrea, which had raged for some two decades. Four years after my departure, the Tigrayan Peoples' Liberation Front and its allies finally toppled Mengistu's regime in 1991, forcing the dictator to flee to Zimbabwe where the late Robert Mugabe, another admirer of Kim Il-sung, granted him asylum. My parents remained in Addis Ababa during the transition to a new government under Prime Minister Meles Zenawi.

As a faculty member of Yonsei University for the last five years (after teaching for over a decade at the University of Hawai'i at Manoa), reflecting on my experiences in Africa during the 1970s and 1980s has given me the opportunity to talk to people, read widely, and reflect critically on the complex postwar history of the two Koreas that profoundly shaped my family's personal history as well as countless others'. This book seeks to give presence to ordinary people who have languished in the dark in the annals of national history, by drawing particularly on microhistory, which narrows the scope and scale of observation. A distinctive feature of this study is its integration of multiple narratives of Korea within the larger processes of globalization and world history. To humanize and concretize this history, each chapter focuses on a feature story drawn from popular culture that captures the key issues of the day. The book also addresses the geopolitics and transnational connections that disrupt ideas of national belonging or citizenship. For instance, it examines the uneasy placement of people into ethnoracial and other sociopolitical categories like *ppalgaeng-i* (commie), *saetomin* (people of a new land), and *damunhwa-in* (a multicultural person), formed out of a convergence of peoples, ideals, and cultural orientations, complicating the semantic domain of what it means to be a Korean. This volume endeavors to provide a compelling and accessible gateway to understanding contemporary North and South Korea and their respective diasporas through the mundane and the everyday, contextualized in broader frameworks.

There is one major caveat. In contrast to the surfeit of sources on the South, there is a dearth of available information on North Korea, as fragmentary, selective, and sometimes unreliable narratives culled from defectors or NGO groups construct a particular discourse about the North. Given the secrecy of official statistics, the difficulty in accessing historical archives, and the tendency of the scholarship to focus on the narratives of elites or of men, the coverage of the North is naturally less detailed compared to the

South. At the same time, this volume employs strategies like reading against the grain and listening carefully to marginalized subjects and their silences to analyze the dominant narratives against which they construct their own.

The study begins in 1953 in the aftermath of a devastating civil war, national division, and the emergence of two very different Korean societies in the north and the south. They are separated by a buffer zone—four kilometers wide and 250 kilometers long— along the thirty-eighth parallel, the Demilitarized Zone (DMZ), which is the most heavily militarized border in the world and the last Cold War frontier. Only an armistice agreement holds together a fragile peace, though the specter of nuclear war on the peninsula still haunts both sides of the border. The book then explores how twins born of the Cold War developed two separate identities in the eyes of the world. The North chafes under its image as an isolated, impoverished pariah state caught up in a time warp, with the world's worst human rights record and a reclusive leader who perennially threatens global security with his clandestine nuclear weapons program. In contrast, the South basks in its reputation as a thriving democratic and capitalist state with the eleventh-largest economy in the world, a model for other countries in the Global South to emulate. The volume ends with the latest developments, giving special attention to the increasing global fascination with everything Korean—from K-pop to Samsung phones, cosmetic surgery, Google map images, and Instagram photos of the Democratic People's Republic of Korea (DPRK). In contrast to standard histories, this study examines not only the internal developments of the two Koreas side-by-side but also the diaspora experience, which has challenged the master narratives of national culture, homogeneity, belongingness, and identity. The epilogue offers a conspectus of the book by examining *Burning,* a recent award-winning film by Lee Chang-dong, one of South Korea's auteurs, in the context of recent regional disputes, from trade to military deployments, that have altered relationships of the peninsula with Japan, China, and the United States and that will certainly influence the future of the two Koreas.

1 *Out of the Ashes of War*

The 1950s

This first chapter examines the social and political realities of national division and the collective traumas and a sense of anxiety and fear caused by internecine hostilities. Themes include the exile experience and the impact of the Cold War on national and cultural developments. It explores how the North branched out, as the Soviet Union did, to engage with Third World countries that were beginning to undergo the complex process of decolonization.

On September 6, 1956, Yi Jungseop (1916–56), widely regarded today as one of Korea's most talented and versatile modern painters, died of hepatitis at the young age of forty at the Red Cross Family Hospital in Seoul. He passed away in abject poverty, without his family at his side. Born in Pyeongwon (in present-day North Korea) to a well-to-do family, Yi became interested in art while studying at Osan High School. He found a mentor in Im Yongryeon, who had studied at Yale University and worked as an artist in Paris. In 1932, Yi gained admission to Teikoku Bijutsu Gakkō, the famous imperial art institute in Tokyo, where he studied Western painting before transferring to the Bunka Gakuen

(Academy of Culture), a progressive school that allowed him to engage in free-style avant-garde techniques like line drawing and other Fauvist forms. As a member of the Association of Free Artists (*Jiyū bijutsuka kyōkai*), he garnered the Second Art Exhibition prize and was recognized by the judges as "a prodigy of the peninsula." Soon several prominent Japanese art magazines like *Mizue* and *Atelier* were featuring his works. He completed his studies in 1941 at the start of the Pacific War and returned to his hometown in Wonsan, a coastal city located in the northeastern part of the peninsula. In May 1945, Yi, affectionately known as Agorisan (Mr. Long Jaw Yi), married Yamamoto Masako, who took on a Korean name, Yi Namdeok. The couple had met at Bunka Gakuen in 1938 and courted for several years, exchanging two hundred or more hand-drawn postcards and letters. Theirs was a unique inter-racial and companionate marriage; they were both very talented artists who shared a genuine love relationship that seemed to tran-scend nationality and culture. Masako hailed from a very wealthy Japanese family. Her father, the president of a subsidiary of Mitsui Stock Company, was open to her marriage to someone from out-side of Japan proper (*gaichi*). Likewise, Yi's immediate family members were all conversant in Japanese and did not oppose their relationship, because Masako was a Christian and a fellow artist. However, the newly married couple could not live in blissful mat-rimony after Emperor Hirohito unexpectedly announced Japan's unconditional surrender and recognition of the terms of the Potsdam Declaration on August 15, 1945, that ended thirty-five years of Japanese colonial rule. Yi's life reflected the experiences of Koreans who found themselves liberated from colonial rule only to be swept into the bloodiest fratricidal war. The Korean War tore the peninsula into two ideologically opposed nations, leaving in its

FIGURE 1. Barbed wire fence on Gangneung Beach, South Korea.

wake unresolved trauma from the gruesome violence, family separations, dislocation, and political retribution on both sides.

As World War II ended, euphoria swept across the Korean peninsula, which was suddenly liberated from decades of colonial rule. Yet the immediate dissolution of the Japanese empire by the Allied Powers created a huge power vacuum, sounding an ominous warning of civil unrest and political uncertainty for the next eight years for those living on the peninsula. The number of Koreans living abroad in 1945, mostly in places like Japan, Manchuria, and Russia, totaled approximately 5 million, comprising more than 20 percent of the total Korean population. By comparison, roughly 6.9 million Japanese civilians and soldiers lived outside of Japan's mainland, complicating the task of the Allied Powers to dismantle this multi-ethnic empire and repatriate its members, especially interracial couples like Masako and Yi (and their children), many of whom got married under the wartime assimilation policy. After the liberation of Korea, such couples became acutely aware of the hostility and risks of remaining on the peninsula, and some Korean wives even divorced their Japanese husbands for fear of reprisals. However, there were Japanese women like Masako who opted to remain despite the cloud of uncertainty that hung over them as former colonizers. The fact that Masako's in-laws were wealthy landowners and well connected in Wonsan may have persuaded her that a future in Korea was possible. Other Japanese expats without relatives willing to sponsor their return to their homeland had no alternative but to remain on the peninsula. A group of nineteen Japanese women, who are now in their nineties, live in Nazarewon, a small nursing home in Gyeongju, South Korea.

When the Allied Forces declared the liberation of the peninsula, the Koreans, who had not achieved victory on their own, were ill prepared to initiate a process that would transfer political power, thus triggering conflicts over the creation of a new government. Despite the struggles between members of the Shanghai-based Provisional Government in exile and those aligned with the Committee for the Preparation of Korean Independence under Yeo Unhyeong (1886–1947), a left-leaning nationalist to whom Governor-General Abe Nobuyuki personally handed over power, national leaders began to make earnest plans for reconstructing their nation. But unbeknown to the majority of Koreans, the great powers—the United States, the Soviet Union, China, and Great Britain—had already discussed a four-power international trusteeship over their country in Cairo in 1943 and later in conferences in Moscow, Yalta, and Potsdam. Korean leaders were conspicuously absent from any of the discussions. To complicate matters, following President Franklin

Roosevelt's untimely death in May 1945, Harry S. Truman sought a more hardline position vis-à-vis the Russians. The midwives to the painful birth of the twin nations from a unified Korea were more concerned with their own Cold War agendas than the fate of the people. In response to Japan's sudden defeat and to increasing distrust of Soviet activities in the north, the Americans unilaterally partitioned the peninsula across the thirty-eighth parallel and started repatriating Japanese officials back home in early September. For their part, the Soviets aimed to set up a Socialist state in the north to secure their sphere of influence.

After thirty-five years of Japanese colonial rule, the Korean leadership in the south was eager to prepare for statehood, but competing claims led to confusion and tensions. Kim Gu (1876–1949), who had led the Shanghai-based Provisional Government, returned to Korea, expecting to take control at the helm, but he found himself sidelined by other leaders. Yeo Unhyeong, who had secretly organized the Korean Restoration Brotherhood during the Japanese occupation, was recently released from prison. He established the Committee for the Preparation of Korean Independence, which formally announced the founding of the Korean People's Republic (KPR) on September 6, 1945. That same day, the United States Army Military Government in Korea (USAMGIK), under Lieutenant General John R. Hodge, proclaimed itself the only legitimate government in the southern part of the Korean peninsula, and outlawed the KPR. A nagging concern for the Americans and right-wing nationalists was the presence of leftists and members of the Korean Communist Party in the south, especially since they had participated in establishing the fledgling nation in cooperation with Yeo. Koreans in the south also kept a wary eye on clashes in the north between the occupying Soviet forces and local Communist

Party, and anti-Soviet and anti-Communist students, many of whom belonged to the Christian Social Democratic Party. Demonstrations in the northern city of Sinuiju during the second week of November resulted in twenty-three deaths and the imprisonment of more than two thousand protestors. Landed families like that of Yi Jungseop (the artist mentioned above) faced severe scrutiny because of their wealth and Christian (often Presbyterian) background and fled to the south, bringing with them a virulent fear and hatred of Communism.

To ensure that such Communist influence would not take root in the south, the USAMGIK outlawed all left-leaning organizations, such as the Korean Communist Party and the Korean Student-Soldier's League, an organization of student conscripts established during the colonial period whose primary aim was to create a national army and disseminate leftist publications. Bypassing the plethora of factions such as the Korean People's Republic—a coalition of leftist, moderate, and rightist groups—the Americans supported the right-wing, pro-American Democratic National Party, composed mainly of English-speaking landowners and businessmen who sought to protect their assets by drawing on anti-Communist rhetoric. To the dismay of opponents, the Democratic National Party embarked on a path that failed to address the most deep-rooted Korean grievances. It not only delayed land reforms, which were already underway in northern Korea, but it supported the USAMGIK's decision to retain most of the colonial police, and appointed collaborators in key administrative and military positions under the pretext that Koreans were not ready for self-governance and needed supervision. The party also supported the suppression of local ad hoc counsels, or people's committees, created to remove the Japanese and collaborators from positions of authority. Ignoring populist demands for justice for past colonial abuses, the United States handpicked an anti-Communist septuagenarian, Syngman Rhee (1875–1965), who lacked any grassroots support, and arranged for him to return from exile in Hawai'i. Rhee stood in stark contrast to the Soviet choice in the north— a Moscow-groomed former anti-Japanese guerrilla fighter named Kim Il-sung.

The postwar north reflected both the external influence of the Soviet Union as well as its own political culture, ideology, and style. At the First Congress of the Workers' Party of North Korea (the forerunner to the Workers' Party of Korea) in Pyeongyang on August 28, 1946, 366,000 members elected Kim Tubong (1889–1958) as chairman and Ju Yeongha (1908–?) and Kim Il-sung as vice presidents. The thirty-four-year-old Kim Il-sung (1912–94) drew on his wartime activities as a leader of a guerrilla faction in Manchuria, fashioning his image as a revolutionary hero and champion of agricultural reforms to impress his Soviet handlers. On August 31, the *Rodong sinmun* (Worker's Newspaper), which would later become North Korea's official newspaper, published its first installment on the historic elections. In the following months, the interim North Korean Provisional People's Committee (established by Kim Il-sung) began to address the agricultural crisis, nationalize key industries, and confiscate the land owned by the landlord class, redistributing it among the peasants. As Kim's government strengthened the political base of the party by eliminating the landed class, these new policies of postcolonial liberation in the north would spell trouble for families like that of the artist Yi Jungseop. His elder brother went missing after being charged by the Wonsan People's Committee of being a capitalist landlord. Yi's dreams of studying abroad in Paris also evaporated when his family fortunes disappeared, along with those of two million Christian landlord families in the north. When Yi discovered that his brother had been executed, he started to contemplate fleeing to the south for fear of more bloody reprisals against his family.

The radicalization of workers was not unique to the north. As right-wing forces started to gain a strong foothold in the south, hyperinflation and food shortages triggered a series of labor strikes staged by leftist groups such as the National Council of Korean Labor Unions, which culminated in a popular uprising in Daegu in the autumn of 1946. As a strike by railroad workers spread throughout North Gyeongsang Province, civilians joined the protests. The USAMGIK and local police worked hand in glove to suppress the strikes violently. By November 14, 1947, the dissolution of the US–Soviet Joint Commission looked inevitable. Disregarding calls for a left-right coalition, the United States presented the Korea Issue to the American-controlled United Nations General Assembly, which in turn quickly established a Temporary Commission on Korea (UNTCOK) under Resolution 112 to oversee separate national elections under UN supervision. When the Soviets refused entry of UN supervisors into the north, the General Assembly drafted a new resolution granting an election to be held in areas accessible to the UN Commission (mainly in the southern half of Korea) to establish a separate government.

The unilateral decision by the United States to create a separate regime through the mechanism of a United Nations resolution triggered large demonstrations across Jeju Island in the south starting in March 1948. Protesters opposed the UN resolution and called for US troops to withdraw from the peninsula. The local police in concert with the Northwest Youth Group, a paramilitary group made up of anti-Communist Korean refugees from the north that had been dispatched by the USAMGIK, began to commit atrocities against the demonstrators. Syngman Rhee in turn declared martial law on the island allegedly to quell armed leftist insurgencies. The US-occupied south forged ahead with general elections on May 10, disregarding the South–North Joint Conference in Pyeongyang where leaders from both sides of the peninsula (representing fifty-seven political parties) convened in a last-ditch effort to boycott the UNTCOK-supervised elections. It bears noting that delegates to the joint conference included English-speaking moderates like Kim Gyusik (1918–50) and rightists like Kim Gu, who met with Kim Il-sung to find a resolution. Following the general elections, the Republic of Korea (ROK) declared statehood on August 25, 1948, with Syngman Rhee as the South's first president. The North declared the Democratic People's Republic of Korea (DPRK) the following month on September 9, with Kim Il-sung at the helm as the premier, thus finalizing the national division. Disregarding the twin births, the United Nations recognized the Republic of Korea as the sole legal government of Korea at the Third General Assembly.

In the South, the state began to implement draconian measures to consolidate the power of the new regime and its military. The ROK military conducted a massive purge of its rank and file suspected of having taken part in or sympathized with the mutinies of roughly three thousand soldiers stationed in the cities of Yeosu and Suncheon in October 1948, who had refused to suppress the uprisings on Jeju Island, where an estimated eighty thousand people were killed in one year. The military purge offered a pretext to draft a new National Security Law in December 1948, outlawing leftist activities and allowing the government to round up opposition lawmakers on trumped-up espionage charges. The state also linked its opponents to Communist organizations, including those who called for the prosecution of pro-Japanese collaborators. By 1950 tens of thousands of people were arrested and imprisoned under the National Security Law, even executed under fabricated charges of treason.

That is exactly what happened to Kim Suim. Born in 1911, Kim went to American missionary schools and graduated from Ewha College, the only women's university in Korea that offered a degree in English literature. Newspapers and journals of the time featured her as a "modern girl" who later worked as an English translator at Severance Hospital. She was romantically involved with Yi Gangguk, a German-educated leftist intellectual who later defected to the North, and she also maintained a secret relationship with Colonel John E. Baird, a fifty-six-year-old American military police chief who sired her son. He eventually cast her off when his American wife joined him in Seoul in 1949. Vilified as a notorious seductress and South Korea's Mata Hari, Kim was charged by the military court with abetting Yi in the theft of classified information from Baird and passing it on to North Korean agents. The state executed her on June 15, 1950. The US military investigators tasked with reviewing Kim's case concluded that Baird had no access to any classified documents and that the South Korean military had concocted everything. Such tactics of bullying opponents into forced confessions and cultivating the spectacle of public executions exacerbated left-right tensions and repressed any large political and social upheavals in the South by leftist groups. Taking advantage of America's ignorance of the political and social realities in the South, right-wing forces engaged in terrorism and assassination of prominent leaders such as Yeo Unhyeong in 1947 and Kim Gu in 1949, both of whom had wanted to play a role in the country's reconstruction after liberation from Japan despite their political orientations. The number of civilians displaced by divisive and oppressive politics ran into the hundreds of thousands as they were forced to flee their towns to avoid political reprisals or arbitrary arrests. More than one hundred thousand civilians were killed even before the Korean War.

Meanwhile, in North Korea, Kim Il-sung resolved to unify the peninsula and liberate the South from what he viewed as a reactionary regime. Initially the Soviet Politburo did not believe that North Korea had the military capabilities to overthrow the South; however, by August 1949 the Soviet leader Joseph Stalin began to see some promising possibilities if there was a quick victory with the support of the newly established People's Republic of China under Mao Zedong. Having secured assurances from the Soviet Union and China, Kim Il-sung ordered a preemptive attack on June 25, 1950. The North Korean People's Army, with eight divisions and 75,000 soldiers, crossed the thirty-eighth parallel, seizing Seoul in three days, and forced the southern government to retreat to Daejon and then to Busan. By the beginning of August, the US and ROK forces had withdrawn behind the Nakdong River, a position which the UN Command maintained until General Douglas MacArthur launched a surprise amphibious raid in Incheon on September 15, 1950, trapping the North Koreans, reversing the battle, and recapturing Seoul on September 26. MacArthur was authorized by President Harry Truman to cross the thirty-eighth parallel to invade North Korea, which dramatically altered the course of the war.

Serious concerns that Mao Zedong might intervene became a reality when 300,000 combat-seasoned Chinese soldiers crossed the Yalu River on November 25, 1950, during the cover of night while the American forces were enjoying their Thanksgiving meals. The Chinese involvement triggered yet another massive exodus of people. More than 1.2 million residents of Seoul started fleeing further south, marking another turning point in the war. Kim Dongni's short story "Heungnam Evacuation" (1955) captures the chaos that ensued when Chinese troops invaded the northern port city, compelling the UN forces to evacuate after President Truman declared a national emergency. Under the code-named Christmas Cargo, approximately 100,000 soldiers and more than 90,000 North Korean civilians boarded 193 merchant vessels and military transports between December 15 and 24, 1950, in subzero temperatures and traveled to Busan and other ports in the South. Among those rescued were the future parents of current South Korean president Moon Jae-in (b. 1953), whose mother, Kang Hanok, was able to board the *SS Meredith Victory* (now known as the Ship of Miracles). This was one of the largest evacuations from land by a single ship under the helm of Captain Leonard LaRue, who ordered the dumping of weapons and cargo to take on hundreds of passengers. In Wonsan, the *SS Lane Victory*, a 455-foot ship with a crew of sixty seamen, took aboard 7,009 refugees and 3,384 troops and transported them to safety in Busan.

The artist Yi Jungseop and his family were some of the fortunate to board the *SS Lane Victory* and escape the North. To avoid conscription into the People's Army during the initial invasion in 1950, Yi had sought refuge in an abandoned mine until the UN forces advanced toward Wonsan later that autumn, defeating North Korean units. Like most refugees from the North, Yi and his family had to settle in the port city of Busan, the nation's southernmost city and the provisional capital, which was teeming with over half a million war refugees from all over the peninsula.

Frequent outbreaks of epidemics in the crowded refugee camps and regular fires caused his family great suffering. Yi had to scrape the bottom to earn money, standing in long lines to secure casual work on the docks or peddling stolen goods from the US military post exchange (PX). Life in Busan deteriorated as the war dragged on, and Yi moved Masako and their two sons to Seogwipo, Jeju Island, where they lived in a tiny room. Here he created his famous paintings of his family. In "A Family on the Road," Yi depicted a father pulling a wagon with his wife and two sons, who throw flowers on the road in search of utopia. The father raises his hands toward the heavens as a dove lands on the hands of one of the sons, perhaps conveying Yi's hope that the family had arrived at their final destination in Jeju Island, free from the horrors of the war's violence. But in July 1952, Yi was forced to make a heart-wrenching decision to send his family back to Japan to protect them from the deprivation of war. The trauma of the war seeped into his solitary life: Yi was haunted by the guilt of leaving his mother behind in Wonsan, horrified at his elder brother's execution, and frustrated by his inability to secure a visa to reunite with his family in Japan. The only outlet for his raw emotions and pain was art. Due to the scarcity of art supplies, he improvised with tinfoil from cigarette packets to create more than three hundred images of his happy family, for whom he desperately longed. He depicted the children in familiar poses—hugging, sleeping, and riding a bicycle. Family intimacy found its way into portraits sketched in some sixty letters and postcards that he sent regularly to his wife and children. These would become his most famous pieces. Like most refugees from the North, Yi could neither return home nor cross the straits, as he once did, to Japan where his beloved family now lived. He was an exile from home and family.

The writer Yi Hocheol (1932–2016) also captured the human tragedy of the Korean War through literature in his debut short story "Far from Home," which was published in *Munhak yesul* (Literary Arts) in 1955. After graduating from high school, Yi was drafted into the Korean People's Army and accompanied his unit to Uljin where he was later captured by the North; by sheer luck, he was later rescued by his brother-in-law, allowing him to return to his village. After learning that the Chinese planned to get involved in the war, Yi fled to the South and eked out a living doing odd jobs on the docks in Busan and working as a security guard at an American military base. In "Far from Home," Yi explored the agony of leaving one's hometown through his four protagonists who sleep in empty freight cars on Pier 4 and the precarious lives of the male refugees in Busan who hustled for cash to survive. Above all, he depicted the homesickness and dislocation of refugees who realized that they could never return to their families in the North.

The Korean War was one of the deadliest in modern world history to end without a peace treaty. The sheer destruction and loss of life on both sides had a devastating psychological impact on civilians, who suffered casualties at a higher rate than in World War II and the Vietnam War. The war also separated ten million Koreans—no less than one quarter of the population—from their family members; Yi Jungseop, for one, left his mother behind in the North. From August 1945 to the signing of the Armistice Agreement on July 27, 1953, thousands of civilians were detained, suddenly disappeared, or executed. Both sides committed horrific atrocities against the civilian population. The retreating forces on both sides often conducted large-scale massacres, eliminating individuals whom they suspected of being Communists or collaborators without any due process. In some instances, North Korean soldiers forcefully recruited civilians to augment their armies, uprooting many young men from their villages and destroying the livelihoods of their families. The scale of abuses on the ground was matched by the devastating destruction from above as American aircraft dropped more tonnage of bombs in the North than they had used in Germany, obliterating many towns, dams, and factories. The devastation shocked even the stoic General MacArthur, who reported to the Senate Armed Services and Foreign Relations Committee, after being released from his command in April 1951, that the utter destruction had caused him to vomit.

There was a forced blanket of silence about the atrocities. From 1961 to 1987, politicians and media outlets that dared to confront the atrocities committed under the military dictatorships in the South faced harsh prosecution. Similarly, in the North bereaved families dared not utter a word about the massacres committed by the Korean People's Army, resulting in a collective amnesia over the tragic episodes of the war. It was only in 2005, when the Truth and Reconciliation Commission of Korea in the South started to examine testimonies and official documents (released later in 2010), that executions of civilians and political prisoners could be confirmed. Even these revelations, however, could not account for the civilians who found themselves conscripted by one side to commit atrocities, or the families of *wolbuk-in* (those who went north) or *wolnammin* (those who went south) who faced suspicion, punishment, or ostracism after the war. Bak Gwangsu's acclaimed film *To the Starry Island*—an important milestone in war cinema—explores unhealed civilian wounds as Mun Jaegu brings his elderly father's body back to his fishing-island town of Gwiseong for burial. The islanders angrily refuse to let the coffin ashore, unable to forgive the deceased man's role in the reprisals against alleged Communists in their village during the Korean War. In a central scene, a single string divides the Communists from the capitalists in the school playground—a metaphor for the artificiality of the thirty-eighth parallel—as nationalist troops masquerading as North Korean soldiers compel the islanders to denounce the capitalists in their community, unmasking their true loyalties. That Mun's father cannot be buried on his island but must be burned out at sea suggests that the trauma of reprisals during the war have not been resolved.

The fate of Yi Jungseop also reveals the private toll that the war had on one artist whose work came to represent the scars of family separation. Hopes of reuniting with his family faded after a brief visit with them in July 1953. Yi worked in Tongyeong at a craft school, teaching students how to make lacquerware with mother-of-pearl, while producing some of his finest oil paintings, which depicted the joys of everyday life—from children frolicking on the beach to marriage ceremonies. This was his way of avoiding the harsh realities of the war. Extreme financial need, coupled with a deep longing for his family, contributed to Yi's mental illness, which was exacerbated by his turn to alcohol for solace. His last attempt to sell his paintings through a private exhibition at the Midopa Department Store Gallery in Seoul in 1955 and another at the US Information Service (USIS) in Daegu failed to bring him the income he so desperately needed. Yi soon succumbed to hepatitis, and a close friend had his body cremated, sending some of the ashes to his wife in Japan. Yi left behind a large body of work, mostly tinfoil drawings and hand-painted postcards. His final series of bull paintings no longer resembled the vigorous, powerful animal that had represented Korea under Japanese colonialism in his first series. The gray colors reflected an animal with all the vitality sapped out of it. Yi's tragic life story provides a glimpse of the tragedy of the war on both the individual and the collective scale. The profound sense of anxiety and fear caused by internecine hostilities, the disorienting experience of dislocation and family separation, and the realization that exile was permanent would have an impact on postwar reconstruction and the trajectory of two separate nations.

2 Dependent Capitalist Development or a Path of Self-Reliance?

This chapter explores the separate paths of economic and social development in the two Koreas. The South resorted to a strict, even draconian, top-down approach to embark on rapid industrialization that meant heavy costs and reliance on imported goods, ideas, and culture from its patron, the United States. The Korean diaspora began to increase exponentially during the 1960s with immigration to America and Germany from the South. In contrast, the North sought a path of self-reliance to achieve economic and political independence through strong leadership at the top and the workers' zeal at the bottom. The North projected its assets and influence in Africa and also welcomed aggrieved minorities such as the Black Panthers from the United States. Both Koreas were drawn further into Cold War politics and war (especially the Vietnam War), resulting in rising hostilities following assassination and infiltration attempts by the North.

From the American People: Dependence and US Patronage in Postwar South Korea

In 1958, Yang Jaehyeon (1926–2001), a thirty-two-year-old master's student at Seoul National University, would leave his wife and two sons behind to embark on a journey of study abroad in the United States to pursue an advanced degree in the sciences. Yang was one of the first students to graduate from Seoul National University, which was founded in 1946 by the American Military Government after it consolidated Keijō (Gyeongseong) Imperial University into a single system and commissioned the University of Minnesota (a land-grant university with strong agricultural, engineering, and medical programs) to restructure its curriculum. While Yang was tempted to study in Minneapolis, where 226 faculty members at Seoul National University would get their degrees by the 1970s, he also looked at other schools in the Midwest for opportunities. During the Korean War, missionaries sponsored the first wave of Korean students to attend American colleges and universities, such as Berea College, University of Louisville, Purdue University, Syracuse University, the University of Wisconsin, and Western Kentucky University. Based on a recommendation by Choe Gyuwon, one of the first Koreans to earn a doctorate at Purdue University, in 1959, and later a professor at Seoul National University, Yang decided to travel to West Lafayette. Purdue was well known among elite circles for its engineering programs and was a popular destination for US military officers and eventually South Korean military cadets to further their training. Because South Korea needed foreign-educated scientists and engineers to develop the country's infrastructure, the government promised students like Choe and Yang positions in government and universities at home if they were not able to secure positions in the United States. Since passports were hard to procure after the war, the South Korean government rarely permitted male students to take their wives, except for a handful of lucky students like Choe, whose wife was allowed to join him in West Lafayette to earn a master's

FIGURE 2. Statue of Admiral Yi in downtown Seoul.

degree in physics. After earning his doctorate in chemistry in 1962 at Purdue, Yang remained in West Lafayette for an additional year as a postdoctoral fellow and returned to South Korea to work at the Korea Institute of Science and Technology, which developed many national industrial initiatives, from energy to petrochemicals, steel, and mechanical industries. Yang advanced to a position at the Korea Institute of Nuclear Fuel Development and then to a professorship in the Department of Chemistry at Dankook University. Seeking to further his country's development, he recruited other

FIGURE 3. Juche Tower in Pyeongyang.

Purdue alumni, such as Yun Yeogyeong, to return to Korea in order to head the Techno-Economics Group in 1968. Yun would later become the president and chairman of the Korea Development Investment Finance Corporation.

Supporting the education of Koreans figured quite prominently in America's aid to South Korea to cultivate and nurture human resources. A report by the UNESCO/UNKRA Educational Planning Mission in 1953 revealed that the war had destroyed most of the existing schools and that military authorities had occupied the extant facilities. Due to the lack of available facilities, skilled workforce, and educated teachers in the South, the US State Department actively recruited specialists from America to teach for short periods and created participant training programs, providing valuable scholarships to Korean students. The Smith-Mundt Act of 1948, for instance, authorized the US State Department to create an exchange-visitor program in which American medical, scientific, and academic institutions could host trainees from developing countries in America. The act also provided grants to students, bureaucrats, and other social leaders from Korea for short-term training and education at universities in the United States. The Nathan Report, an independent study conducted by the American firm, highlighted the importance of sending Korean students abroad, noting that the prestige and knowledge attached to an American education would address the skilled workforce South Korea desperately needed. Between 1950 and 1966, the United States Operations Mission sent 6,700 Koreans to the United States for training, and the United States Information Service (USIS) sponsored 940 students to study at institutes of higher education. Many of the students were already professionals such as medical doctors, lawyers, and professors and were able to solicit additional funds through the East-West Center, Fulbright Program, Ford Foundation, and Asia Foundation. They eventually spearheaded research and teaching at the universities and developed the medical, scientific, and political and legal fields in South Korea. American missionaries continued to play a key role in sponsoring hundreds of these students, who were disproportionately Christian and found support from a church or church-related organization.

The US government wielded education as a tool to ensure that future leaders of the fledgling Korean state adopted American political culture and mores. From 1952, the US Army offered to tailor programs of its own and sponsored several thousand enlisted officers for short-term training in America, where grantees received instruction in proper military etiquette and decorum. Likewise, in 1955, the US State Department launched an educational exchange program that targeted Korean journalists as part of its public diplomacy project to teach them about the American media and professionalism. It entrusted the Medill School of Journalism at Northwestern University to groom pro-American journalists through academic courses and internships, and even provided Korean journalists internships to work at assigned newspaper companies in America to gain experience. The American embassy in Seoul actively supported participants of this program, especially through USIS publications such as *Free World,* a magazine established by Earl J. Wilson that was the most widely circulated in the Asian region. The United States also provided financial support for scholarly publications like *Sasanggye* (The World of Thought), the leading intellectual journal in South Korea at the time, which produced thirty tons of newsprint annually. They were freely distributed to various agencies. The State Department maintained that these publications would serve as a great vehicle for promoting US policies among certain student and artist groups and steer them away from Communism. On a larger scale, the United States could use South Korea as an example to promote democracy in other countries.

The impact of soft and hard American patronage would shape the contours of South Korean postwar development. From 1946 to 1976, the United States allocated $12.6 billion in economic and military aid to Korea. For Americans, food aid became the means by which it converted Korea's tastes and food system to become dependent on the United States—first through aid food, then through commercial exports such as grain. In the aftermath of the war, unemployment and a shortage of basic goods led to soaring prices on rice and triggered an ongoing spiral of inflation. The deficit of the ROK, which exported far less than it imported, was only sustainable because of US aid. The US Public Law 480 program began to send surplus agricultural products to Korea in 1955, and by 1971 this aid amounted to $646 million, which bankrolled the ROK's consumer goods industry, or "three white industries," consisting of wheat flour, sugar, and cotton. In 1961, CARE (Cooperative for Assistance and Relief Everywhere, formerly Cooperative for American Remittances to Europe) donated 24.5 million pounds of cornmeal and 5 million pounds of powdered milk, which transformed the diet and eating habits of Korean children, though not without some bumps along the way. During the early years, the donated dried milk earned a terrible reputation for causing Korean children to have diarrhea (because they ate it instead of dissolving it in water), and most of it ended up as livestock feed. Cornmeal was to be prepared as a gruel, but it was difficult and expensive to prepare because many schools lacked decent kitchens. Mass-produced bread was first baked successfully in Busan in 1963 using cornmeal along with powdered milk and a small amount of sugar, and it was distributed to 95,000 children in sixty-six schools; soon bread became a staple in school lunch programs.

The donation of surplus wheat flour to Korea in 1966 by the United States Agency for International Development (USAID) allowed for larger distributions among children at schools, especially those living in impoverished remote areas. Koreans developed a preference for white bread, which had a softer texture and satisfied the palate of children more than the cornmeal-based *geonppang* (hard tack). In reality, before the boatloads of wheat and cornmeal ever made it to their tables, many Koreans had already gotten their first taste of "Yankee food" through American military rations during the Korean War, when children scavenged army dumpsters, collecting anything edible. They were eager to find canned food (such as beans and corn) but especially SPAM, which they sold to restaurants that mixed this new meat with *kimchi.* During times of privation, these inexpensive and precooked tins of pork meat became a prized commodity for *budae jjigae* (army base stew), also known as Johnson's stew after Lyndon B. Johnson, the thirty-sixth president, who visited Korea in 1966 and promised to continue American food aid. The customary practice of communal side dishes and a simmering bowl of something like army base stew had become commonplace during the war as food became scarcer. In disregard of health risks such as gastrointestinal infections, unhygienic habits of communal stew eating have been part of the culinary experience in South Korean cuisine.

By August 1966, the new regime under Park Chung-hee was actively aiming to change the eating habits of Koreans by replacing rice with wheat-based diets to address food shortages. The politics of food became a symbol of Park's coercive tactics through controversial social policies. As cheap flour imports poured in from the United States, the majority of brewers started substituting wheat powder for nonglutinous rice to brew *makgeolli,* a popular rice wine, which made the drink much thicker and heavier while emitting a peculiar odor and leaving an unpleasant aftertaste. The regime further imposed a series of draconian laws, designating days on which markets could not sell any rice and making it a patriotic duty to allot two rice-free days as a means to promote wheat consumption. The state also promoted flour-based meals such as the bread-and-noodles-only day, opened flour-based meal consultation centers under the guise of scientific improvement, and even held daily inspections of children's lunchboxes for excess rice. Given such restrictions, brewers resorted to using artificial sweetening additives such as saccharin and aspartame as well as ethyl alcohol and calcium carbide to speed up the fermenting process, but as Koreans discovered, these chemicals caused a lot of gas and bloating.

In addition to changes in promoting new foodways, the Americans first became involved in facilitating large-scale international adoption with the airlift of German and Japanese orphans at the end of World War II. Fueled by a desire to demonstrate American goodwill and a positive image to the rest of the world, these baby lift mercy missions became an important part of America's foreign policy. Over the next six decades, more than 200,000 Korean children would be sent abroad as international adoptees to more than fifteen countries, the vast majority to the United States through the Holt Organization, an agency created by an Oregon farmer, Harry Holt, and his wife, Bertha (a nurse and fundamentalist Christian). In 1954, the couple attended a local presentation by World Vision, a Christian relief organization, on the topic of Korean War orphans and felt the call to rescue these helpless children. At the time, US federal law prohibited the adoption of two children from abroad, but after Congress passed the Bill for Relief of Certain Korean War Orphans, sponsored by the two senators from Oregon, the Holts were able to adopt four boys and four girls from Korea.

The images of Harry Holt disembarking from the plane with eight children from South Korea appeared in newspapers around the country as more American couples expressed a willingness to adopt and offer a home to Korean War orphans. Two years later, in

1956, the couple established the Holt Adoption Program in the United States, which is still one of the largest international adoption agencies, with a big office (Holt Korea) in Seoul. Some scholars have viewed the Holt Adoption Program as another guise under which US imperialism operated in Korea. Many children who were available for adoption in Korea during the 1950s and 1960s came from a mixed-race background. Unmarried mothers who became pregnant by American soldiers gave up their children for adoption to the Holt Agency; they were motivated in part by the stigma they would inevitably face in South Korea but also by the agency's promise of a better future for their children in the United States. In recent years, the experiences of Korean adoptees have come into the spotlight; their narratives of displacement and alienation growing up in white families or communities with little if any exposure to their Korean heritage have led to painful discussions and soul-searching. Since the 1990s, a growing number of adoptees who have found each other online and created new global networks have opted as adults to return to Korea or visit in search of their biological and cultural roots. One remarkable story involved identical twins separated at birth. One day, Anaïs Bordier, a fashion designer in London who grew up in Paris and Brussels, stared at a mirror image of herself on a YouTube video that her friend sent to her. Her lookalike was twenty-seven-year-old Samantha Futerman, who lived across the ocean in New York. Coincidentally, they were both born on November 19, 1987, in the Korean city of Busan and were adopted. Like a scene out of *The Parent Trap,* the twins contacted each other. They took a DNA test that confirmed their relationship, and made a documentary called *Twinsters* (2015) about their journey together to discover one another and their adoption stories. Even years after the Korean War, the Holt Agency continues to operate in Korea, and twins like Bordier and Futerman seek answers about their birth mother, whose privacy they have chosen to respect because she does not want to meet them (at least for now).

The adoption story is linked at least in part to another aspect of the patron-client relationship between the United States and Korea. Conspicuously absent in the American records are the thousands of Korean women who serviced American GIs as sex workers. In 1953, after the signing of the U.S.-ROK Mutual Defense Treaty, the Americans stationed approximately 37,000 troops in South Korea, which became one of the most militarized regions in the world with ninety-nine bases and installations, each with *gijicheon* (camptowns). In the war film *Flower in Hell* (1958), Sin Sang-ok (1926–2006) uses documentary footage to give viewers a glimpse of daily life in postwar Seoul, panning his camera on American soldiers to show how Koreans had to forge relationships with American GIs to procure US dollars to survive poverty. In another classic film, *The Stray Bullet* (1961), Yu Hyeonmok also features American GIs exclusively in relation to Korean sex workers. In this film, an accountant and his refugee family from the North struggle to scrape by in Liberty Village, a shantytown in Seoul. Rejected by her disabled fiancé and desperate for money, Myeongsuk, the protagonist's sister, turns to prostitution. In one poignant scene, she solicits an American GI, clad in her Western outfit in the part of town occupied by the American army—the 640-acre Yongsan Garrison built initially by Japanese colonizers and known colloquially by GIs as Hooker Hill. The relationships between Korean women and GIs resembled European-style colonial concubinage, and the cohabitating marriages continued to be a widespread practice under US occupation as it was under the Japanese.

Under Park Chung-hee's regime, the state created legally recognized special districts for the sex industry designated to cater to US soldiers. The state regulated the sex trade by distributing health inspection cards to sex workers and treating those infected with sexually transmitted diseases at detention centers such as the infamous monkey houses, which had barred windows. Hailed as dollar-earning patriots, these women earned derogatory appellations as U.N. madam, Yankee wife, Yankee princess, or Yankee whore—a change from the euphemistic term "comfort women," which referred to women who were coerced into becoming sex slaves for the Imperial Japanese Army. The terms "wife," "princess," and "whore" somehow suggested greater agency on the part of the women but elided the nature of coercive necessity that drove women to work as sex workers. The camptown economy peaked during the 1960s when the country was in desperate need of foreign currency to rebuild its war-torn economy. The livelihoods of Koreans involved in this illicit economy depended heavily on the GIs who became a permanent fixture on the postwar Korean landscape.

To entertain a large number of troops, the US Eighth Army Show also required a continuous supply of Korean musicians and big-band shows to boost morale. To be considered for a gig, Korean bands, who modeled themselves after the likes of Benny Goodman, Duke Ellington, Glenn Miller, and Billy Vaughn, had to audition every three to six months before a committee sent by the Pentagon. Because of the intense competition to earn registration cards, Korean musicians adapted quickly by learning American jazz style from the AFKN (American Forces Korea Network) radio station, which started disseminating Western pop songs in 1957. In 1959, the Kim Sisters entered the US market, becoming the first female act to release an album; they also appeared on various television programs like the *Ed Sullivan Show* and toured multiple cities in the United States and Europe. Because AFKN radio attracted many listeners, KBS (Korean Broadcast System) also began to air programs dedicated to Western pop. Korean musicians who had performed for the US Eighth Army Shows came of age in the 1960s—a time when they started to experiment with a wide range of genres from country music to rock 'n' roll. As Western music dominated the airwaves and the street, all things America seeped into daily life, profoundly shaping youth culture.

American patronage played a significant role in the reconstruction of postwar South Korea, leaving its imprint on every aspect of Korean life. The public sphere was shaped by journalists who received their education and work experience in America. Knowledge and culture carried over by graduates of American higher education filtered into the nation's universities, medical facilities, and scientific centers. The South depended on scientists like Yang Jaehyeon, who had benefited from his studies abroad in chemistry to transform the petrochemical and nuclear industries in South Korea. Surplus American food (from SPAM to white bread) and pop music found their way to Korea, changing diets and listening habits of the public, while Korean war infants, whether given up by their mothers voluntarily or as a result of coercion, made their journey to the United States to be adopted by American parents. These Korean transnational experiences were painful, leaving scars, even as the leaders were determined to leave the nation's impoverished past behind.

The Self-Development-First Principle
and the Great Victory: The DPRK

Transnational crossings were not limited to the South. On April 12, 1957, Georgeta Mircioiu (b. 1932) finally married Jo Jeongho in Bucharest. Mircioiu met Jo in 1952, but they waited five years for their marriage certificate to be approved by both governments. Their union was reported as the first international marriage in North Korea. Jo was a teacher assigned to oversee North Korean orphans in Romania, while Mircioiu worked as an art teacher in Siret at a school for these orphans. The couple returned to Pyeongyang in 1960, but Mircioiu was forced to return two years later to Bucharest to seek medical treatment for their daughter, who suffered from calcium deficiency, and was subsequently denied a return visa to reunite with her husband, who was accused of associating with a foreigner and sentenced to a labor camp.

Between 1951 and 1959, some thirty thousand war orphans from North Korea were sent to Eastern bloc countries in East Germany, Hungary, Poland, and Romania, as well as to China and Mongolia. The Socialist Republic of Romania not only offered fraternal diplomatic and material support to the DPRK but also agreed to take care of three thousand North Korean war orphans—the largest group adopted by one country—under a covert program among the Socialist bloc to "help a friend." Poland, for example, housed orphans in remote towns like Świder, Otwock, Gołotczyzna, and Płakowice away from the public eye. In 1958, a Red Cross delegation from North Korea visited the children, mostly ages four to thirteen, encouraging them to work hard so that they could play an active role in rebuilding their homeland in the future. After their return to North Korea in 1959 with the completion of North Korea's

Five-Year Plan, the fortunate ones were sent to foreign language high schools or colleges, or to study fine arts and film, but the majority were not able to use their language skills and instead were sent to factories, coal mines, or the military.

The adoption of North Korean orphans by Eastern European countries marked a high point in Socialist bloc cooperation and fraternal aid in the reconstruction of North Korea—one of the first large-scale, multilateral development projects during the Cold War. The Soviet occupation of the North from 1945 to 1948, which included direct military assistance and support from Joseph Stalin, played a crucial role in its early years as a fledgling nation. The status of the DPRK, however, differed from Eastern European countries like Poland that were completely under Soviet domination; the North could shift positions vis-à-vis the Chinese and Soviets. As both discovered quickly, neither was unable to stop the purge of Kim Il-sung's domestic opponents or his move toward a one-man Stalinist autocracy and relations. The strained Sino-Soviet relations and rivalry paradoxically offered Kim space to consolidate his power by eliminating rivals like Jo Mansik (1883–1950), whom the Soviets initially supported to run the North. Kim also purged others tied to the Soviet faction—members from the South Korean Workers' Party, who were mostly Communists who had arrived from the South; and the Yenan faction, a group of pro-China Communists who endorsed Nikita Khrushchev's revisionist line in criticizing Stalin. It was during the purges of the Yenan faction that Kim began to push his *juche* (self-reliance) ideology and cult of personality while preventing any groups from advocating de-Stalinization.

North Korea's successful postwar reconstruction, which surpassed South Korea's economic development until the early 1970s, was due partly to the fraternal support of Socialist countries and partly to domestic ideologies that stressed self-reliance, hard work, and responsibility. In 1953, Kim Il-sung led a delegation to Moscow to settle the terms of assistance. The Soviets, who were still recovering from World War II, agreed to cancel repayment of North Korea's outstanding debts and offered one billion rubles in outright aid, both monetary and in the form of industrial equipment and consumer goods. Soviet technicians soon arrived in North Korea to help with the rehabilitation efforts. Kim also visited Beijing in November 1958 shortly after the withdrawal of thousands of Chinese troops who had remained in the North after the war to help provide human resources for rebuilding its war-torn infrastructure. He successfully received equally generous pledges from Mao Zedong as China canceled North Korea's debts, mostly incurred from the war, and offered 800 million *yuan* between 1954 and 1957, reflecting the Chinese interest in competing with the Soviet Union for influence in North Korea.

Pyeongyang also received aid from the Mongolian People's Republic, which sent some 86,500 head of livestock. East Germany, the third-largest contributor of external assistance after the Soviet Union and China, played a significant role in rebuilding Hamheung (North Korea's second-largest port city) and also contributed telephones and switchboards to restore Pyeongyang's tattered communication services. For its part, Albania donated asphalt for paving roads, while Czechoslovakia provided buses. Poland built the West Pyeongyang Railway Factory, and Romania, which had taken in North Korean war orphans, volunteered to construct the Pyeongyang Central Hospital. Official visits by Otto Grotewohl of East Germany, Enver Hoxha of Albania, and Gheorghe Gheorghiu-Dej of Romania played an essential role in reinforcing solidarity between the DPRK and its allies in Eastern Europe, a historical high point of international socialist solidarity, as relations between the Soviets and the Chinese would deteriorate in the early 1960s.

Within days of the armistice, Kim began to devise a Three-Year Economic Reconstruction Plan, which he implemented in 1954. The challenges were monumental. The North's industry had sustained significantly more damage than the South's because the United States had leveled virtually all of its significant cities through aerial bombings. Most of its factories and hydroelectric dams were destroyed, transportation networks cut off, and food crops ruined by massive flooding. But by 1956, the Tass Russian Agency reported that the North had not only achieved its goal of attaining prewar output levels in state and cooperative industries, but had even overfulfilled its target, except for chemical fertilizers, carbides, and sulfuric acid. The recovery of these industrial commodities took longer because most of the factories were obliterated during the war and had to be rebuilt from the ground up. The party prioritized the development of heavy industry but also paid attention to the need to produce consumer goods, especially the textile industry.

One important ideology that Kim Il-sung articulated during the early recovery period was *juche*, which was first advanced as a slogan on December 28, 1955, in a speech titled "On Eliminating Dogmatism and Formalism and Establishing Juche in Ideological Work." While this was purportedly a critique of Khrushchev's de-Stalinization projects, Kim would later incorporate the ideas of the individual, the nation-state, and its sovereignty from Marxism-Leninism to create his version of self-reliance, emphasizing independence, national economy, and self-defense. For example, by 1949, North Korea abolished the use of Chinese characters and promoted the Korean national language, basing it mainly on the

Pyeongyang dialect and speech patterns of the working class. Kim claims to have preserved Korean traditions by converting most loan words into pure Korean words except for a few Russian loan words (in contrast to the English and Japanese words that had crept into the South Korean language).

The next Five-Year Plan of 1957–60, which continued to stress rapid industrialization, addressed the devastating damage of the war on land and agricultural infrastructure. Although the country had recovered to its prewar level of agricultural production by 1956, the party began to outline measures to modernize production by investing in large-scale construction of irrigation systems, river dams, and reservoirs, as well as machinery and fertilizer. It was also critical for the North to coordinate agricultural production with Socialist reform: under the Land Reform Act (1946), the state had confiscated all cultivated land in private ownership and began to introduce collectivized farming. By August 1958, after the integration of all individual peasant farmers into newly created collectives, the country launched a major program to expand the scale of farming through mechanization. Unlike its counterparts in the South, the North implemented progressive labor laws for women, eliminating the old family registry system based on male lineage and private property and replacing it with a nuclear family system. It also stipulated greater rights for mothers and pregnant women, such as maternity leave and other benefits. On one of his "on the spot guidance" trips to the Cheongsan-ri Cooperative Farm in Gangseo County (South Pyeongan Province) in February 1960, Kim Il-sung proposed the Cheongsan-ri Spirit and Method to guide economic management. He called on higher institutions to support lower-level organizations to promote party directives and policies. When a sense of responsibility was instilled among the workers, they would hold a stake in the management of their farm or factory. This new approach echoed the spirit of top-down and bottom-up management that had helped to bring the DPRK into existence. First employed in the agricultural sector (and later in the rest of the economy), Kim's new method facilitated the merging of the traditional village unit into a single collective in each district. The Cheongsan-ri method of management was a personalized, on-the-spot approach that required management committees to help farmers improve production through incentives and social reforms. As a result, each cooperative farm established nonagricultural institutions as well, such as state-subsidized medical services, free and secondary school education, kindergartens, and communal dining halls. This system of responsibility also helped to solve the problem of food insecurity, as it required farmers to hand over a large portion of their crops to the government, which then reallocated the surplus to urban areas. Since the 1950s, about 70 percent of the North Korean population, including the entire urban population, received food through this government-run system. Even after the state allowed peasants to cultivate private garden plots in the late 1980s, most households were dependent on this public distribution system, which allotted rations of food and other consumer goods like clothing on the basis of one's position (which is semihereditary)—until the system broke down during the mid-1990s famine.

Although the North enjoyed short-term benefits from aid and trading agreements with other Communist countries, which accepted raw materials in exchange for oil and steel, it longed for greater autonomy. Kim Il-sung sought to promote greater self-reliance when he introduced a new ambitious slogan in his announcement of the first Five-Year Plan in December 1956: "Rush as the Speed of the Cheollima." The *cheollima* referred to a mythical winged horse from the Chinese classics that could travel one thousand *li* (400 km)—a symbol representing Kim's optimistic belief in the perseverance and speed of the workers to build the country in the face of impossible odds. Kim offered ideological incentives for working at a dizzying pace to rebuild the nation rather than employing rational modes of economic management, as he turned to the elaborate mechanisms of mass mobilization to galvanize a rapid economic recovery and build a state-controlled, collective economy. The Cheollima movement, which began two years before China's Great Leap Forward (1958–60), shared many of the same goals of transforming an agrarian country into an advanced industrial nation. By the end of the 1950s, the North declared that it had achieved self-reliance, a striking accomplishment compared with its southern rival, which still relied heavily on foreign assistance. Notably, all previous North Korean experiences became filtered through its narrative of self-reliance, and the role of foreign countries like the Soviets or Chinese in postwar reconstruction was rarely if ever mentioned.

The different paths of economic recovery on the peninsula cannot be explained by foreign aid alone. South Korea did in fact receive far greater assistance in absolute terms than the North, and while fraternal aid from Socialist countries was massive, diverse, and crucial, especially to the reconstruction of Pyeongyang, there were other important factors. First, the regime's ability to mobilize the North Korean population was indispensable for the success of this project. Sheer human will and mass participation were also critical to the fulfillment of the Five-Year Plan in four years. By 1960, North Korea was the second-most industrialized country in Asia next to Japan; heavy industry accounted for more than 70 percent of the North's economy, with a 20 percent annual growth rate during this period. Second, by nationalizing its industries and agriculture, the North became mostly self-sufficient in its production of food and clothing and its provision of housing for all of its citizens. Pyeongyang looked like a modern city with its major boulevards and high-rise residential buildings, accommodating various cultural facilities, statues, and public squares for leisure activities. It outpaced the South in the production of steel, machinery, mining, chemicals, and electricity. Kim attributed these successes to the Cheollima movement; for instance, he had called on workers at the Gangseon steel plant in Gangseo County to produce an extra ten thousand tons of steel at a factory with a capacity to produce only sixty thousand tons of steel. The workers doubled the steel output. Like Soviet miner Aleksei Stakhanov, who allegedly extracted 102 tons of coal in less than six hours (fourteen times his quota) in 1935 and gave birth to the phenomenon of ultraproductive Stakhanovite workers, Korean workers who surpassed their targeted goals of production received the title "Cheollima rider."

The Cheollima movement organized the labor force into work teams and brigades to compete for increased production. The campaign focused on industrial and agricultural workers as well as those employed in education, science, sanitation and health, and culture. Other work units eligible for Cheollima citations included entire factories, factory workshops, and self-contained sectors such as ships or railroad stations. To celebrate Kim Il-sung's forty-ninth birthday, the Mansudae Art Studio constructed the Cheollima Statue, which it unveiled on April 15, 1961, on Mansu Hill in Pyeongyang. The bronze sculpture, now a significant landmark in the capital city, stands at fifteen meters; a male worker raises a document from the Central Committee of the Workers' Party of Korea, and a female peasant holds a bundle of rice—both are riding the *cheollima,* symbolizing the speed and perseverance of the people.

Like the Stakhanovite phenomenon in the Soviet Union, the Cheollima movement created significant disruptions in the economy, making it necessary to set aside 1959 as a buffer year to restore balance in the economy. Although growth rates were high, state rewards for those who met production quotas often created imbalances as competition to fulfill annual plan targets led to haphazard growth when some industries performed better than others. For instance, while steel production did well, the transportation system, which enjoyed little clout, suffered bottlenecks and breakdown. The lack of coordination among sectors and regions prompted the state to introduce a one-man management system, modeled after the Soviet system, in December 1961. Under this system, large nationalized enterprises operated under the auspices of a central control to address the problem of imbalances. The Daean Work System applied agricultural management techniques (which grew out of the Cheongsan-ri method) to the industrial sector. In 1991, Kim Il-sung lauded the Daean Work System during his New Year's address for its more rational approach to industrial management—which had achieved targeted outcomes—where engineers and technical experts shouldered more of the burden in areas they could contribute to most. Although the state replaced the Cheollima movement with the Cheongsan-ri method and the Daean Work System, the North's reliance on mass ideological campaigns continued into the 1990s.

From the early days of North Korean statehood, propaganda served as an essential political tool to educate and mobilize the masses. Kim Il-sung's image as a rugged guerrilla fighter who led the Manchurian partisan struggles in the 1930s, and a paternal figure of the Victorious Fatherland Liberation War served as the model for the heroic worker, who took on a more militaristic form and nationalistic character. The establishment of the *suryeongje* (a leader dominant system) included frequent on-the-spot guidance tours by Kim Il-sung, a signature of modern pageantry, which helped to create the illusion that there were no boundaries between the country's leader and ordinary people. Prince Norodom Sihanouk of Cambodia, who spent some time in the North, observed that by showing a personal interest in the lives of workers, Kim was able to use his charismatic personality to forge relationships with the people. Visits by Kim resulted in a large number of film clips, documentaries, and statues or plaques at local sites after his visit. More importantly, while workers might have viewed a personal tour by Kim to their factory or farm as merely an acknowledgment of their service and labor, each visit played a more significant role in intensifying his personality cult and promoting a monolithic ideological system. As the state cultivated the image of Kim as a heroic fighter and father of the nation, it also developed the *seongbun* system, a new sociopolitical classification that determined one's status on the basis of the perceived loyalty of one's family to the government. Ultimately, the establishment of three groups—the core, wavering, and hostile classes—created a hereditary caste system. People closest to Kim and select anti-Japanese resistance fighters became part of the core class, while peasants, laborers, and workers stood one rung lower in the hierarchy. The bottom of the ladder included the hostile class, who were primarily Japanese collaborators, landowners, and intellectuals. Many of these were relocated to impoverished and isolated areas and relegated to work in farming, mining, and other menial occupations.

There were a few exceptions to the rules of social hierarchy. One individual who did not face charges as a collaborator despite his problematic history was the chemist Yi Seunggi. In 1939, Yi and several other scientists from Japan invented vinalon, a chemical fiber of the polyvinyl alcohol family made from limestone and anthracite, large deposits of which could be found in the North. Although he worked with Japanese scientists, Yi's development of a synthetic process for creating this polymer exemplified the key ideological platform of economic self-reliance. Yi was born in Damyang, South Jeolla Province, in 1905 and attended high school in Japan; he then enrolled at Kyoto Imperial University and graduated with a degree in chemical engineering. He worked closely with Professor Ichiro Sakurada and a team of researchers to develop and patent a water-insoluble fiber based on liquid PVA (polyvinyl acetate) solution in 1939; by the late 1940s, Japan was producing vinalon from PVA-based fibers. While it is unclear whether Yi defected to the North after serving as the dean of engineering at Keijō (Gyeongseong) Imperial University in 1945, he did enjoy a connection to Yi Jong-ok (1905–99), who became the vice president of the DPRK. The latter courted Yi Seunggi by showing him how technicians at a chemical plant were able to produce alcohol from carbide, a critical step in producing vinalon, otherwise known as the *juche* fiber. It would later become a popular choice of fabric in the North. Impressed by Yi Jong-ok's recommendation, Kim Il-sung offered Yi Seunggi a laboratory built inside a cave in Jeongsu-ri to conduct research. He started to produce vinalon products in 1954 at a chemical factory in Sakju, North Pyeong-an Province. Later, Yi oversaw the first large manufacturing complex for vinalon in Hamheung City in 1961, which was funded by Kim Il-sung himself. For Kim, the production of vinalon without significant foreign input represented the essence of *juche;* it also had useful purposes in making clothing, fishing nets, various resins, and films. Yi also allegedly produced chemical weapons in the April 25th Vinalon Factory, the February 8th Vinalon Factory, and the Suncheon Vinalon Complex. All this illustrated that in a land where self-reliance was the dominant ideology, some exceptions (very few, admittedly) could be made in a strictly hierarchical society for the good of the nation.

Standing Up to the Americans: Rikidōzan and the *Zainichi* Koreans

While Yi Seunggi was researching vinalon, another story unfolded that reflected the challenges of the North Korean diaspora in Japan. In 1952, Rikidōzan (Kim Sinrak) retired as a sumo wrestler to debut as a professional wrestler by challenging America's Bobby Burns to the ring. Rikidōzan became known as the father of Japanese professional wrestling. In the early days of television, he captured the nation's attention by humiliating American "villains," knocking them down in the ring with his trademark karate chop. He emerged as a national hero in the 1950s and early 1960s, helping to restore Japan's pride and self-esteem after its defeat in World War II. Throughout his career, Rikidōzan guarded the secret of his Korean origins, which would have subjected him to discrimination in Japan as a *zainichi* ([a foreigner] residing in Japan) Korean. He was born in 1924 as Kim Sinrak in northern Korea when it was under Japanese colonial rule. After his father's death he was adopted by a family in Nagasaki (Japan), and to protect him from any racist treatment his adoptive family changed his name to Mitsuhiro Momota. Kim joined the Nishonoseki sumo stable and debuted in 1940. Weighing over 130 kilograms, he stood out with his quickness and agility, earning him the ring name Rikidōzan, which translates as "rugged mountain road," a phrase that reflected his eight-hundred-mile trek from Nagasaki to Tokyo to become a sumo wrestler. By the age of twenty-three he was on the verge of becoming an *ozeki* (champion), when he abruptly quit sumo following a heated argument with an official over a bout in the ring. He had fought in two dozen sumo tournaments and finished with a career record of 135–82.

In 1951, after watching an American pro wrestling show in Tokyo (sponsored by the Japanese Red Cross to entertain occupying American troops), Rikidōzan and a group of professional judoka decide to transform themselves and become professional wrestlers in 1952—the year the US occupation of Japan ended. Rikidōzan worked as a construction worker to make ends meet, training in martial arts during his free time and getting into shape. He traveled to the United States in 1952 to train in Hawai'i and won his first match at the Cow Palace in Daly City, California, that summer, defeating Ike Aikens in one of the 260 matches he participated in during his thirteen-month tour. In July 1953, Rikidōzan founded the Japan Pro Wrestling Alliance (JWA) with the assistance of Nick Zapetti; in November of that year, Rikidōzan returned to Hawai'i again, where he would win an eight-man tournament to challenge Lou Thesz, the NWA World Heavyweight Champion.

The JWA also promoted a series of fights in 1954 featuring Rikidōzan, which were broadcast by Japan's national television networks. His popularity as a sumo wrestler helped him to build a strong fan base. As he clashed with the best, including a host of villainous American opponents, he gained more coverage in the press. Rikidōzan defeated "Classy" Freddie Blassie in Los Angeles in 1962 to win the WWA World Heavyweight title, making him the first Asian wrestler to win a World Heavyweight Championship. In May 1962, Rikidōzan had the opportunity to wrestle Lou Thesz, the nineteenth and final time the latter would defend his world title. Following an exciting period of success, tragedy ensued. On December 8, 1963, Katsuji Murata (a yakuza gangster) stabbed Rikidōzan in the abdomen with a urine-soaked switchblade in the men's room at a Tokyo nightclub. Rikidōzan died a week later of peritonitis at the age of thirty-nine. In the wake of his death, rumors swirled that the wrestler's ownership of hotels, nightclubs, golf courses, and apartment complexes had brought him into contact with Japanese mobsters; similarly, his association with North Korea gave rise to rumors that he had been assassinated by the US Central Intelligence Agency.

None of Rikidōzan's Japanese fans knew that he was a first-generation ethnic Korean resident in Japan; his struggles, identity, and experiences of racism were invisible to them. On January 7, 1950, the Japanese government announced a decree forcing 620,000 ethnic Koreans living in Japan to register with the government. They would lose their Japanese citizenship after Japan regained sovereignty on April 28, 1952, on signing the Treaty of San Francisco and renouncing its territorial claims to the Korean peninsula. In 1955, a law required all registered foreigners to be fingerprinted. At this time, the constitutional rights extended to non-nationals did not apply to ethnic Koreans. As a result, they faced significant discrimination, deprived of welfare benefits and civil service jobs and marginalized as second-class citizens. Their status differed remarkably from ethnic Koreans in China, for example, where the state granted them partial autonomy and the right to maintain their cultural heritage and language. To survive, Koreans who remained in Japan pursued jobs in the informal sector or engaged in illegal activities and crime while resisting Japan's naturalization system, which required assimilation and the adoption of Japanese identification. Others joined the pro-North organization Chongryeon (General Association of Korean Residents), established in 1955. Efforts to repatriate ethnic Koreans from Japan to North Korea led to the migration of more than 93,000 individuals between 1959 and 1984, lured by the promise of a better life and freedom from discrimination. This campaign also included a few thousand Japanese spouses and their children who left for North Korea.

When Rikidōzan's Korean identity was revealed in the 1980s, the memory and image of this beloved wrestler shifted. He went from being the ethnic hero of Japan to an ethnic Korean hero. For some, he represented an international figure who transcended nationality and ethnicity. In North Korea, Rikidōzan, the orphan who was later abandoned by his adoptive Japanese family at the age of thirteen, was a son of the fatherland. A North Korean biography, *I Am a Korean* (1989), attributed Rikidōzan's accomplishments to the warm care of Kim Il-sung and the Workers' Party, suggesting that the North had helped him overcome the threats of the US imperialists and Japanese reactionaries. Kim Il-sung even ordered the building of a tomb for him, even though he was buried in the Honmonji Temple cemetery in Tokyo, Japan. A North Korean children's comic book, *World Professional Wrestling King, Rikidōzan,* was published in 1995, and a fifteen-cassette video series and full-length novel on Rikidōzan's life in 2001. Rikidōzan exemplified the North's narrative of the people's bitter struggle against the oppressive forces of the world.

Yi Seunggi and Rikidōzan—both natives of North Korea—had left to live in Japan but found themselves embraced by the Communist regime, the former as a hero of North Korea's ideology of *juche* and the latter, posthumously, as a wrestling champion.

They represented the unique symbolic achievements of the North, which had struggled to recover after the devastating Korean War. Although it had initially relied on the assistance of the Soviet Union, China, and the Socialist bloc countries, the North forged its own independent economic path. Until the 1960s, the North Korean economy grew much faster than its southern counterpart. As the North stressed its nationalistic and autonomous character, it became an increasingly closed society. At the same time, it would take the valuable lessons from its recovery and seek to become the beacon to postcolonial states in Africa and the vanguard of the struggling masses of the world.

"Let's Give Up Our Freedom for a Better Life": Korea, Inc.

On November 29, 1954, the South Korean parliament passed the controversial Amendment to the Constitution by Rounding Off to the Nearest Integer to extend Syngman Rhee's presidency. The National Assembly put the bill to a vote, and support for the amendment totaled 135 out of 203 votes, one short of the two-thirds majority necessary for its passage. However, the ruling Liberal Party claimed that it had passed, arguing that 135 votes accounted for two-thirds of 203 (regardless of the math) since they had consulted with a mathematics professor at Seoul National University. On May 15, 1956, under the newly revised Constitution, the South Korean government announced that the third presidential election would take place. The constitutional amendment process reflected the corrupt political culture of South Korea. For the past decade, Rhee's extremely ruthless regime ruled the South, failing to solve Korea's economic backwardness. Park Chung-hee's authoritarian military rule followed, touting its achievement of an economic miracle (often referred to as the Miracle on the Han). Both exploited fears of a Communist threat in order to repress democracy and suppress voices of opposition at any cost.

After the Korean War, Rhee failed to bring economic or political stability to the South. Supported by the military and right-wing organizations like the White Skull Squad and Korean Youth Corps, Rhee's regime used an anti-Communist veneer to harass opposition groups and routinely arrest or execute individuals on trumped-up charges. After the controversial amendment, all the lawmakers who were against Rhee joined forces to establish the opposition Democratic Party and nominated Sin Ikhui (1892–1956) as their candidate. Meanwhile, the ruling Liberal Party, as anticipated, nominated Rhee for the presidency again. Jo Bong-am (1898–1959), an advocate of radical and egalitarian land reforms who served as the minister for agriculture under Rhee's first government, announced his presidential aspiration again with the backing of his left-leaning Progressive Party. Scholars often cite the success of Jo's land reforms as one of the factors that laid the groundwork for the economic miracle, an unprecedented transformation of Korea during the 1960s and 1970s from a rural and impoverished land into a modern and developed nation. The Farmland Reform Act, which was enacted in March 1950, allowed the government to purchase 40 percent of all arable land, which at the time was owned by roughly 3 percent of the population, and redistribute it among farmers. By 1957, close to 90 percent of the land was owned by rural Koreans, effectively dismantling the landed class, who had been the backbone of traditional Korean society for centuries.

In a terrible twist of fate, the Democratic Party nominee Sin Ikhui died of a heart attack during the height of the elections, allowing Syngman Rhee to defeat the Progressive Party's nominee Jo Bong-am, who won one third of the votes. Their histories could not have been more different. During the Korean War, Rhee had fled the capital during the northern offensive, while Jo remained behind to oversee the evacuation of the city, where he tragically lost his wife, Kim Jo-i, who disappeared during the chaos. Paranoid over his opponent's popularity, President Rhee and the Liberal Party exploited Jo's radical past (although he had publically broken with the Communists in 1946 for their lack of independence from the Soviet Union and open disregard for democracy) and the Progressive Party's calls for a peaceful reunification with the North to charge his rival with espionage. In July 1959, the Supreme Court ordered Jo's execution on charges of high treason, indicting him with making illicit contact with North Korean spies. Rhee also outlawed the Progressive Party after the trial under the New National Security Law created in December 1958, and instigated the ostracism of Jo's family. After the lifelong efforts of his daughter Jo Hojeong to clear his name, the Supreme Court exonerated Jo in 2011, describing his execution as the nation's first judicial murder. As for the vice presidential race, despite all-out efforts to rig the elections and fake the returns, the ruling liberals suffered a humiliating defeat when the majority of people cast their votes for Chang Myon (1899–1966), the leader of the New Group in the Democratic Party, putting Rhee in a very awkward position by forcing him to accept the top opposition politician as his chief deputy.

South Korean elections in March 1960 yet again exposed the corruption of Rhee and his political party. To the dismay of opposition voters, Jo Byeong-ok (1894–1960), the Democratic Party presidential nominee, died at Walter Reed Army Hospital in Washington, DC, on February 15, 1960, leaving Rhee as the only contestant in the presidential race. The government removed opposition observers at the polls, allowing the Liberal Party to manipulate the ballots freely. Not surprisingly, President Rhee won the fourth presidential election again with an implausible 88.7 percent of the votes. The blatant election fraud and, more immediate, the gruesome discovery of the body of an antigovernment high school protester floating in the sea with the shrapnel of a tear gas canister lodged in his eye shocked the nation. Protests broke out in Masan (a city in South Gyeongsang Province) over the vote rigging, which snowballed into more massive demonstrations across the country. Rhee's regime sent the Korean Anticommunist Youth Association to attack students from Seoul National University who were protesting police violence and calling for new elections to be held on April 28, 1960. The attackers met with resistance when students from the country's prominent universities joined together for a massive antigovernment protest set for the next day—better known as the April 19 Revolution. On April 25, professors of universities in Seoul issued a statement denouncing the regime. When an armed crackdown failed to subdue the demonstrations, Rhee issued a formal resignation on April 26 and went into self-imposed exile in Hawai'i, ending twelve years of dictatorship. His government handed power over to the interim government of Heo Jeong (1896–1988) for a brief time as the National Assembly voted for a constitutional arrangement that would give the prime minister full responsibility for governing the nation.

Yun Boseon (1897–1990) was elected as the next president under a new parliamentary system on August 13, 1960, with Prime Minister Chang Myon as the de facto head of state, who sought to establish a democratic government and designed the first five-year economic development plan. The toppling of Rhee's regime sparked massive demonstrations by university students and labor organizations, further fueling the fire among radical and progressive intellectuals over the issue of reunification. At the same time, North Korea began to advocate for a federation of South and North Korea and the neutralization of the entire peninsula. This idea even appealed to Senator Mike Mansfield, who argued that the United States must consider the possibility of reunifying the two Koreas in consultation with the great powers. Different student groups and leftist organizations called on Prime Minister Chang to visit the United States and the Soviet Union to discuss reunification and the permanent neutralization of the peninsula. Despite efforts by Chang's fledgling government to bring order by drafting a long-term economic development plan (which the next regime would follow), it failed to address deep-seated grievances. The military was increasingly uneasy over calls to investigate the wrongdoings of Syngman Rhee's government, which threatened to rip open painful scars. The high unemployment rates, factory work stoppages, the rise of an unruly working class, militancy of leftist groups aligned with the North, and radical vocal students seeking a North-South Student Meeting in Panmunjeom: all fueled unrest and instability.

In the predawn hours of May 16, 1961, military columns led by Major General Park Chung-hee, Kim Jongpil, Kim Dongha, and key members of the eighth class of the Korean Military Academy, who were disgruntled over corruption in the military, toppled the Second Republic and seized power in Seoul. Justifying the coup d'état as its national responsibility to crush Communist elements to restore order, the junta called for the reaffirmation of South Korea's alliance with the United States and other liberal democracies and advocated for economic reconstruction as the means to end social turmoil. While the current literature points to Park as the mastermind behind the coup, it was really Major General Kim Dongha of the Marine Corps who played the crucial role in furnishing most of the troops to take over Seoul. Both Kim Dongha and his accomplice, Kim Jongpil (1926–2018), a lieutenant colonel who served in the Army Headquarters G-2 Intelligence Section, would be forced to resign from their positions after clashing with their superiors over corruption and financial irregularities, which allowed Park to solidify his position as he imposed martial law. This forced Prime Minister Chang Myon to tender his resignation and led to the establishment of the Supreme Council for National Reconstruction, which secured plenipotentiary legislative and administrative powers. On March 24, 1962, two days after President Yun Boseon announced his resignation, the Supreme Council empowered its chairman, Park Chung-hee, to act as de facto president until the government would concede power to a civilian government. The junta had no intention of keeping its word and declared its right to participate in civilian government. Park openly doffed his military outfit and won the presidential election in 1963 as the candidate of the Democratic Republican Party.

Park's Third Republic was built on a foundation of the economy first, mobilization of the population, and the invention of a national spirit and tradition. Employing slogans like "Let's give up our freedom for a better life" or "Useless rumors harm national security," which he plastered on placards all over Seoul, Park modeled his nationalist agenda on Japan's Imperial Edict on Education issued by Emperor Meiji in 1890 to strengthen patriotism among schoolchildren. Based on his experiences in Manchuria as a soldier in the Japanese Kwantung Army, Park aimed to rule with an iron fist, melding traditional values of sacrifice, filial loyalty, and duty with strong ethnonational pageantry and patriotism. It became mandatory for citizens to pledge allegiance to the national flag and participate in anti-Communist contests while the country focused on building memorial monuments as reminders of mutual suffering and victories. The military state now centered on two institutions: the Supreme Council for National Reconstruction (SCNR) and the Korean Central Intelligence Agency (KCIA), with Park as the chairman of the first and Kim Jongpil as director of the notorious spy agency. The latter would coordinate both international and domestic intelligence activities, its primary aim being to suppress local opposition to Park's regime, monitor activities of the North, and deflect attention from reunification through social engineering—in essence, to control every aspect of life through violence and coercion.

In 1957, the United States unexpectedly announced that it was phasing out its development assistance (which effectively started to decline from 1958), propelling the South to adopt new economic plans. Park changed the country's national development policy from import substitution to export promotion based on the aspiration for national autonomy. President Park established the Economic Planning Board in July 1961 to develop a five-year Economic Development Plan, charging the new Korea Trade Investment Promotion Agency (which reported directly to the president) to oversee an export strategy. This resulted in rapid growth during the 1960s and 1970s. The plan relied on intensive government intervention to protect and promote private investment in fledgling industries in selected sectors, such as electrical and coal energy and synthetic fibers. The Central Bank came under state control, regulating interest rates, subsidizing credit, and providing special government guarantees for small and medium-sized enterprises.

Park's economic program, which sought to create vital industrial centers in several major metropolitan centers, such as Seoul, Busan, and Daegu, significantly impacted life in rural Korea. The emphasis on industry triggered significant out-migration from the rural areas during the 1960s and 1970s. As men began to migrate to the cities, older women in rural areas started to shoulder the agricultural work, resulting in the feminization of the agrarian population. More significantly, young women between the ages of fifteen and twenty-four had the highest urban migration rate of any other age group. Job opportunities were abundant in industrial cities as factories sought cheap, unskilled female laborers with flexible working hours. For example, the workers in the Peace Market in Seoul were primarily young women between the ages of twelve and twenty-four who engaged in pressing, threading, and ironing. Although city jobs paid better than rural work, remittances did not flow from urban centers to the villages.

On the contrary, rural families supported their children (mainly sons) in the cities by sending money, not only for their daily expenses but also for their education. Single female migrants, who earned considerably less than men, remitted most of their earnings to subsidize the education of their brothers in the city. When they got married, women usually left the urban workforce, not merely due to social norms but because employers used marriage as a pretext to offer lower wages, citing fears of job turnover and unreliability.

The South's prioritization of economic development and rapid urbanization was accompanied by numerous challenges. The outskirts of Seoul, which had not previously been developed for residential habitation, were now teeming with workers from the countryside. As a result, Gangnam and several northeastern regions became part of the burgeoning metropolis in 1963. The sudden population growth, which caused significant traffic congestion, overcrowding in residential areas, and the rise of many unauthorized shantytowns, led to the Basic Seoul Urban Plan in 1966. This ambitious plan aimed to disperse 60 percent of the population south of the Han River through redevelopment schemes, such as the construction of four hundred apartment buildings in 1969 alone and the building of the Hannam Bridge and the Gyeongbu Expressway to connect the city center to the new districts across the river. Impressed with the *Autobahn* during his visit to West Germany in 1964, Park envisioned a highway connecting Seoul with Busan and other cities like Daejeon and Daegu. After roughly two and a half years of construction, which included drilling twelve tunnels, 305 bridges, and 428 kilometers of paved road, Park's military engineer squads and 8.9 million people had created Korea's infrastructure with a budget of $35 million, or roughly 24 percent of the annual budget. Just like the revolutionary changes the Gyeongbu Expressway brought to Korea, the construction of the Mapo Apartments (1962), Han-gang Public Official Apartments (1966), and Citizens' Apartments (1967–70) profoundly changed the everyday lives of urbanites. The new vertical urbanity—with Western-style apartments and apartment-centered, multifamily housing complexes—gave rise to concerns about safety, privacy, and neighborly relations and created unique spatial formations like playgrounds, neighborhood parks, and parking lots that shaped daily life. In 1964, Park proclaimed the completion of South Korea's first multistory residential complex (ten six-story buildings) as a symbol of progress and affluence, but also as useful propaganda against the North. The state also passed the Building Act (1962) and the Public Housing Act (1963) to facilitate the rapid construction of buildings, and founded the Korea Housing Corporation to encourage people to move into these apartments rather than the many makeshift shantytowns located next to hillsides, which posed a significant challenge to the government's urbanization drive. Today more than half of Korean families live in apartments, leading South Korea to be called the Republic of Apartments. Despite attempts to pass strict legislation metrifying the country and banning the use of traditional Korean measurements like the *li* (393 meters) and the *pyeong* (3.3 square meters), South Koreans continued to use the old system of measurement until June 2001, while the North continues to employ the traditional method.

Urban planners continued to expand Seoul, creating new industrial centers in the outskirts of the city. By 1967, the Guro Industrial Complex housed factories in light industries such as sewing, textiles, and wigs. Jo Sehui's critically acclaimed novel *A Dwarf Launches a Ball,* published in 1978, features a site like Guro; namely, the fictional Eun-gang Industrial Complex, a group of squatter settlements and factories where female workers labored. The novel delivers a scathing critique of the tyranny of Park's regime and the reckless industrialization mounted on the backs of the most vulnerable inhabitants of the city. Their collective plight is embodied in the disfigured dwarf, whose family is evicted from their home to accommodate the forced redevelopment of the district. Today the Guro site still houses marginalized groups such as many *Joseonjok* (ethnic Korean Chinese) and other foreign migrant residents.

Concerned about the health of the workforce, military, and the nation as a whole, the regime began to implement new metrics and policies for promoting public health among the Korean population. The state became mainly preoccupied with the health of the male population, which it linked to national security. A new conscription law (enacted in 1957) required a mandatory two-year military service for all able-bodied and healthy South Korean men from ages eighteen to twenty-eight. To promote hygiene, the regime also drafted Korean doctors and advice columnists to launch a campaign urging parents to circumcise their sons during the winter break before middle school. By the 1970s, the practice of circumcision, introduced by US military doctors and accepted by a majority of Koreans, became almost universal. It evolved into a rite of passage for young boys entering middle school to participate in a "whale hunt," a play on the word "foreskin" in Korean. Newspaper columnists also encouraged urban populations to invest in childhood appendectomies and tonsillectomies, two popular surgeries in the United States among middle-class families.

The population explosion became another pressing social issue following the Korean War and rapid urbanization. Park's regime sought to lower birth rates (the total fertility rate exceeded six children per woman in the early 1950s) to promote fast economic growth and modernization. Formed in 1961, the Planned Population Federation of Korea partnered up with the state to reduce the birth rate through the provision of information, contraception, and family planning services. Aware of a successful program in Taichung, Taiwan, the government launched two pilot studies in Goyang, a rural city in Gyeonggi Province, in 1963, and Seongdong, a district in southeast Seoul, from 1964 to 1966, before implementing the program nationwide. The studies showed that the key to success was the mass mobilization of women. Family planning offered new forms of birth control technology, such as the Lippes Loop IUD (intrauterine device) in 1964. The successful distribution of IUDs can be attributed to the fact that they were free of charge and advertised widely in radio and print. The following decade, the dissemination of IUDs would be linked to the Saemaeul (New Village) movement and its ambitious program to transform rural society. Family planning clinics also offered other options such as condoms and contraceptive foam tablets. In 1966, the 3-3-35 campaign urged Korean women to have only three children, one every three years, until they reached thirty-five. By the 1970s, the slogan had changed to "Sons or daughters? Let's have two and raise them well." The United States was eager to help Korea reduce its birth rate. USAID provided mobile clinics that offered free abortions all over the peninsula, so that by 1977 there were 2.75 abortions for every live birth. Sterilization rates, which had been relatively low in the 1960s, began to rise dramatically during the 1970s as married women and men sought tubal ligations and vasectomies. This rise was attributed to a simple outpatient procedure and the tripling of payments to physicians who performed the procedure. The efforts to reduce the birth rates were so successful that by 1984 the total fertility rate (TFR) was down to 1.74; by 2005, the state began to express alarm when the TFR reached the historic global low of 1.08, well below replacement levels. In a country where antinatalist policies had long dominated, the ultralow fertility rates would demand a new approach to female fertility.

Park's government also began to address environmental problems that impacted the health of citizens, especially the unexpected plague of intestinal parasites. While Korea explored ways to send its workers abroad to labor as miners in West Germany in 1963, shocking test results found that applicants had roundworms in their stomachs, which led to the denial of work visas and a temporary quarantine. The breaking story in German newspapers embarrassed the Park regime, which was acutely conscious of poor hygienic practices among Koreans. As early as 1960, the government passed the Parasitic Disease Prevention Act. Aware of Korea's image as rural, poor, and backward, Park sought to make ascariasis (roundworms) more visible and shameful to Koreans. News stories about Koreans infested with parasites—even photographs of a nine-year-old girl with 1,063 worms—galvanized a group of scientists and activists to create a grassroots program, the Korea Anti-Parasite Eradication program, in 1964. As an agricultural nation that lacked chemical fertilizers (since most factories were in the North and had been obliterated during the war), Korea needed to do something, as farmers still used night soil, or human excrement, in the fields. A national antiparasite campaign launched in 1969 mandated that all schoolchildren bring their stool samples in small paper bags twice a year to their teachers, who in turn passed them to state laboratories for inspection. This kind of self-policing and frequent testing often induced children to offer fake samples to avoid scrutiny. As the state laboratories became more sophisticated, children who were identified as infected with parasites had to endure the humiliation of ingesting anthelminics, leading to a significant decline in the rate of infection.

Alongside these health interventions, the government imposed strict austerity measures that transformed the everyday lives of people. To discourage people from celebrating the new year twice, Park removed the Lunar New Year as a public holiday and even cracked down on mills that produced *tteok* (rice cake), the staple ingredient for the Lunar New Year soup which symbolized that a person was now a year older. Park not only wanted to decrease the consumption of rice; he also sought to limit festive events that would distract from the development of the nation. After heated polemic debates in 1985 about Park's destruction of tradition, the

National Assembly agreed to grant the people a one-day holiday again on the Lunar New Year. Additional austerity measures introduced by the Saemaeul (New Village) movement in the countryside, as well as investment in the heavy industries, also transformed how Koreans ate their meals. Established in 1968 with money from Japan, the Pohang Iron and Steel Company (POSCO), created by Park through directed funds, operated two integrated steel mills in South Korea. POSCO introduced the cutlery set, which included a pair of chopsticks and a spoon made from stainless steel; they were touted for their resistance to corrosion and staining and their durability. The use of stainless ware like rice bowls to keep rice hot for a longer time proved to be quite useful in large-scale serving operations such as factory dining halls and cafeterias. For housewives, these highly durable utensils and bowls, which did not rust or stain and proved easy to wash, were highly appealing for practical purposes, especially for the budget-conscious.

Protests against the Park regime's ruthless policies—from intrusion into everyday domestic life to repression of political speech—found expression in literature, whose authors discovered that they were not immune to the state's long arm of retribution. "Land of Excrement"—Nam Jeonghyeon's (b. 1933) short story in *Hyeondae munhak* (Contemporary Literature) in 1965—represents both an allegory of Park's brutal dictatorship and an undisguised critique of American imperialism. Nam, who first made his literary debut with his short story "Warning Zone" in 1959, was arrested for violating the Anti-Communist Law two months after the publication of "Land of Excrement." During his trial in 1966, the prosecution charged Nam with inflaming anti-US sentiments, while his lawyer protested against the draconian state censorship laws.

Despite valiant efforts by fellow writers and activists, the court found Nam guilty and sentenced him to six months in prison and a seven-year ban on publishing. Nam's other writings had brought him into conflict with the government, but it was "Land of Excrement," reprinted in the North Korean journal *Tong-il jeonseon* (Unification Front), that landed him in trouble. Written as a monologue, the story's protagonist, Hong Mansu, addresses his dead mother, who died of shame after her brutal rape by American GIs whom she had gone to welcome, carrying Korean and American flags. Mansu, whose proud lineage includes Hong Gildong (a heroic bandit with supreme intelligence and supernatural powers, often compared to Robin Hood) and a resistance fighter against the Japanese, seeks revenge not only for his mother but for his younger sister, Bun-i. Unlike her mother, who died after her rape, Bun-i continues to suffer sexual abuse at the hands of Mr. Speed, an American sergeant. While selling American goods in the black market, which his sister procures for his survival, Mansu learns that Mrs. Speed has come to visit her husband. Mansu deceptively invites the American woman to tour a mountain, where as an act of vengeance he rapes her—an eye for an eye. Disregarding its own history of sexual assault, the US military blows up the mountain with its entire arsenal, including a nuclear bomb, as retribution. In "Land of Excrement," the South is the defiled land, raped and exploited by its politicians and Americans, who have turned it into excrement. After his release in 1967, Nam once again returned to jail in 1974 after being tried by a special military committee for violating the Presidential Emergency Ordinance no. 1, which prohibited criticism of the government. The deprivation of Nam's right to free speech was one of the hallmarks of Park's regime, which relied on silencing opponents through state violence.

Two Postcolonial Paths: Self-Sufficiency and Normalization

In his speech titled "On Socialist Construction and the South Korean Revolution in the Democratic People's Republic of Korea," on April 14, 1965, Kim Il-sung outlined the fundamental tenets of *juche*, which included political independence, economic self-sustenance, and self-reliance in defense. While *juche* was just an ideal in the 1950s when the North received aid from the Soviet Union, China, and Socialist bloc countries, by the 1960s it represented the revolutionary ideology that would guide the North's global aspirations and diplomacy with the Third World. Two months after Kim's *juche* speech, South Korea signed the Korea-Japan Basic Treaty on June 22, 1965, reestablishing diplomatic relations with its former colonial rulers, and received a total of $800 million from Japan, including $300 million in grants, $200 million in Japanese government loans (both specified in the claims agreement), and another $300 million in private commercial loans. The final amount had been decided in a secret agreement between KCIA director Kim Jongpil—President Park Chung-hee's right-hand man—and Japan's foreign minister Masayoshi Ōhira in 1962. Both men went on to become prime ministers. The Japanese also offered technological and business expertise to South Korea, which helped incorporate South Korea into the Japanese economic zones. Such separate approaches to their economies set the two Koreas on divergent postcolonial paths during the age of globalization, when the world markets experienced a significant upsurge in trade. Whereas the South hitched its fortunes on the developments of the global economy and on compensation from America for its participation in the Vietnam War, the North increasingly turned inward toward self-sustainment, even as it reached out to Third World countries, which would have significant ramifications for its future.

After fourteen years of hard negotiations and intense pressure from the United States on both sides, the Japan-Korea Treaty affirmed that the government of South Korea was the only lawful government on the peninsula. It also reestablished normal diplomatic and economic relations and a generous package of grants and loans in return for a promise that South Korea would drop its demand to be compensated for Japan's colonization of Korea between 1910 and 1945. Five supplementary bilateral agreements covered specific issues: fisheries, the status of Koreans residing in Japan, property claims and economic cooperation, cultural matters, and the mechanism for settlement of disputes. The US ambassador to Japan, Edwin Reischauer, released a statement welcoming the move toward normalization of relations. But his endorsement did not quell fears among Koreans that Japan would again dominate their country, not to mention deep-rooted anger that erupted even before the signing of the treaty. Student demonstrations warned of a second Japanese takeover, while opposition leaders argued that the Dokdo (Takeshima) sovereignty issue had never been resolved during the discussions. Moreover, victims who had suffered under colonial rule—comfort women, forced laborers in Sakhalin, and Korean conscripts in Hiroshima and Nagasaki who perished during the atomic strike—never received an official apology from Japan, which they had long demanded. The Japanese government had proposed to compensate individual victims directly, but the South Korean government insisted on receiving the whole amount of grants on behalf of the victims, which it never distributed as promised.

Park, who intended to exploit the new resources to compete with Japan, recognized that he could also exploit another lucrative source of revenue for Korea—the Vietnam War. When the United States failed to garner support from its European allies for its unpopular war, the Lyndon Johnson administration looked to dependent developing countries to contribute troops. The US More Flags campaign in 1964 elicited enthusiastic support from Park, who was eager to take advantage of the opportunities for loans, subsidies, and technologies to fuel Korea's economic growth, and also the chance to build up his military-industrial complex. Park prioritized the vote on sending troops to Vietnam, which took place a day before the National Assembly passed the Japan-Korea Treaty, stifling voices that protested the sacrifice of young Korean lives for economic gain. For the United States, enlisting free-world forces in the Cold War against Communism added to its propaganda fodder.

The operative document, the so-called Brown Memorandum of March 4, 1966, defined the quid pro quo relationship between the United States and Korea in terms of economic and military obligations. Park shocked Ambassador Winthrop Brown with his expensive list of demands, which included paying for the modernization of Korea's military-industrial complex (i.e., aircraft) and the cost of troop deployment, including equipment and salaries for Korean soldiers serving in Vietnam (which exceeded anything they made at home) among other things. In total, the memorandum specified at least one billion dollars in American payments (constituting more than 3.5 percent of the South's GNP) in the period 1965–70, representing a reversal of the decline of American assistance during the early Park years. Despite Park's terrible human rights record, the United States recognized South Korea as a critical ally in Vietnam and signed an administrative agreement concerning the status of US troops in Korea (SOFA) in August 1965.

The Vietnam War generated a bonanza for Korean enterprises (especially construction companies), which received contracts to support the American war effort. The United States promised to procure as much from Korea as possible without seeking bids from other sources and offered to find new markets for Korean exports. Some 100,000 Korean civilians found employment in Vietnam performing a variety of services for the Americans. Between October 1965 and March 1973, over 300,000 South Korean soldiers fought in the Vietnam conflict as mercenaries. Some of the best Korean divisions—the White Horse Division, the Tiger Division, and the elite Blue Dragon Marine Corps—served in Vietnam, its soldiers motivated by the lucrative combat pay.

As Park anticipated, Korea's economic growth skyrocketed as a result of the windfall from America's unpopular war. By 1970, the war income had transformed Korea from an import-only country to a nation whose exports had increased some twenty-six times since 1960. While the South overtook the North in its exports, it also paid a heavy price for its involvement in a deadly war that devastated lives. Over five thousand Korean soldiers died in the nine years of fighting; some ten thousand were wounded, which included victims of the forty million liters of defoliant Agent Orange that the US military sprayed in South Vietnam. Korea also became a target of international criticism for its participation in horrific war crimes. As in the American military, Korean soldiers engaged in atrocities against civilians, perpetrating appalling massacres that are not as well known as the Mỹ Lai massacre in March 1968, one of the most tragic episodes of the Vietnam War. One such incident took place in Hà My, a small coastal settlement of Quảng Nam Province in central Vietnam, where Korean troops killed some 135 women, children, and elderly persons and bulldozed their corpses in a mass grave, later destroying the site with napalm bombs to cover up their crimes. Korean soldiers also left behind *Lai Daihan* (Vietnamese fathered by Koreans)—an unknown number who were conceived through rape. In recent years, South Korea has sought to atone for the killing of more than nine thousand Vietnamese civilians during the war. In 2018, the People's Tribunal on War Crimes by South Korean Troops during the Vietnam War, organized by Korean social groups, focused on the two most infamous massacres, in the villages of Phong Nhi and Phong Nhất, as well as in Hà My, mentioned above. Two survivors of the massacres gave testimonies during the tribunal hearings. The goal was to prepare a lawsuit against the Korean government to press for an official apology and compensation for the victims. The first citizens' tribunal has opened up fresh wounds and demanded an accounting of the decisions of the Park regime to support the American war effort in Vietnam.

Meanwhile, the North found itself becoming increasingly isolated on the international stage as relations with traditional allies such as the Soviet Union and China began to deteriorate. Nikita Khrushchev's critique of Stalin's cult of personality and desire for coexistence with the West threatened Kim Il-sung, who continued to model his regime on Stalinist norms. The North decided to focus on achieving symbolic victories on the world stage that would give it greater visibility, starting with its winning streak at the 1964 Winter Olympics in Innsbruck (Austria), the first time the North had sent thirteen athletes. Han Pilhwa (b. 1942) became the first Korean Winter Olympic medalist as she caught the speed-skating world by surprise. Standing 170 centimeters and relatively unknown in the women's field in 1964, Han gave the Russian Lidiya Skoblikova, the defending champion, a run for her money, earning the silver medal.

Two years later, in perhaps one of the biggest upsets in World Cup history, the unheralded team from North Korea (with 1,000:1 odds placed against them) stunned the heavily favored Azzurri, the Italian team, at Ayresome Park in the 1966 FIFA World Cup, by beating them 1–0 when Bak Doik scored the shocking goal. This was the first time that a nation outside Europe or the Americas had qualified past the first round of the tourney. The DPRK relished its victory over its ideological enemies in the Cold War. Propelled into the quarterfinal, the North Korean team drew a huge fan base at its training base in Middlesbrough, bringing the unlikeliest people together. Portugal, a favorite of the tourney with one of the world's greatest strikers, Eusébio da Silva Ferreira, ended North Korea's miraculous run by defeating the mighty Cheollima warriors by a score of 5–3, but only after Korea took an early 3–0 lead. Soccer commentators and fans were thoroughly impressed by the team's attack style, technical abilities, and mannerisms, which the North proudly claimed were part of the aforementioned Spirit of Cheollima, the symbol of North Korea's revolutionary spirit. The route to the quarterfinal was challenging, but it paled in difficulty to qualifying for the tourney. FIFA's decision to ban South Africa due to its apartheid regime left no slot for an African team when all fifteen eligible nations from the continent withdrew in protest, leaving Australia, North Korea, and South Korea to play a round-robin tournament in Japan. In a twist of fate, when FIFA switched the venue to Cambodia, the South Koreans withdrew for political reasons, leaving the North Koreans to play only two games, defeating Australia. Despite all odds, the squad was allowed to train at the ICI chemicals plant in Middlesbrough, which at the time had a large workforce of over thirty thousand people. While the initial crowds came out of curiosity to watch the team train, the win over the Italians led the town to admire the spirit and speed of the Cheollima warriors. Daniel Gordon and Nick Bonner captured that spirit in their documentary *The Game of Their Lives* (2002).

But the North quickly realized that sports laurels could not compete with the South's active engagement in geopolitics. Its intense militarization was a direct response to South Korea's normalization of relations with Japan and entry into the Vietnam War. In 1965, Kim Il-sung assured the Democratic Republic of Vietnam (DRV) that he was ready to send material aid, even some volunteers, to help with the war effort. The following year, a Vietnamese delegation headed by Lê Thanh Nghi arrived in Pyeongyang to arrange for the shipment of construction materials, small arms, ammunition, food, and clothing. The North then negotiated with China on the transportation of this aid. At the same time, Kim met with Leonid Brezhnev, who reported back to the Politburo in 1966 that North Korea rejected the Chinese slander that Russia had sent insufficient aid to Vietnam, and who pushed for greater protection of the DRV against bombardment. Brezhnev observed that Kim filtered all the events in Vietnam from the perspective of the DPRK's security, because of the American imperialist aggression in Asia as well as its ambitions to instigate revolutionary movements in the South. Navigating the sensitive Sino-Soviet split, the North cautiously held both countries at arm's length while maintaining a militant position against the United States. Kim saw an opportunity to conduct a proxy war against the South in Vietnam by dispatching his air force pilots to engage in air combat and by disseminating Korean language propaganda to weaken the morale of South Korean soldiers. Closer to home, Kim increased provocations across the DMZ border on the peninsula to express strong opposition to the South's involvement in Vietnam.

The year 1968 witnessed two of the most serious incidents on the Korean peninsula since the end of the Korean War. Although skirmishes had become common along the DMZ since 1967, none was more brazen than the attempt by North Korean commandos to assassinate the president of South Korea, Park Chung-hee. On January 21, 1968, a thirty-one-member commando team, disguised as South Korean soldiers and civilians, infiltrated the Blue House and came within one hundred meters of Park's residence before South Korean police intercepted them. This handpicked, special operation commando unit trained for two years and spent its final fifteen days rehearsing plans within a full-scale mockup of the Blue House. The men (also known as Unit 124) had received extensive training in infiltration and exfiltration tactics. Kim Il-sung took the gamble that the US military forces would be too preoccupied with Vietnam to take retaliatory measures. When South Korean troops arrived at the scene of the plot, a gun battle ensued that led to the deaths of dozens of South Korean soldiers and civilians and three American soldiers. A school bus also got caught in the crossfire. Twenty-nine commandos committed suicide or were killed, leaving only two survivors. One survivor found a way back to the North and later became a general. The South captured the other alive; Kim Sinjo (b. 1942) received a pardon after a year of interrogations because he had not fired his gun. Reborn, first as a South Korean citizen and then as a Presbyterian minister, Kim represented the repentant Communist who could be rehabilitated in the right environment. Decades later, President Lee Myung-bak appointed him to serve as a human rights adviser to the governing Grand National Party. The assassination attempt heightened security fears and served as a pretext for violently suppressing the pro-democracy movement. It also led to the introduction of a reserve force and military training at schools that would prepare soldiers to protect the nation, and to the creation of the 684 Corps, a special combat unit trained to infiltrate the North.

The North also felt emboldened to undertake another mission. Just two days after the failed raid of the Blue House, on January 23, 1968, a North Korean patrol intercepted the *USS Pueblo,* a Navy intelligence vessel that was engaged in a surveillance mission (tracking Soviet submarines). The North Korean navy took the ship to the port of Wonsan, where the eighty-two-man crew found themselves bound, blindfolded, and then transported to Pyeongyang. With the Tet Offensive raging two thousand miles to the south in Vietnam, President Lyndon Johnson ordered no direct retaliation, opting for secret negotiations for the release of the crew. The North Korean authorities coerced a confession and apology out of the commander and the crew under threat of torture and forced them to study propaganda materials in a compound in Pyeongyang. In August, the North Koreans staged a news conference in which the prisoners praised their captors for their humane treatment; however, crewmembers subversively inserted innuendoes and sarcastic language into their statements. Some prisoners even rebelled in photo shoots by casually sticking out their middle finger, claiming that it was a Hawaiian good-luck sign. On December 23, 1968, eleven months after the *Pueblo*'s capture, US negotiators reached a settlement with their North Korean counterparts. The United States apologized for the ship's intrusion into North Korean territory and pledged to cease such actions in the future. The North released the eighty-two crewmen at the Bridge of No Return in Panmunjeom to South Korea. The capture of the *USS Pueblo* was the most significant crisis in two years of increased tension and skirmishes between the United States and North Korea. Today the ship, which has yet to be decommissioned and remains the only US naval vessel in captivity, is still displayed proudly on the Daedong River in Pyeongyang as a tourist attraction.

Exploiting the paranoia over infiltration by the North, Park Chung-hee's regime intensified its search for Communist sympathizers, targeting antigovernment dissidents and social movements. On August 24, 1968, the KCIA unveiled what it claimed to be a severe espionage case, charging Kim Jongtae, Kim Jilrak (the chief editor of *Cheonmaek* and nephew of Kim Jongtae), and several university students with secretly establishing the Revolutionary Party for Reunification and accepting money from the North to fund the publication of Communist propaganda to help overthrow Park and form a Communist government. They had little chance for a fair trial, as their lawyers complained that they were often hindered in visiting their clients, making it impossible to mount a proper defense. The high court charged five members of this alleged organization (including Kim Jongtae and Kim Jilrak) with espionage and immediately executed them. The students also faced stiff sentences for engaging in espionage and violating the Anti-Communist Law. The trial was a warning that Park's regime would be even more vigilant than the Americans in rooting out Communist infiltrators from the body politic.

The South's obsession with Communist propaganda also concerned the Americans after four of their soldiers defected to North Korea between 1962 and 1965: James Dresnok (age twenty-one), Charles Robert Jenkins (twenty-four), Larry Allen Abshier (nineteen), and Jerry Wayne Parish (nineteen). While the motives of the latter two are unknown because they died of illness before they could tell their stories, Dresnok, a Virginia native, blamed his painful childhood, unsuccessful marriage, and fears about an impending court-martial for his decision to run across a minefield into North Korea. Jenkins, in an interview with the *New Yorker* in 2008, claimed that after ten beers he made a stupid decision, but in his memoir, *The Reluctant Communist* (2008), he also admitted that fear of being forced to fight in Vietnam was another motive.

Life in the North was more complicated than the four defectors had anticipated. They worked as English teachers, translators, and even stars who played villainous Americans in propaganda films like *Unsung Heroes*—which signaled to the outside world that they were still alive. Although the North portrayed the Americans as content and living together in idyllic conditions, in reality they chafed under constant surveillance and were forced to read and even memorize entire passages from Kim Il-sung's oeuvre. The North arranged marriages for them with foreign women who were either abducted or voluntarily came to the North. For instance, Jenkins married Hitomi Soga, a Japanese woman twenty years his junior, who was kidnapped by North Korean agents in 1978 and compelled to teach Japanese language and customs to North Korean spies. In 2004, Jenkins moved with his daughters and wife (who was repatriated in 2002) to Sado Island after the North Koreans released them. The documentary *Crossing the Line* (2006) captures their stories and includes interviews with Dresnok, who still lived in Pyeongyang with his family at the time and rejected the idea of leaving (whether voluntarily or out of coercion).

The North was quick to understand that if four white American soldiers chose to renounce their citizenship and defect to the North, aggrieved racial minorities in America might be easy to pull into its orbit. Deemed by the FBI as one of the greatest threats to the United States, the Black Panther Party, founded in 1966 by Bobby Seale and Huey Newton, represented a powerful force of resistance against segregation and racial oppression. Just like Che Guevara, who was inspired after his visit to Pyeongyang in 1960, the early Black Panthers' leader Eldridge Cleaver viewed the North as a viable alternative to China or the Soviet Union. In his personal papers, he declared that it was Kim's nation that was the first to bring the US Imperialists trembling to their knees. Drawn to Kim's ideology of *juche,* Cleaver visited Pyeongyang twice in 1969 and 1970, describing the city as an earthly paradise and the North as a vanguard of the international Communist movement for oppressed masses of the world. But Cleaver's support for the North was neither blind nor naïve, as he employed his public support as a form of protest against the policies of the American government. For its part, the North appreciated the Black Panthers' understanding of its rival South Korea as a mere puppet of the United States and regarded the radical Black group as an essential link in the worldwide struggle against American imperialism.

The North's engagement with the Black Panthers exemplified its aspiration to expand its influence more globally in the 1960s. It sponsored full-page advertisements in the *Guardian,* the *New York Times,* and the *Washington Post* to promote Kim Il-sung's ideology of *juche.* While critics mocked the North's efforts as wasteful, the DPRK not only succeeded in reaching radical groups in America but also established full diplomatic relations with over twenty nations, the majority of which were from newly independent nation-states in Africa and the Middle East. The North began to develop a more ambitious goal of engaging actively in Third World diplomacy. Buoyed by the founding of the Non-Aligned Movement in Belgrade in 1961 (spearheaded by the leaders of Yugoslavia, Egypt, India, Ghana, and Indonesia), the North felt that it was critical to address the annual Korea Question in the United Nations General Assembly. By creating a voting bloc sympathetic to the North, Kim believed that he could elicit support for reunification and the permanent withdrawal of the United Nations forces from the Korean peninsula. This was a strategic game of chess, seeking diplomatic relations with newly independent and developing world nations, to gain votes in the General Assembly. Not to be outdone, South Koreans invoked the Hallstein Doctrine—no relations with any state having relations with North Korea—to counter the North's activities. The seeds sown by the North in the 1960s would bear fruit in the 1970s, especially in countries in Africa where it sought to spread its revolutionary message.

South Korea also reached outward in its quest to develop its economy, leading to the creation of a widely flung diaspora. On December 10, 1964, some three hundred miners and nurses gathered in the hall of a mining company in Hamborn in North Rhine-Westphalia to welcome President Park Chung-hee during his state visit to West Germany. In an emotional speech, he urged his countrymen to work for the honor of the country and look to the future so that their children could live in prosperity. President John F. Kennedy's cessation of US gratuitous aid, with the offering of smaller loans, was a massive blow for the South Korean economy heavily dependent on the United States. Unable to rely on the Americans to fund his ambitious economic programs, Park planned to send Korean workers abroad to countries that suffered from labor shortages. This would solve simultaneously the problems of unemployment at home and the government's need for foreign currency, which migrant workers could send back home in the form of remittances. For the next two decades, the government dispatched workers, first to Vietnam and Germany and then Saudi Arabia during the Middle East construction boom following the oil price hikes of the 1970s.

The first country to accept South Korean migrant workers was West Germany; between 1963 and 1965, South Korea sent 3,809 miners and female nurses. By 1977, this largely overlooked group of migrants in Germany totaled 7,936 Korean miners and 10,723 registered nurses. Roughly 60 percent of them either remained abroad in West Germany or immigrated to North America. Their remittances—a total of $101,503,000—represented approximately 2 percent of the Korean GDP. Under the *Gastarbeiter* program, German employers deliberately hired only single Korean females with no children to avoid paying maternal benefits to migrant workers. Although the German media portrayed these nurses as Angels from the Land of the Morning Calm, the serene imagery masked the difficulties that Korean women faced in Germany. The work of nursing care was grueling, and the compensation was low, due not only to the specific line of work but also to discrimination. Korean nurses often worked the night shifts because they did not protest. As a general pattern about one third returned to South Korea after three years while another third traveled to other destinations including the United States. The final third settled in Germany, becoming first-generation Korean female immigrants. Those who married Korean miners complained that their husbands did not adapt to German society as well as they had; this was in part because the miners were isolated in underground tunnels for eight hours a day while nurses formed direct, close relations with German patients and made house calls in the community. Many of these nurses aspired to be like Jeon Hyerin (1934–65), an intellectual and writer who gave up studying law in Seoul to pursue a degree in German literature at the Ludwig Maximilian University of Munich from 1955 to 1959. Her existentialist works, inspired by Jean-Paul Sartre and Simone de Beauvoir, inspired and challenged many Korean nurses in Germany to pursue a different lifestyle from that in Korea, where a dictatorship controlled the lives of people. Despite her tragic suicide in 1965 at the age of thirty-one, Jeon's inner conflicts and struggles, captured in her writings, became an inspiration to many. Her essays published posthumously in 1966 would become a best seller back at home.

The first group of Korean coal miners arrived in Germany on December 16, 1963, under a miner-for-aid swap. The Korean government paid travel costs for these men while the German enterprises were responsible for wages and language training. Dispatched miners were usually better educated, with at least one in four in possession of a college diploma. A total of 7,987 men in their twenties and thirties worked in 140 coal mines across the Ruhr Valley on three-year contracts; their pay was significantly higher than in South Korea, where the per capita income stood at eighty-seven dollars. To deal with labor shortages as domestic demand for coal soared in the wake of an industrial boom, West Germany decided to hire Koreans, one of the few non-European groups permitted in the country under strict immigration laws. Mining was a hazardous enterprise, and the South Korean government estimated that some 117 Korean miners died in accidents in mine tunnels that stretched seven to eight hundred meters underground. Nonetheless, miners competed for the opportunity to work in Germany where they could earn as much as one thousand Deutsche marks, or roughly fifty thousand *won* a month—a hundred times higher than the salary of a banker or other professional in Seoul.

Throughout the 1970s, Koreans staged protests demanding the right to remain after their contracts ended. They cited their contributions to the German economy. In the end, they received permission to settle in Germany, where some miners became sailors or shop owners, for example, while others took advantage of the relatively inexpensive education system to attend German universities. Not all workers had traveled to Germany out of economic motives; at this time, Koreans held an intense curiosity and fantasy about German culture, language, and the land of Hermann Hesse and Ludwig van Beethoven. In 1973, the immigrants formed Glück Auf (Good Luck), an association that provided community and support to Korean miners who remained in Germany. As the first oil shock hit Europe, West Germany's economy suffered, and high unemployment rates led German men back to the mines, which spelled an end to the *Gastarbeiter* program in 1978.

The South Korean government's aim to earn foreign currency and relieve pressure on the domestic economy also became possible through the 1962 Emigration Act; the government encouraged emigration as part of its national development plan to secure overseas remittances as adult emigration followed the labor migration policies of receiving countries. Between 1962 and1982, out of 516,156 Koreans who emigrated to foreign countries, 416,679 selected the United States as their final destination. Latin American countries like Brazil, starting in 1962, and Argentina in 1965 attracted Korean migrants to work in agriculture. The ethnic Korean population in Iran numbered up to 25,000 in the 1970s before the revolution; the new government repatriated virtually all of them. Canada's relatively open immigration policy during the 1960s and Australia's pro-Asian immigration policy turned these countries into a popular destination for Koreans as well. What began as short-term stays frequently turned into permanent settlement in these countries.

The historic political, economic, and military relationship between Korea and the United States led to three waves of migration to America. The first Koreans landed in Hawai'i in 1903, and immigrants continued to arrive to work in the sugar and pineapple plantations until the migration ended abruptly with the Chinese Exclusion Act of 1924 (which also excluded other Asians) and with Japanese colonization. The only exceptions were some political refugees and Korean students who managed to study in the United States before World War II. Between 1950 and 1965, some fifteen thousand Koreans moved to America in the second wave, especially after the McCarran-Walter Act made Asians eligible for citizenship. This group consisted of women married to American GIs, adopted children (many of mixed-race descent), and students and businesspeople. Following the passage of the Immigration and Nationality Act of 1965 (also known as the Hart–Celler Act), the third and largest wave of Korean immigrants arrived in America. The new act eliminated separate quotas for each country and gave preference to gifted professionals, scientists, and artists as the United States sought to recruit educated experts from abroad. Another part of the law, known as the Brothers and Sisters Act, facilitated family reunification; it allowed immediate relatives of US permanent residents and citizens to join them. Importantly, relatives of US citizens were allowed to immigrate without being counted against the overall immigration quota. The act had a dramatic impact, paving the way for tens of thousands of South Koreans—particularly those from middle-class and upper-class families—to come to the United States. These numbers included doctors, nurses, scientists, and technical workers who helped to create the image of the model minority. Some immigrants sought to flee their poverty and escape South Korea's authoritarian politics and social instability.

Many educated immigrants were unable to use their professional or educational credentials, so like earlier European migrants they opened their own urban enterprises as greengrocers and dry cleaners. In Los Angeles, immigrants settled among other minorities in West Adams; due to racially restrictive covenants, they were not permitted to live elsewhere. The tight-knit Korean Presbyterian Church on Jefferson Boulevard, the crowded Olympic Market at 3122 West Olympic, as well as barbershops and bookshops turned drab stretches of Los Angeles into a veritable Koreatown. Koreans nurtured a two-generation strategy by taking their earnings and investing heavily in their children's education. Some have argued that the educational successes of the next generation contributed to the image of Koreans as a model minority, although overall statistics temper this optimistic generalization. By the 1980s, the growing prosperity in South Korea led to less-educated migrants. The 1992 Los Angeles riots sparked widespread recognition that the American Dream as it was imagined in South Korea was far too rose-colored. Racial and ethnic tensions flared up in violence, marking a turning point in South Korean emigration to the United States.

The 1962 emigration policy was successful in generating funds to finance Park's economic projects, but it also created paranoia as North and South Korea vied for influence among the new Korean diaspora communities. Rumors of North Korean operatives in West Germany, disguised as professors who were out to recruit Koreans, culminated in the East Berlin Incident on July 8, 1967. Given the freedom of mobility and access to North Koreans in Berlin, some South Koreans had reached out to obtain news about relatives who still remained in the North or to engage in cultural exchanges. These interactions provided the ideal pretext for the KCIA to fabricate a sensational spy case. Park's security forces rounded up some 194 cultural and academic figures, employing deceptive and coercive tactics, even resorting to kidnapping. Among the detained was famous composer Yun Isang (1917–95), the renowned painter Yi Eungno (1904–89), and philosopher Im Seokjin (1932–2018). Under torture and threats to family back home, they made false confessions about their espionage activities for the North. Loud outcries from prominent artists, civic groups, and even the German government did little to deter the KCIA, which abducted or forcefully repatriated from West Germany and France thirty additional Koreans (including three miners), for espionage. Three of the arrested received the death penalty, which the state eventually changed to life imprisonment. West Germany expelled three South Korean diplomats for violating its rights as a sovereign nation and seriously considered breaking off diplomatic relations. The souring of relations between the two countries contributed to a gradual decrease in the number of Korean miners and nurses who traveled to Germany for work in the 1970s.

The story of Yi Eungno captured the paranoia and fear under which Korean émigrés lived in Europe in the 1960 and 1970s. A graduate of Gawabata Art School and one of best Western painters in South Korea, Yi was appointed dean at Hongik University in Seoul; he decided to leave for France in 1958 to engage more deeply in Art Informel and European abstractionism. In Paris, this gifted artist developed a reputation for his modern painting skills using traditional Korean materials. He worked with Galerie Paul Facchetti in Paris and garnered critical global acclaim after he participated in the 1965 São Paulo international biennale. Yi traveled back and forth to East Germany to meet his son, who had been in the North during the Korean War. The Park regime charged Yi with spying for the North, pointing out these interactions as evidence of his Communist leanings. After two and a half years in a Korean jail, Yi returned to France with the support of the French government, which had advocated for his release. Despite his innocence, artists in Korea ignored him and refused to curate Yi's private art exhibition in Seoul. He mounted his exhibition in Paris instead in 1975 and became a naturalized French citizen in 1983.

In contrast, the North offered to host Yi's art exhibition in Pyeongyang, where his son resided. Yi's life as a father and artist—separated from his kin by the Korean War, and his homeland by Park's anti-Communist rampage—reflected a life torn apart by the two Koreas. In the end, the state failed to produce concrete evidence that expatriates like Yi harbored North Korean sympathies, let alone engaged in espionage. The Berlin Incident exposed Park's ruthless authoritarian tactics to the world and alienated Koreans living abroad, some of whom never returned to their homeland—like Yi, who suffered a heart attack and died without ever seeing his works exhibited in Seoul.

Choe Inhun's (1936–2013) novel *The Square* (1960) engages the trauma of national division by drawing parallels between the two Koreas, both of which have developed into repressive police states. His own biography mirrors the traumatic national separation at birth. Choe joined his family and escaped to the South on a US naval ship. Instead of finding a democratic state in the South, Choe lived under one of the most authoritarian regimes, witnessing the momentous April 19 Revolution (1960), which became the theme of his most famous work. The novel focuses on a South Korean protagonist, Yi Myeongjun, who is stunned by his father's decision to move to the North without any forewarning. Yi lives a privileged life in the home of his father's friend, a banker with two children who become Yi's bosom friends. A philosophy student, Yi conceptualizes two spaces of life: the private chamber (the mental refuge of individuals) and the square (a public forum for engagement in society that is essential for humanity). He initially believes that humanity cannot survive in a closed room, that it needs the square for a healthy, fulfilled life. Disillusioned by the cruelty of society and the South's lack of a moral compass, Yi retreats to a closed room. When his father appears in a North Korean propaganda broadcast, the authorities arrest and beat Yi mercilessly. What troubles Yi about the violence is the limitless power that the police state has over the individual. As the detective reminds him, he could kill a "Red bastard" like Yi and dump his body in some obscure place without any fear of reprisals. Yi flees north, only to discover that the North is just an "ash-grey republic," devoid of its blood-red revolutionary passion. The North was just another form of corrupt dictatorship supported by mindless citizens. Yi is forced to join the northern army when the Korean War breaks out, and he finds himself once again a prisoner. At the end of the novel, Yi decides to return neither to the North nor the South but rather to live in a neutral state, a space where empty ideology and brute force do not govern people's lives. Unable to find such a place, Yi's only option is to commit suicide. It is an indictment of the two Koreas, where dictatorship and repression of dissent kill the best of the young.

3 *Sex, Hair, and Flower Power*

The 1970s

The 1970s have often been depicted as the dark age for democracy in Korea. In the South, the military regime's intrusive regulation of daily life—from strict surveillance over women's clothing to nightly curfews and social purification campaigns—created an atmosphere of repression. At the same time, this could not impede the emergence of a dynamic urban culture and unorthodox religious and social movements. This period saw the rise of the notorious camptowns, where American soldiers and Korean prostitutes intermingled. These colonized spaces continually reminded Koreans that the women and land of Korea were spoils of war for American consumption and entertainment. The South also worked with diasporic groups to corner the market for wigs and beauty supplies in urban America. The North, in contrast, sought to showcase its selfless ideals, primarily through the media of film, while attempting to spread its ideals to Europe and Africa.

Social Purification and Unorthodox Movements

On December 5, 1975, the Seoul Metropolitan Police arrested Sin Junghyeon (b. 1938), known today as the godfather of Korean rock

FIGURE 4. South Korean container freighter in the North Sea.

music, for possession of marijuana. Sin listened to American pop music on a homemade radio, learning various genres from blues to psychedelic music on the American Forces Korea Network (AFKN). His debut in a variety show was at the US Eighth Army base in 1957. In 1972, at the height of his singing career, the President's Office asked Sin to pen an ode to President Park Chung-hee and his ruling Republican Party. When Sin refused the dictator's request, the South Korean music industry blacklisted him and banned his songs, including his "Beautiful Girl." Before his arrest, he wrote an article in the popular weekly magazine *Sunday Seoul* in 1973 about his experience smoking marijuana, which he claimed hurt his head. The state declared that his music—like all pop music—was a menace to South Korean decency and morality. Park's regime became suspicious of the effects of "happy smoke," an integral part of the youth and radical culture. He had already imposed curfews and regulations on hairstyles, outfits, and even white rice consumption; censorship and control over various forms of entertainment also became the norm. Korean-grown weed remained an outlier; it was

FIGURE 5. Monument of Father and Son (Pyeongyang).

still unregulated. During his four months in prison, Sin was forced to cut his hair, was subjected to waterboarding, and later sent to a mental institution. The government-controlled press smeared his reputation, calling him a degenerate and a drug addict. When Sin was finally released from the psychiatric ward, the government banned him from performing music for life. The arrest of Sin symbolized the regime's obsession with control, especially any form of unorthodox expression or movement that threatened the state.

Historians have characterized the 1970s as a decade of pivotal change in world history: the decade of detente, a shift from postwar economic policies to neoliberalism, the flowering of progressive values and the feminist movement, and more. But for South Koreans, the 1970s were defined by the Yushin Constitution, which granted Park broad dictatorial powers with no limits on reelection. He implemented the Declaration of the State of National Emergency and the Martial Law Decree on October 17,

1972, which banned all assemblies and demonstrations for political activities. It also restricted speeches, publications, the press, and broadcasts, further limiting the media's ability to provide unbiased news coverage. The Yushin constitution, coincidentally enacted on the same day as North Korea's Socialist constitution on December 27, 1972, declared that the freedom of speech could be restricted when deemed necessary. This allowed Park to ban all activities of the National Federation of Democratic Youths and Students, a group that Park's government declared to be illegal for its anti-establishment stance and for allegedly being controlled by North Korea.

Under this draconian system, Park also sought to purify Korean pop music as part of his effort to create a healthy society. Like Sin, famous trot singers Nam Jin (b. 1946) and Na Hun-a (b. 1950) found themselves banned from television when the Song Clean-Up Campaign classified trot as a remnant of Japanese enka. Introduced during the colonial occupation as music for the urban elite, trot was used by the Japanese in military songs produced during World War II to spread its propaganda. The music featured a two-part structure with a downbeat and backbeat. Na Hun-a, the King of Trot, was primarily responsible for its final adoption into Korean culture with new time signatures (like the three-part time that emulated Korean folk music) and the replacement of the minor pentatonic scale used by the Japanese with a major heptatonic scale. According to some scholars, trot inaugurated Korean pop music. Even after liberation from Japan, trot remained immensely popular in Korea. Na Hun-a's "The Hometown Station" was the iconic song of the early 1970s, whose lyrics now reflected the everyday experiences of ordinary people, such as romance, friendship, and the occasional reference to one's hometown. For middle-aged

Koreans, trot was a nostalgic reminder of their youth, the music that had comforted them during the Korean War. The most popular song banned by the government for being *waesaek* (Japanese influence) was Yi Mija's "Lady Camellia." The song, which had sold millions of copies, was a hit for thirty-five weeks in its heyday. Although the melody was reminiscent of Japanese enka, music lovers of the time argued that it was authentically Korean because it captured the feeling of sorrow.

Park's Song Clean-Up Campaign took place at a time when American popular music thrived in Seoul, especially in the military camptowns and on the radio. However, due in part to government repression but also to quotidian living conditions, which precluded listening to loud music, rock did not become an integral part of Korean music in the 1970s outside of small groups of urban youth. Most youths did not have access to radio as they did in the West—a critical factor that helped to popularize rock music. Instead, politicized Korean youth were drawn to folk music known at the time as *tong* guitar. In the tradition of Bob Dylan, the music was mellow, accessible, and simple, produced only with the voice and a guitar or two. Folk music provided the venue through which antigovernment youth expressed their dissent. For example, Kim Min-gi's (b. 1951) "Morning Dew"—a song full of resolve in spite of the sorrows of life's trials—was the ideal anthem for the dark days of political turmoil. "Like the morning dew after a long sleepy night," the songwriter climbs on "the morning hill to learn a little smile." Though the song contained no clear political lines, Park's censors banned it along with Kim's other songs, and he found himself under police surveillance. Another popular song was Han Daesu's (b. 1948) "To the Land of Happiness," which called on youth to forge their own path with optimism: "Come with your head up, hand in hand" to the land of happiness where the "wilderness is vast, and the sky is blue." Having traveled with his father (a nuclear physicist) to the United States, Han, who was familiar with American counterculture music, infused the free spirit and optimism of the youth into his lyrics. To censor folk songs that were so popular among dissidents, Park established the Broadcasting Ethics Commission to identify and ban subversive music. In its place, Park promoted sentimental "healthy popular music" like "My Homeland," which held little appeal for the masses.

The state also imposed nationwide nightly curfews from midnight to 4 A.M., while the so-called fashion police patrolled the streets, carrying rulers to measure the length of women's skirts and men's hair, and cited offenders for violating the Minor Offenses Act—daily outrages captured in Kim Hoseon's film *Yeongja's Heydays* (1975). Just like the model Twiggy, who rocked the Western world with her iconic style, the singer Yun Bokhui (b. 1946) created her sensation in Seoul with her bobbed hair and ultrashort A-line skirts, modeling six miniskirts created by the designer Bak Yunjeong. Korean men donned the hippie look that originated in the United States during the Vietnam War, and denim jeans came to symbolize defiance against the state among the youth. At midnight, the police set up barricades in the streets after the sounding of a siren, which contributed to the Korean "do it quickly" mentality—businessmen quickly downed bomb shots of hard liquor to sign off on deals before the start of the curfew.

In May 1970, the police arrested the poet Kim Jiha (b. 1941) after the journal *Sasanggye* (The World of Thought) published his poem "Five Bandits," a scathing critique of Park's government and his policies. Drawing on the "Five Eulsa Traitors" (those who signed the 1905 protectorate treaty turning Korea over to Japan),

Kim parodied a list of lawmakers, high-ranking officials, military generals, and owners of *jaebeol* (conglomerates), calling them the "five major bandits" who preyed on the people. Park's authoritarian regime collaborated closely with these conglomerates to push its export-oriented economic plans in exchange for concessionary loans, tax cuts, and subsidies—all at the expense of ordinary people, who were excluded from the benefits of rapid industrialization. One of the generals Kim lampooned resembled Park, a sycophant of Japan and a traitor of the worst kind. The state suspended publication of the magazine and jailed the editors and the poet Kim on charges of violating the Anti-Communist Law, even though the poem had nothing to do with Communism or North Korea. Like his predecessor Syngman Rhee, Park used the draconian National Security Law as a powerful ideological and institutional tool to suppress political opposition to his authoritarian regime.

The corruption captured by Kim's poem, the growing gap between the rich and poor in the urban centers, and the collapse of rural society as a result of rapid industrialization became salient themes in Korean fiction in the 1970s. For example, Hwang Seokyeong's (b. 1943) "Far from Home" examines the lives of migrant workers who labor on a land reclamation project. By the 1970s, more than 50 percent of the residents of Seoul came from rural areas, providing labor for factories in the urban centers. Unable to eke out a living on their low wages, the workers in Hwang's short story voice their grievances against their miserable working conditions. The protagonist, Yi Donghyeok, ends up being the only person on the picket line because the company hires thugs to intimidate the workers. In the final scene, Yi stands alone with a stick of dynamite strapped on his chest, representing the futile yet real conditions of laborers. Another common trope in the literature and film of this era was the "hostess," young women who migrated from the rural areas to find work, only to encounter sexual harassment and rape in the factories. Some even ended up in brothels, which is captured poignantly in Kim Hoseon's film *Yeongja's Heydays* (1975). The South Korean government regulated local prostitutes through an elaborate scheme that involved camptown installations for US servicemen and Gisaeng Tours, which catered to Japanese male tourists following the 1965 Treaty of Basic Relations. The sex industry represented the dark underbelly of South Korea's economic development, in which the state took a direct hand by encouraging prostitution and with policies to promote sex trafficking of women—all to procure a foreign currency to fund state-driven initiatives. *Yeongja's Heydays* reflects the hypocrisy of morals under the Park regime. Like many young rural migrants, the protagonist is forced to endure rape and injury at work but then is condemned for working in the sex industry.

The Future Is Now: The Southern Eccentrics, Nam June Paik, and the Reverend Sun Myung Moon

Two controversial Korean figures in the arts and religion captured the world's attention in the 1970s. In 1974, the artist Nam June Paik coined the term "electronic superhighway" and presciently envisioned a global community that would have access to videos for free in a Video Common Market. His ideas galvanized the field of telecommunications and video art, making Korea a leader in the global artist revolution. In the realm of religion, the Reverend Sun Myung Moon emerged as a popular religious cult figure, not only in Korea but also in the United States and Japan, with his unorthodox message of world peace and mass marriages. At its peak in the

1970s, Moon's Unification Church boasted more than five million followers and owned vast tracts of land all over the world, a university, and several media organizations. Korea was now linked to the most innovative art concept and popular cult religion.

Described as "the father of video art" who conceptualized the "electronic superhighway," Nam June Paik (1932–2006) was a Korean American artist born into a prominent family in Seoul in 1932 during the Japanese occupation. In 1949, he left his homeland with his family for Hong Kong and eventually settled in Japan where he studied music and aesthetics at the University of Tokyo, completing a thesis on the modernist composer Arnold Schoenberg. Paik then moved to West Germany to study modern composition at the University of Munich and the Academy of Music at Freiberg. His acquaintance with Karl-Heintz Stockhausen (an electronic music composer) and friendship with the American experimental composer John Cage profoundly influenced his career. Meeting these two figures kindled Paik's interest in the spontaneous, theatrical elements in musical performance—in part influenced by the idea of free exploration in Zen (an interest he shared with Cage). As a result, Paik was drawn to the iconoclastic Fluxus movement—a neo-Dadaist collective of artists who rejected elite aesthetics in favor of living art that collapsed the boundaries between art and life. This avant-garde movement, which revolved around Cage, valued random creativity, simplicity (but also the burlesque), and collaborations between artists. In 1962, Paik performed his "One for Violin Solo," which involved smashing a violin, a symbol of high culture and the classical composers.

Paik's artistic output was prodigious. He made his debut in 1963 at the Exposition of Music-Electronic Television at the Galerie Parnass in Wuppertal where he modified television sets (which represented a form of middle-class life) and magnets to distort the images, refusing to screen the standard broadcast. Paik sought to transcend the materiality of the televisions and emphasize the detached images and their meaning. After he moved to the United States in 1964, Paik began to engage with the New York art scene.

A pivotal moment in Paik's career occurred when he purchased his first portable Sony video camera in 1965; when he got stuck in traffic due to Pope Paul VI's procession, he proceeded to tape. Paik screened the footage that afternoon for friends in Greenwich Village—a moment that some identify as the birth of video art. He soon met the classical cellist Charlotte Moorman, who would collaborate with him on various projects. One of his legendary pieces was "Opera Sextronique" (1967), in which Moorman stripped as she played her cello. She was arrested in the middle of her performance, earning her the notorious sobriquet "the topless cellist," while Paik was labeled a cultural terrorist. In "TV Bra for Living Sculpture" (1969) Moorman donned a bra made of miniature TV sets, while in another adaption Paik built a cello out of television sets, which Moorman played in "TV Cello" (1971). With the help of the Japanese engineer Shuye Abe, he created new visual techniques on his synthesizer. Paik's work, with his focus on mass media and iconic imagery, explored the changing relationship between a complex humanity and technology.

Paik was best known for his fifty-one-video installation "Electronic Super Highway: Continental U.S., Alaska, Hawaii" (1995)—a map made of television screens playing videos representing each state, such as a clip of *The Wizard of Oz* for Kansas. America's superhighway was almost a decade old when Paik arrived in the United States, and it beckoned drivers to "see the U.S.A. in your Chevrolet." Paik—who was the first to use the title of his

installation—imagined what he called a broadband communication network that would include all forms of technology, from
audio cassettes to telex, satellites to fiber optics. His idea was a precursor to the World Wide Web. Paik also imagined a global community of viewers, what he called the Video Common Market, in
which one could disseminate videos freely. Some have seen this as
a precursor to video-sharing platforms such as YouTube. Whether
it was his incredible use of video art in "Video Fish" (1975), "Positive
Egg" (1975), "Something Pacific" (1986), or his fifty-nine-minute
political video performance "Guadalcanal Requiem" (1979), which
sought to raise awareness of the victims of the war in the Solomon
Islands, Paik's works defied borders and boundaries. He challenged
social taboos, and his revolutionary works laid the groundwork for
artists in media art today, being prophetic of how art functions in
our contemporary information age.

On the religious front, Korea became known for the charismatic
figure of Sun Myung Moon (1920–2012) and his Unification
Church—a group popularly known as the Moonies, who claimed
millions of members. In 1936, Moon claimed that he met Jesus
Christ on a Korean hillside and received instructions to establish the
kingdom of heaven on earth. His early biography could not have
predicted his life trajectory. An electrical engineering student at
Waseda University in Japan in 1941, Moon became active in the
Communist Party to fight for Korea's independence. He served a
five-year sentence in a North Korean labor camp for allegedly spying for the South in 1947. He escaped during a United Nations attack
and fled to Busan. In the South, Moon became an ardent anti-
Communist and advocated for reunification. His teachings on the
Cold War pitted Democracy and Communism as the final conflict
between God and Satan. In 1954, Moon founded the *Tongilgyo* (the

Holy Spirit Association for the Unification of World Christianity), calling himself the Second Messiah. Drawing on Christianity, Confucianism, Shamanism, and anti-Communism, Moon developed the Divine Principle (1957), arguing that Jesus would have married the ideal wife and created a perfect family, and giving the task of unifying all religions and societies under his personal rule, as he took a second bride, seventeen-year-old Han Hakja.

In 1971, the Reverend Moon moved to the United States and in 1972 founded the International Conferences on the Unity of Sciences to support the world's largest academic conference, which included Nobel laureates who Moon believed would help unify science and religion. Moon also established the Professors World Peace Academy in 1973 to gain access to media and university professors, and later the Assembly of the World's Religions in 1985 to promote his cult more broadly. In 1974, Moon actively supported President Richard Nixon during the Watergate scandal, extending the Unification Church into the realm of politics in the United States. Moon's conviction for tax evasion and conspiracy, which landed him in prison for thirteen months, did little to hamper the expansion of his enormous spiritual and business empire. Moon's diverse enterprises were prominent in South Korea, Japan, South America, and the United States and included newspapers like the *Washington Times* (which he founded in 1982) and Chicago-based True World Food, which supplies most of the raw fish to Japanese restaurants in the United States. Moon also held a controlling stake in the University of Bridgeport in Connecticut and owned a small arms manufacturing company, a soccer team, a ballet company, a pharmaceutical company, and various resorts. But perhaps the most famous global event was Moon's mass wedding ceremony in 1995, where he played matchmaker to some ten thousand couples of different nationalities, cultures, and languages. In one fell swoop, these couples, who did not know each other before the ceremony, tied the knot, reciting the Family Pledge that reiterated the church's core beliefs. Despite all the controversy and criticism of being a dangerous cult, Moon's church still has an estimated one million followers around the world, attesting to the tenacity of this mega institution.

Revitalization? To Saemaeul! To the World! To the Future!

On the economic front, South Korea began to industrialize rapidly, but it came at a hefty price. On November 13, 1970, Jeon Taeil (1948–70), a twenty-two-year-old textile worker at a sweatshop in Seoul and a labor activist, immolated himself at the Peace Market, demanding that management and government observe the Labor Standards Law. Infuriated by the exploitation of workers who were forced to work more than fourteen hours a day, Jeon dedicated himself to the labor movement after studying the labor laws on his own. Shocked at his self-immolation, workers and intellectuals began to forge alliances to create an energized labor movement. As a result, about 2,500 new labor unions organized across the nation in the 1970s alone. The rise of the labor movement coincided with Park's decision to clamp down on human rights. As mentioned above, the new Yushin Constitution, which empowered the president to enforce emergency measures over all matters of the state, restricted people's freedoms and rights. Emergency Decree Number Nine, in particular, curtailed dissent, banning all expressions and acts that "oppos[ed], distort[ed] and vilif[ied]" the Yushin Constitution or called for its revision. The state relied on this repressive decree to arrest many intellectuals and students, outlawing rallies and demonstrations on college campuses. Park also used his expansive powers to target the press and used special military courts to punish opponents without any due process of law. His regime announced death penalties, as in the Inhyokdang Incident (April 9, 1975). The state charged eight defendants with creating the People's Revolutionary Party, which allegedly planned to overthrow Park; the defendants were all tortured and executed in less than eighteen hours after they heard their verdict.

In tandem with the Yushin Constitution, Park launched the Saemaeul (New Village) movement in 1970 to modernize the rural South Korean economy. The goal was to bring up the standard of living in the countryside to urban standards. In his speech, Park stressed the slogan "diligence, self-help, and cooperation." Although the state touted its role in the success of the movement, it needed the participation of rural society for the plan to work. Even though the state contributed the resources, it expected each community to use them for its collective welfare; for example, 33,267 villages received 336 bags of cement gratis to construct roads, buildings, and so forth. A critical feature of the movement was the autonomy of each community to choose its leaders. These local leaders—many of whom were young and well educated—formed an essential link between state and society. Due to their close relationships with villagers, local leaders were successful in persuading them to participate in the new projects. Despite providing much-needed infrastructure—from electricity and irrigation systems to bridges and roads—reducing poverty, and improving the standard of living in certain areas, the movement failed to prevent the problem of rural flight to the cities by the youth. Likewise, as modern orange tiles replaced the traditional straw-thatched roofs and as reformers ordered the old zelkova trees, which served as guardian deities, to be chopped down, the villagers began to question the motives of the state, which had little regard for local customs and beliefs. In both the country and the city Park pushed his modernization program, driven by a single-minded desire to modernize at any cost, even the cost of human lives and cherished traditions.

Made in South Korea: Wigs, Textiles, Shoes, and Plywood

Korea's rapid economic development prompted it to look for new markets and ways to bypass American quotas that would be imposed on Korean goods. In the 1970s, Bangladesh's primary export was jute, a rough fiber made from a tropical herbaceous plant, which was used for making twine and rope or burlap sacks. On the other side of the world, clothing and textiles from South Korea began to flood the US markets, threating local industries. To protect American markets, President Richard Nixon negotiated with European leaders to pass the Multi-Fiber Arrangement (MFA), setting firm quotas on imported clothing sold to the United States. As South Korea hit its American quotas, textile companies like Daewoo sought out alternative markets. The goal was to manufacture Korean products in Bangladesh and sell them under the auspices of Bangladesh. For Abdul Majid Chowdhury, an entrepreneur in Bangladesh, this was a godsend, as a lucrative offer from Daewoo would allow him to build Korean companies to make clothes for export to the United States. In 1980, Daewoo dispatched several representatives to Bangladesh to help set up the country's first export-oriented garment factory, Desh Garments. Chowdhury also dispatched 128 workers to train at Daewoo in South Korea for six months. Today, Bangladesh is one of the world's largest exporters of apparel with more than four thousand garment factories.

Before South Korea became the leading exporter of semiconductors and cell phones, textiles along with plywood, shoes, and wigs were the pillars of Korea's exports in the 1970s, until cheap-labor countries entered the market. In 1967, South Korea became the largest exporter of plywood to North America, and by the 1970s it controlled more than half of the market as Japanese manufacturers moved to more high-tech ventures, allowing the Koreans to fill the niche. State tax relief and preferential interest rates, as well as low technological requirements and low wage costs, led South Korean manufacturers to develop a critical edge in their export drive. During the 1970s, shoemaking manufacturers set up factories in South Korea, attracted mainly by the cheap labor and production costs. Production of South Korean shoes rose from 180 million pairs in 1975 to 326 million in 1978 as brand names like Nike, Adidas, and Converse set up shop in Korea as well as retailers J.C. Penney and Sears, Roebuck. Like the MFA quota set by Nixon, the United States International Trade Commission began to restrict the number of shoes South Korea could export each year to the United States, starting in 1977.

During the 1960s, thousands of female workers stitched hair in Guro, a district of southwestern Seoul, and wigs, a state-sponsored industry, comprised roughly one tenth of South Korea's total exports by revenue. Hair cost around 7,000 *won* ($6) for 3.75 kilograms of hair in 1964, which fetched 40,000 *won* ($40) in the 1970s. One third of the wigs worn by Americans during the 1960s and 1970s came from South Korea as retail sales jumped to $500 million in 1969, and a vast majority of young women over seventeen possessed at least one wig. YH Trade, a wig company founded in 1966 with ten workers, had expanded to four thousand within four years, earning a state prize for Excellence in Exports. Korean immigrants became the conduit for selling wigs in the United States in the early 1970s to African Americans. In 1967, the Japanese invented a synthetic thread called Kanekalon, revolutionizing the wig market. Through successful negotiation, Korean manufacturers acquired exclusive rights over this material. Cheap Korean-made synthetic wigs sold for less than thirty dollars to African Americans, and YH Trade exported more than $100 million of wigs between 1965 to 1978 until it closed down the following year after the company started to lose money and clashed with labor unions.

Hyundai, Inc.

Korean industry also began to emerge as a world player starting in the 1970s. Today, Hyundai ("modernity") Group is the largest company in South Korea, with significant political and economic power. Its founder Jeong Juyeong (1915–2001) was born to an impoverished peasant family in Gangwon Province in North Korea and was the eldest of seven children. He started out doing menial labor as a stevedore at Incheon Harbor, a construction worker at Boseong Professional School, and a handyman for a starch syrup factory before landing a job as a deliveryman at the Bokheung Rice Store in Seoul. In 1937, the owner of the rice store became ill and offered the business to Jeong, a twenty-two-year-old at the time. However, this enterprise was not successful since the Japanese government monopolized the rice industry on the peninsula under its colonial rule. Jeong then decided to enter the automobile repair business, but he was unable to make any money during wartime. These early failures nonetheless provided Jeong the entrepreneurial skills and experience that he needed to begin his own business one day.

After the war, Jeong launched Hyundai and Hyundai Civil Industries, aware of the need to rebuild the nation's infrastructure. He won several government contracts to build the multipurpose dam on the Soyang River in Gangwon Province (1973), the Gyeongbu Expressway connecting Seoul to Busan (1968), and a shipyard in Ulsan (1972). Soon Jeong became the most sought-after contractor by the American military, allowing him to merge his Hyundai Civil Works Company with Hyundai Engineering and Company. In 1967 Jeong and his brother Jeong Seyeong established the Hyundai Motor Company and began assembling the Ford Cortina sedan in their Ulsan plant in 1968. As members of the first Korean company to sign an overseas assembling agreement with Ford, Jeong's engineers were able to gain the requisite knowledge and expertise in building cars. Sourcing engine and transmission parts from Ford and Mitsubishi, Jeong's engineers worked with a group of British engineers and produced the Hyundai Pony in 1976, the first mass-produced sedan designed by Giorgetto Giugiaro, a world-renowned Italian coachbuilder. In 1978, Hyundai started to ship its cars to Latin America as well as Belgium and the Netherlands, and by 1982 the Pony appeared in the UK market and then in Canada the following year. The relatively inexpensive Korean car filled a niche market for affordable sedans, selling more than 25,000 vehicles that year, a huge bonanza for the company.

In 1977, Jeong founded the Asan Foundation with a scope of activities comparable to the Rockefeller Foundation in the United States. To tout his influence, he sponsored various philanthropic and research projects, including the establishment of nine hospitals, a medical college, and Life Sciences Research Institute. By the 1990s, Jeong's conglomerate comprised more than sixty subsidiaries, from automobile manufacturing to chemicals, shipbuilding, construction, and financial services. The group would undergo significant restructuring during the 1997 Asian financial crisis but remains one of the biggest conglomerates in the world today—a symbol of Korea's rise from the ashes of colonization and war.

The Flower Girl: The DPRK and the World

In the North, filmmakers had been busy crafting their trade for the world to admire. In 1972, at the Karlovy Vary International Festival in Czechoslovakia, the film *The Flower Girl* secured the Prix Special Award from an international jury. Based on a revolutionary theatrical performance allegedly written by Kim Il-sung and produced by his son Kim Jong-il, *The Flower Girl* garnered critical acclaim at home and abroad. Choe Ikgyu (b. 1934), who would later become the head of the Ministry of Culture, was one of the finest directors in the North. As an antifeudal period piece set in the late 1920s, *The Flower Girl* has been widely regarded as an immortal classic, along with the 1968 four-hour epic *Sea of Blood*. A veritable stage director and lover of cinema, Kim Jong-il played a critical role in reshaping North Korean films. When he joined the party's Central Committee in 1964, he became involved in the arts (especially in film), and from the late 1960s he oversaw the Propaganda and Agitation Department. Kim viewed North Korean cinema and other state-sponsored art—from public spectacles to visual media—as powerful ideological tools to control and build consensus in the DPRK. Like the Soviets in the 1930s, the North Koreans learned how to exploit the emotional power of film to mobilize the masses.

Set against the brutal backdrop of a Japanese-occupied Korea during the 1930s, *The Flower Girl* follows a young woman, Kkotbun, who picks flowers on the mountain every day to sell at the market to care for her ailing, widowed mother and blind sister. Their heartless landlord harasses them mercilessly for money, driving the blind sister to sing on the street. In desperation, Kkotbun sells flowers in a nearby town, hoping to afford medicine for her mother, who tragically dies in her absence. When the landlord's wife falls ill, she blames Kkotbun's blind sister, who she believes has been possessed by her deceased mother's spirit, and tries to freeze her in the snow. When the flower girl returns home, the vengeful landlord binds her in chains. At that moment, her brother, who she assumed had perished in the anticolonial struggle against the Japanese in the Revolutionary Army, returns home to visit the family. When he realizes that Kkotbun is missing, he organizes a group of villagers to overthrow the landlord. According to Kim Il-sung, he conceptualized these powerful scenes in Jilin, China, during his anticolonial struggle in the 1930s. Only Kim Il-sung (who is never mentioned in the dialogue) and his Communist army, arriving heroically at the end of the film to liberate the village, can save the flower girl's family. The film has been so popular that a statue of Kim Il-sung with the film's cast and crew still stands near the entrance of the Pyeongyang Film Studio, and the star of the film, Hong Yeonghui, adorns the one-*won* banknote in North Korea, revered as a national hero. The film's success in the Eastern bloc and China reflected the common goals of Socialism and anti-imperialism.

Kim Jong-il, who watched foreign films in the 1960s following the collapse of the Korean film industry during the war, aspired to change North Korean cinema from its overformulaic scripts. He envisioned creating epic dramas and compelling stories that evoked strong emotional identification. In his treatise *On the Art of Cinema* (1973), Kim emphasized his seed theory, which sought to filter all artistic creation through a single ideological foundation or seed that provided the underlying ideological message. One popular genre was the heroic epic film that relied on pathos, exemplified by Kim's film *Sea of Blood,* which was based on a play that his father allegedly wrote in China as a soldier in the anti-Japanese guerrilla army. The film follows the life of the protagonist Sunnyeo and her family as they join the Communist revolution to fight the Japanese, who have inflicted countless tragedies on their lives. The film, later adapted into a revolutionary opera and a story, conveys the *juche* ideology of self-reliance through a female resistance fighter who loses her husband and child "in a sea of blood." The opera was North Korea's longest-running production, staged several thousand times and presented three to four times a week at Pyeongyang's main theater, marking a high point in North Korean artistic production, which mixed music with dance and spectacle, popular melodies with folk song, and traditional instruments with a Western orchestra. The message that oppressed people could free themselves to become the happiest people in the world (under the constant care of the party) became part of the state's propaganda scheme at home in the 1970s, but it also extended to those living in postcolonial Africa—a place where Kim's message was actively being exported.

In 1979, seven-year-old Monica Macías and her two siblings, Maribel and Paco, traveled from Malabon, Equatorial Guinea, to Pyeongyang so that her mother could have surgery. Four months later, rebel forces toppled her father, Francisco Macías Nguema, the first president of Equatorial Guinea. His nephew and successor tried and executed him, charging him with mass murder, embezzlement, and treason. In 1969, the North had established diplomatic relations with this small West African country, a year after it gained independence from Spain. Struggling with little if any support from its former colonizer, Nguema had welcomed the offers of aid from North Korea. Kim sent provisions as well as advisers from the Korean People's Army to lend military and technical assistance. The relationship between North Korea and Equatorial Guinea was not unusual; in fact, the North sought to build alliances with smaller postcolonial African countries as a strategy to spread its ideology and influence in the world. Before his death, Macías Nguema asked Kim to take care of his family—a request that Kim honored like a doting grandfather.

After her husband's execution, Monica's mother headed home to protect her eldest son, while Kim enrolled her two daughters in the prestigious Mangyongdae Revolutionary School in Pyeongyang, reserved for the children of functionaries and those in Kim's elite circles. Monica not only mastered Korean but learned how to strip, clean, and assemble a Kalashnikov rifle. She recalled in her autobiography that Kim never reneged on his pledge to his old friend to take care of his children, and treated them like family. Upon graduating from high school, she enrolled at Pyeongyang University of Light Industry and lived in a hotel that housed students mostly from China and Syria. Monica surreptitiously watched films from the United States and listened to music from South Korea that the international students had smuggled into the country. After a two-week trip to Beijing in 1988 to visit a cousin whose father was working at the Equatorial Guinea consulate, she began to field queries about her future and proposals to move to Spain, which the North Korean authorities did not prevent. In 1994, several months before Kim Il-sung's death, Monica received a plane ticket to Madrid where she and her siblings would live for ten years before moving to the United States, then to South Korea in 2007 before returning home to Equatorial Guinea. Monica Macías had spent a total of fifteen years in North Korea.

The North Korean presence in Monica's home country of Equatorial Guinea was part of Kim's vision of building solidarity with Third World countries as a bulwark against imperialism. As early as 1958, North Korea established relations with the non-Marxist Algerian National Liberation Front, which was waging war against the French. Although neither North nor South Korea were invited to the 1955 Bandung Conference, which established the foundation for the Non-Aligned Movement, the DPRK responded positively to the burgeoning Third World solidarity. With the growing visibility of the newly decolonized nations in global politics, the DPRK began to build ties to Africa and Asia, especially in countries where China had already established economic and diplomatic influence. In turn, South Korea ended its policy of maintaining diplomatic ties only with states that did not recognize the North, as the two countries became embroiled in a fierce struggle for recognition as *the* legitimate Korean government in the United Nations. By the 1970s and 1980s, hundreds of North Koreans served in numerous African countries from Benin to Ethiopia, Libya to Uganda, Zambia to Zimbabwe, and more. They went as technical experts, propagandists, agricultural engineers, and military advisers, providing economic, cultural, and military assistance on a wide scale. The DPRK also became a major education destination for students from developing African nations, and it would claim a vital role in the "south-to-south cooperation" and Non-Aligned Movement (1976). In a different arena, North Korea also began to engage with certain Western nations like Sweden, and countries with active left-wing parties such as Portugal and Denmark, as well as neutral countries such as Austria and Switzerland, to improve its economy. The North also joined several international organizations such as the World Health Organization on May 17, 1973.

The DPRK, which presented its struggle for reunification as identical to the struggle of Third World and proletarian internationalism, conducted a soft war against the South, which it denigrated as an imperial client state. On one level, North Korea directly aided some of its Third World allies by providing military training and assistance and promoted its *juche* ideology, albeit with little success. For example, North Korea supported Robert Mugabe's guerrilla forces during Zimbabwe's liberation movement. Mugabe, who visited Pyeongyang in 1980, was allegedly so impressed with Kim's personality cult that he requested training for his Fifth Brigade to eliminate his opposition, the Zimbabwe African People's Union. In 1975, during the Angolan civil war, North Korea provided military support to the National Front for the Liberation, as well as military instructors to Zaire to train guerrillas in military camps. Kim dispatched more military advisers than the Cubans to train the armed forces of many African nations; and by the early 1980s there were more than two thousand North Koreans working in Africa, whom their client states deemed "less invasive than Chinese, Cuban, or Russian advisors."

On another level, the North resorted to symbolic iconography to assert its presence. For decades, the public spaces of Ethiopia, Senegal, Zimbabwe, and elsewhere bore the signs of North Korea's soft war. From 1969, Pyeongyang's Mansudae Art Studio exported statues and other monuments, many of them free of charge, to at least sixteen African countries. These included memorials that repudiated the colonial past and Socialist realist statues of leaders who took the helm after independence. This was the same studio, founded under Kim Il-sung, that contributed 38,000 statues and 170,000 other monuments throughout North Korea. One notable structure that the North Koreans supported in Madagascar was the Iavoloha Palace, the presidential residence.

On January 10, 2001, the Gold Star Children's Press in North Korea published a comic book, *Blizzard in the Jungle,* by Jo Hakrae and Ri Jeolgeum. In this action-packed comic, a group of North Koreans and Americans are stranded in a jungle in an African country (possibly the Congo or Equatorial Guinea) after their airplane crashes. Inspired by the revolutionary ideals of Kim Il-sung's *juche* ideology, the two North Korean protagonists work collectively with the natives to lead the survivors and outwit a group of gangsters who want to snatch a briefcase containing secret documents. In contrast, the individualistic Americans selfishly break away from the group only to be devoured by crocodiles in a nearby river (probably the Congo River). While the African setting of this comic may come as a surprise to many, Kim Il-sung sought to advance his *juche* ideology in Africa as an alternative vision to the capitalist model. He desired to destroy the imperialist forces and their economic foothold around the world, encouraging dictators like Mengistu Haile Mariam from downtrodden countries like Ethiopia to reclaim their "usurped natural resources." While the search for natural resources was not successful, the DPRK offered technical assistance and machines to dig for iron ore deposits in the small town of Welga, north of Addis Ababa. They also sent a group of agricultural experts to create a substantial collective cotton farm in the fertile lower Omo Valley as well as small-scale irrigation facilities, sewage systems, hydropower stations, and even equipment to build a shipyard on the Red Sea to develop Ethiopia's fishing industry. The legacy of North Korea's presence on the African continent can still be felt today. The statues, monuments, and imperial palaces built by North Korea's Mansudae artists can be seen from Harare to Addis Ababa to Dakar. The very ambitious spirit that invested so much in the postcolonial states of Africa was the same spirit that took in Monica Macías of Equatorial Guinea and provided her shelter and education. The North wanted more than one big win in a sports game; it aspired to become the only recognized and legitimate Korea.

Reflection on the 1970s

As normalization talks between the United States and China began in earnest, the North and South also started to engage in peaceful dialogue, pledging in 1972 to seek a path toward reunification. Despite some hopeful beginnings, especially Inter-Korean Red Cross talks, several armed provocations and discoveries of infiltration tunnels would end any hope for reconciliation. The North also engaged more energetically in its campaigns to attract countries associated with the Non-Aligned Movement, using "people-to-people diplomacy," to create a bloc to support their case for entry into the United Nations. While the North attempted to package *juche* in foreign diplomacy, the ideology's lack of appeal abroad only strengthened its importance at home as the official creed for creating unity and countering the rise of the South and its industrialization program. In the South, talks of reunification with the North generated critiques of the South's rural underdevelopment, its gaps between rich and poor, and the breakdown of agricultural society under Park Chung-hee's dictatorship, while farming communities collapsed as family members left for the cities to join the new working class and urban poor. Despite strong opposition, President Park's authoritarian leadership resulted in an industrial policy aimed at developing heavy and chemical industries with a select group of conglomerates and political elites at the helm. In this system, business and political elites exchanged bribes for political favors. The Rural Revitalization Program initiated by Park in the 1970s was not about improving the quality of rural life but about cronyism. Big conglomerates like Hyundai, LG, Samsung, and Daewoo donated billions of *won* to improve their standing with the state at the expense of the people. In the diaspora, Korean artists like Nam June Paik sought to break down boundaries and barriers by experimenting with new genres; he imagined the creation of a new type of media technology where numerous television stations would challenge the monopoly of large broadcast studios but also create a two-way medium inviting audiences to participate—a utopian world that seemed so prescient of the World Wide Web today. As a new decade approached, the lessons of the 1970s propelled the two Koreas on even more divergent paths, leading the North toward isolation and the South toward greater global engagement.

4 *The Long 1980s*

The year 1980 ushered in a decade of radical transformation. In the South, the social movements that had their roots in the 1970s bloomed into maturity in this decade, generating mass protests against the military dictatorship and leading to the nation's first free elections. A few decades removed from the devastating Korean War and well on the way to becoming an economic success, the South began to confront the haunting memories of the past and the unresolved trauma of family separation. The painful division of the peninsula found expression in television, film, and the arts, which thrived during this period. The North maintained its initiatives in Africa as well as the Middle East but also became increasingly isolated from the rest of the Communist bloc. Tensions with the South worsened as a result of President Ronald Reagan's anti-Communist crusades worldwide.

The Gwangju Uprising and the Rise of the 386 Generation

In *Human Acts* (2014), Han Kang, the Man Booker International Prize winner and fictional writer, provides a haunting glimpse into

FIGURE 6. North Korean subway (Pyeongyang).

the popular uprising and violent government suppression in Gwangju. On October 26, 1979, President Park Chung-hee and his eighteen-year military dictatorship came to an end after Kim Jaegyu (1926–80), a former South Korean Army lieutenant general and the director of the Korean Central Intelligence Agency (KCIA), fatally shot Park and his security chief during an argument at a KCIA safe house inside the Blue House presidential compound. At issue was a proposed armed crackdown on the demonstrations in Busan and Masan and how to handle the opposition leaders, Kim Young-sam and Kim Dae-jung. The state violence perpetrated against the 386 Generation (people in their thirties during the 1990s, who were radicals in the 1980s, and born in the 1960s), who

FIGURE 7. South Korean subway (Seoul).

led the pro-democracy movement, was a moment brutally carved into the historical conscience of the nation.

In Han Kang's novel, set against the backdrop of a student uprising, fifteen-year-old Dongho is sent to look for his missing neighbor and ends up volunteering with two others to watch over the growing number of unidentified corpses decomposing in the municipal gymnasium, as the city has run out of coffins. In a sequence of interconnected chapters narrated by different characters (all connected to the murdered Dongho), Han delivers a shocking psychological autopsy. The brutality of the events eerily mirrors the bloodbath on Jeju Island some thirty years earlier, and the soldiers this time are seasoned Vietnam veterans who have perpetrated unspeakable violence against the Vietnamese people. Employing a second-person narrative to create intimacy and immediacy, Han makes her readers feel what it means to be the victim and the bereaved. Whether it is depicting Dongho's friend, who is also killed, or his grief-stricken mother, the novel is unsparing in its depiction of the intensity and scale of brutality and the dehumanizing impact of the repression. But equally important, Han illustrates how human beings can die for a principle, witness death, and bear the weight of grief as a survivor.

The abrupt end to Park's eighteen-year authoritarian rule led to confusion over constitutional procedures, but soon a transitional government led by Prime Minister Choe Gyuha (1919–2006) stepped in to fill the power vacuum. Chun Doo-hwan (b. 1931), a major general of the South Korean army appointed to investigate Park's assassination, exploited his charge and arrested several suspects, including several rivals. On December 12, a mere six days after Choe's inauguration, Chun engineered a military mutiny with the help of Major General Roh Tae-woo (b. 1932), the commander of the Ninth Division, and with other members of Hanahoe (Group of One), a private group of military officers; Chun then appointed himself as head of the KCIA. Under the pretext that North Koreans had infiltrated the South, Chun imposed martial law on May 17, 1980, as a means to quell demonstrations.

As the new semester began in March 1980, professors and students who had been expelled for their pro-democracy activities returned to their classes. However, students continued their activism, forming unions to orchestrate nationwide demonstrations to demand an end to martial law, to guarantee the freedom of the press, and other reforms. In response to protests across the nation, which reached their peak in early May, Chun extended martial law and deployed paratroopers to crush demonstrations in Gwangju, a southwestern city that was a hotbed of political opposition.

Ordinary Koreans who witnessed the violent crackdown on students from Jeonnam University, who were protesting the closure of their campus, joined them as the conflict escalated. To protect themselves, the protestors raided police stations to form a militia and succeeded in repelling the government forces to the suburban areas; a commune was established, which lasted from May 21 to 26. After negotiations failed, the paratroopers blocked all access and communication to Gwangju. Chun ordered troops from five divisions to conduct a violent crackdown, which resulted in a massacre of several hundred people. On May 24, the state executed Kim Jaegyu and four others for their alleged involvement in the assassination of President Park Chung-hee.

Contrary to the triumphalist narrative of the Miracle on the Han River, this horrific event galvanized the 386 Generation to become active participants in the democratic movement. There is no universally accepted death toll for the 1980 Gwangju Uprising, but the official figures released by the Martial Law Command put the death toll at 144 civilians, 22 troops, and 4 police officers, and an additional 127 civilians, 109 soldiers, and 144 police officers who were wounded. More people were massacred in Gwangju under a US-sponsored dictatorship than at Tiananmen Square nine years later in Beijing. The human acts of heroism and sacrifice in the Gwangju Communes became an important origins story for the pro-democracy movement.

Following the Gwangju Uprising, Chun Doo-hwan inaugurated his seven-year presidency as the head of the Fifth Republic, pledging to bring change and build the economy; yet his repressive measures suggested that he was no different from the previous authoritarian leaders, if not worse. He silenced his critics and banned all forms of political activities and labor strikes by immediately imposing Martial Law Decree No. 10; he arrested leaders of the Park Chung-hee regime, charging them with corruption, as well as two politicians who would be future presidents: Kim Young-sam and Kim Dae-jung. A military tribunal sentenced the latter to death on charges of treason, but petitions (e.g., by Pope John Paul II) for clemency led to the commutation of his sentence to life in prison; eventually, the government allowed Kim to go to the United States for medical treatment. Altogether, Chun banned 567 politicians from engaging in political activity until 1988.

State surveillance over public opinion became even stricter under Chun; he imposed censorship on the press and television and closed down 617 publishing companies by canceling their registrations with the Ministry of Culture. By reorganizing the KCIA into the Agency for National Security Planning (known colloquially as the *angibu,* or Agency) in 1981, the state expanded its reach beyond collecting intelligence on North Korea and became heavily invested in monitoring domestic politics, especially student activists and labor groups. The regime subjected citizens to organized state violence in the name of social cleansing, claiming that it only sought to eliminate social ills; however, the campaign targeted critics of the regime without proper warrants. Some 42,000 victims found themselves in the notorious Samchung Education Camp for "purification education."

A dictator at home, Chun nonetheless gained the confidence of his allies abroad and much of the military and business elite at home. His regime gained a boost when on September 30, 1981, the International Olympic Committee selected Seoul as the host of the 1988 Summer Olympic Games by 52 votes to 27. This decision came as a surprise to Japan, which having successfully staged the 1964 Tokyo Summer Olympics and the 1972 Sapporo Winter Games, had fully expected Nagoya to host the games. An international committee also selected Seoul for the 1986 Asian Games. To ensure the successful preparations of these two global events, Chun needed to appease his citizens after two successive illegal military coup d'états and the horrific massacre in Gwangju. Chun's olive branch took the form a large festival in Yeouido, Seoul, from May 28 to June 1 in 1981 called Gukpung 81 (Wind of the Nation) to promote Korean culture, but the public largely ignored this empty gesture. The regime also sought a safe outlet for public opinion, which took the form of the 3S Policy (Sex, Sports, and Screen)—an investment in public entertainment to deflect scrutiny from politics to popular culture. It also lifted a thirty-seven-year curfew, which contributed to the reemergence of the red-light districts and the rise of the "love hotel," a type of short-stay hotel that provided privacy for sexual activities. These so-called Parktels in Korea originated from the Hotel Love in Osaka.

In contrast to the epic films that the North promoted for its population, the South advertised a large number of B-films with sexually explicit posters and titles to draw audiences back to the movie theaters again. On February 6, 1982, Jeong Inyeop released his B-film *Madame Aema,* an erotic romance, to a packed Seoul Cinema Theater in Jongno. Inspired by *Emmanuelle,* an erotic classic from France in 1974, this was the first Korean film to be screened after the rescinding of the curfew on January 6. It inspired ten additional sequels to satisfy the insatiable appetites of male fans who could not get enough of the seductive An Soyeong, who played the lead role.

Color Television and Attempts at Reconciliation

On June 30, 1983, the Korean Broadcasting System (KBS) aired a series of live broadcasts over 138 days, featuring South Koreans who had lost family members during the Korean War. *Finding Dispersed Families* had the highest viewer ratings and resulted in the reunion of 10,189 separated families. These were the golden years of Korea's television industry with the introduction of color television in 1981, and the number of television sets in individual households increased from four million in 1978 to roughly six million by 1989.

Designed to help commemorate the thirty-third anniversary of the outbreak of the Korean War, the KBS Special Live Broadcast aired daily on channel KBS. *Finding Dispersed Families* documented reunions of long-lost relatives in almost 454 hours of live broadcasting. KBS had initially planned to mark the war anniversary with the segment "I Still Haven't Found My Family," which was broadcast on the morning program *Studio 830* on June 21, 1983. However, producers at KBS became aware of the trauma and intense longing of separated families torn apart by war: the original plan had been to feature 200 people, but when the studio received one thousand applications it decided to present 850 cases on TV. The program made a significant impact from the very beginning, as the phones began to ring incessantly and those who could not get through to the TV station came to the KBS studio in person. TV producers held an emergency meeting while the broadcast was still in progress and decided to extend it beyond its originally intended run of two hours.

Emotions ran high as family members described a lost sibling, child, or parent. In the process, a deluge of war stories poured out. On the first day of broadcasting *Finding Dispersed Families*, thirty-six people were reunited with their families—the first being Sin Yeongsuk, a forty-year-old woman who had been separated from her family in Busan during the Korean War. Her successful reunion prompted people to swarm in front of the KBS headquarters near Yeouido Plaza in search of relatives. The growing crowds required more assistance, prompting KBS to establish the Finding Dispersed Families Headquarters. The second broadcast, on July 1, introduced cases sent to nine regional branches of KBS. One woman fainted the moment she heard the voice of her older brother, from whom she had been separated for forty-two years. A brother and sister burst into tears when they recognized each other after exchanging a few words at the registration counter before they even appeared on television. But not everyone found a happy ending; the dredging up of painful memories led some to contemplate suicide when they thought about their families left behind in North Korea. Meanwhile, people outside the studio came up with ingenious ways to attract attention to their stories. One brought a goat, while another wore a gold crown; people wrote their stories on an E.T. doll or on a car—all trying hard to draw the camera to themselves. Most who appeared on the program were ordinary working- and middle-class Koreans. Unlike the wealthy who employed their resources for newspaper advertisements and phone calls to search for lost family members, the Koreans who surged into the KBS studio lacked the means or technology to do so.

Due to the dire political instability and economic deprivation of the immediate postwar decades, the state had not placed a high priority on reuniting displaced families. Moreover, technology was not accessible to most Koreans. Very few households owned television sets in the 1970s. However, during the early 1980s many households could now afford to purchase televisions of their own. Seventy-eight percent of all Korean television viewers tuned in to watch the live reunions, the highest ratings for any single show in Korean history. Applicants for the *Finding Dispersed Families* program totaled 100,952; the show broadcasted 53,536 cases, which, again, resulted in 10,189 reunions. At the Sixth World Media Conference in Cartagena, Colombia, journalists named the KBS Special Live Broadcast as the "most humanitarian program of 1983." It also received the Gold Mercury International Award. The show had such a profound impact that even US president Ronald Reagan, in his address to the Korean National Assembly in November 1983, commented on the success of the program and urged the North's cooperation. Two years after the airing, a North Korean delegation visited KBS in May 1985, culminating in the historic first South–North family reunions in September of that year. Today the archives of the KBS Special Live Broadcast *Finding Dispersed Families* comprise 20,522 records of live broadcasts by the Korean Broadcasting System.

Memories of the past war, dredged up by the KBS program, collided with the harsh reality of the North-South divide when the Soviet Union shot down a Korean Air Lines jet in September 1983 as it flew over the Pacific Ocean, killing all 269 onboard. The following month, in October, North Korea carried out a bomb attack targeting Chun Doo-hwan during a state visit in Rangoon, killing twenty-one South Korean officials and injuring forty others. Four years later, in 1987, agents bombed Korean Air flight 858 as it flew from Baghdad to Seoul, crashing in the Andaman Sea and killing all 115 passengers and crew. If the North designed these bombings to scare tourists away from Seoul's 1988 Summer Olympic Games, it would fail. However, the world also became aware of the growing civil unrest in the South, which intensified as the labor movement and student activists allied against Chun Doo-hwan's regime, culminating in the massive June Struggle of 1987 that overwhelmed the military dictatorship and led to democratic rule.

Restive Dictators: Terror at Home and Abroad

After the general elections in 1985, opposition groups denounced the Chun Doo-hwan government as illegitimate for engineering a coup and conducting a massacre in Gwangju, among other crimes. When they called for a constitutional amendment and direct presidential elections, the regime was quick to respond with violence. On January 14, 1987, Bak Jongcheol (1964–87), the president of the student council at Seoul National University, died from police waterboarding and electric shock torture when he refused to reveal the location of other activists. Despite the state's attempts to cover up the killing, a group of Catholic priests revealed the truth behind Bak's murder, sparking angry protests. Conditions deteriorated when Chun Doo-hwan passed the Measure to Protect the Constitution on April 13, 1987, and announced that he planned to hand over power to another military ruler without direct elections. Massive rallies led to the June Struggle to push for a constitutional amendment. Another tragedy inflamed the already tense mood in Seoul. On June 9, Yi Hanyeol (1966–87) collapsed after shrapnel from a tear gas grenade tore into his skull while he participated in a demonstration at Yonsei University; he succumbed to his wounds on July 5. Over 1.6 million citizens attended his funeral, which became a political spectacle of grief. In response to the brutality of the state, activists organized a national rally to banish tear gas grenades; 1.5 million people took to the streets in some sixteen cities across the peninsula. Even white-collar workers, who had remained on the sidelines, joined the protests, throwing rolls of toilet paper and voicing their support. On June 19, Chun issued orders to mobilize the army, but fearing a reprise of the violent Gwangju uprising, he rescinded them within hours. On June 26, the Great National

March of Peace took place near Gukbon (National Movement Headquarters for the Adoption of a Democratic Constitution) where over one million people in thirty-four cities participated. The police detained 3,467 protestors.

As the 1988 Olympic Games approached, Chun was increasingly reluctant to resort to violence and mar the image of his regime; he also believed that Roh Tae-woo, his handpicked candidate and the leader of the ruling Democratic Liberal Party, would win the elections because the opposition was divided. Alarmed by the massive antigovernment protests, the United States also pressured Chun to concede to the opposition's demands. Roh announced in the June 29 Declaration that the government accepted the appeals for democratization and direct presidential elections, repealing an electoral college that had indirectly elected the South Korean presidents since the Yushin Constitution in 1972. While there was just enough support among the Korean electorate for Roh to win in the first free direct presidential elections on December 16, 1987, narrowly defeating Kim Young-sam, it bears noting that he garnered only 36.6 percent of the votes. This meant that the June Struggle, a critical catalyst behind the democratization movement, had made a difference.

The June Struggle helped to remobilize the unification movement, which the military regime had repressed in the name of public security. Student activists of the University Student Council and dissidents in art, cultural, and religious circles popularized an anti-American platform that emphasized self-reliance and national unification and called for inter-Korean exchanges. Kim Junggi (b. 1966), a candidate for president of the Student Council at Seoul National University, even wrote an open letter to the students of Kim Il-sung University in which he proposed a joint march across the peninsula and hosting sports events at their respective campuses. In May 1988, Jo Seongman (1964–88), a chemistry major at Seoul National University, leaped to his death from the Myeongdong Cathedral during an event commemorating the eighth anniversary of the Gwangju uprising, urging fellow compatriots to expel the American imperialists who were responsible for national division, and to allow the North to cohost the Olympics. Before his death, Jo also called on the regime to release all prisoners of conscience and political dissidents.

Chun's rule mirrored Park, for they were of the same ilk—in a word, they were military dictators. Even as he vowed to bring democracy, Chun ruled South Korea with an iron fist, torturing and imprisoning thousands of dissidents, and he meddled in domestic politics. His draconian approach to the opposition culminated in mass protests in 1987, involving tens of thousands of civilians who protested on the streets on the eve of South Korea's Olympic debut. With the specter of a violent confrontation between the state and protestors erupting before the eyes of the entire world, Chun agreed to step down, ushering in the first free elections in the country's modern history.

Coming-Out Party: The 1988 Summer Olympics

On November 29, 1984, President Fidel Castro (1926–2016) sent a letter to Mr. Juan Antonio Samaranch, the president of the International Olympic Committee (IOC), in response to the Mexico Declaration, which sought pledges to ensure the participation of all Communist and Eastern bloc countries. The IOC did not want to see a repeat of the political boycotts of the Moscow and Los Angeles games in 1980 and 1984, respectively. While East

Germany and the USSR pledged to take part in the games, Castro, who was critical of the American military presence in South Korea, supported the North's proposal to share the games, which he believed would facilitate dialogue and peace in the divided peninsula. Two years later, on January 8, 1986, in Lausanne, North Korea requested only eleven of the twenty-three events, on the condition that the opening and closing ceremonies be held in Pyeongyang. Kim Il-sung also expressed his desire for creating a joint Olympic organizing committee and proposed fielding a united team, all of which fell on deaf ears in the South.

After winning the bid for the Olympics, Chun appointed General Roh Tae-woo to head the Seoul Olympic Organizing Committee. Employing euphemisms like city environment improvement and city beautification, the campaign cleared the slums to accommodate the expected visitors. The urban poor still rented one-story houses with cold tap water, coal briquette heating, outhouses, and public bathhouses in the 1980s. The state now needed their neighborhoods, such as Sadangdong, Mokdong, and Sanggyedong, for its massive reconstruction and forcibly evicted hundreds of thousands of residents. For three years, a young filmmaker documented the violence and human rights violations behind the so-called beautification projects in his documentary, *Sanggyedong Olympics*. Resistance was to no avail against powerful cranes that demolished homes, forcing the residents to resettle on the outskirts of the capital. Even before they could settle down, the regime tore down the new shantytowns in the dead of winter so that the foreigners would not see the urban poor along the Olympic torch route. Seoul changed almost overnight: tall office buildings sprouted in the central downtown commercial districts, and waterworks and sewage infrastructure underwent an upgrade. There was new construction on the Olympic Expressway, Olympic Park, and Athletes' Village. The Ministry of Transportation and Construction invested in a new subway line to reach the southern half of Seoul—the site of sports facilities. In the lead-up to the 1988 games, the residents of Sanggyedong fought against riot police officers and thugs hired to evict them for redevelopment.

Roh Tae-woo, who was democratically elected in December 1987 in the first free elections, declared the Olympics open to the world on September 17, 1988. The elaborate pageantry, artistic displays, modern stadiums, and Western amenities—deemed the best in Olympic history—marked South Korea's ascendancy over the North. The Chinese, who refused to join the boycott by the North, received a stirring welcome when their team entered the Olympic Stadium. For the first time, the South Koreans did not openly embrace their longtime patron, the United States; in fact, anti-American sentiment ran rampant over displays of American arrogance throughout the games. Simmering tensions exploded over NBC's excessive coverage of Korean boxing officials pummeling a referee over a disputed call, and of two American gold medal swimmers caught stealing a stone mask from the Seoul Hyatt Hotel. Behind the veneer of progress at the summer games lay the human costs of the regime's lightning reconstruction. The state extracted Seoul's "vagrants" (many of them small children) from the street after evicting them from their homes and incarcerated them in facilities like the Brothers Home, where they were abused and exploited for their labor. The police and local officials hunted down disabled people, panhandlers, the homeless, and dissidents, drafting them to work in factories or construction sites, while the owners of these institutions received citations of merit for their "social welfare programs."

The year of the Seoul Olympics, 1988, marked dramatic changes for the South as it emerged out of the shadows of war. But Korean modernization came at a high price, as captured in Bak Gwangsu's (b. 1955) directorial debut film, *Chilsu and Mansu,* in 1988. The film exposes the hypocrisy of government censorship. Loosely based on *The Two Sign Painters,* a story by the Taiwanese dissident writer Huang Chunming, whose writings were banned by Chun Doo-hwan's regime, the film revolves around the protagonist Chilsu (played by Bak Junghun), a struggling billboard painter who hails from an American military camptown. His sister labors as a sex worker for the GIs, who Chilsu expects will invite him to the United States. Struggling to eke out a living, Chilsu develops an unlikely friendship with Mansu, a very talented, intelligent, yet marginalized worker who lives under the shadow of his father, an unreformed Communist sympathizer with a history of state incarceration. Members of the working class, the two friends decide to work together painting construction projects and advertising billboards, living off cheap ramen and soju. One day, while painting a beer advertisement on a huge billboard, the friends begin to share their disdain for the wealthy, educated members of Korean society; their spouting off expletives draws the attention of police officers on the street. The film ends with a standoff leading to the death of one and the imprisonment of the other. It is a harsh indictment of the Miracle on the Han River narrative, and a backstory to South Korea's rapid development in hosting the 1988 Olympics.

The Olympics were not the only grand-scale undertaking of the South. Religion, specifically Korean Christianity, also grew exponentially, leading to the rise of megachurches that helped shape Korean culture and mores.

Assemblies of God: How South Korea Embraced Christianity

On May 15, 1958, David Yonggi Jo (b. 1936) held his first worship service in the home of his friend, Choe Jasil, who would become one of his closest associates, as well as his mother-in-law. Jo began a vigorous campaign to draw people to his church, knocking on doors and praying for the sick. Within a month, the church had grown to fifty members. Worship services moved to a tent pitched in the backyard. By 1961, Jo's church had expanded to four hundred members, leading him to purchase a small plot of land in the Seodaemun district in Seoul. Jo was the eldest of nine siblings and could only enroll at a technical trade school after his father's business went bankrupt. Passionate about learning, he learned English from American soldiers and became an interpreter for a commander at an army base near his home. At the age of seventeen, Jo contracted tuberculosis; during his recuperation, his sister's friend introduced him to the Bible, and he converted. He started to work as an interpreter for Ken Tize, whom he had met at a crusade in Busan, and he translated various Christian books. He then had a religious awakening and felt the call to study theology. After seven months of compulsory military service, he was honorably discharged, which allowed him to continue building his church, now having three thousand members. Unable to manage such a huge congregation, Jo divided Seoul into twenty cells and trained leaders to hold services in their homes. The church, which had grown to eight thousand members in 1968, now held three Sunday services. In 1973, Jo moved his church to Yeouido Island on the Han River during the height of the oil shock. Despite significant financial setbacks in construction, the Full Gospel Church was finally complete, taking up an entire riverfront block of the island, with a ten-thousand-seat auditorium. It was the largest megachurch in South Korea. The success of his church coincided with the Korean economic miracle, which shaped his theology of prosperity.

One of the distinctive teachings of Jo was his belief, influenced partially by shamanism, in the Three-Fold Blessing (the blessing of the spirit, soul, and body), which emphasized physical health and financial prosperity as part of God's will. For Jo, South Korea's rapid rise to wealth was linked to God's work; as he reminded his parishioners, God blessed his followers with material blessings. Another feature of Jo's charismatic ministry involved people speaking in tongues, falling into trances, and loudly proclaiming their desires in the belief that emotional expression would reap benefits from God. In 1981, Jo's church had more than 200,000 members and was recognized as the single largest evangelical Protestant congregation in the world, with seven Sunday services. Christian adherents in South Korea during the Conversion Boom period, especially in Protestant churches, grew from roughly six to ten million by 1989. Jo began to create satellite churches and even a television show. Jo's message of hope and monetary wealth had a particular influence on Korean mores, social organization, daily life, and culture.

Moreover, Christianity meshed well with the authoritarian regime in the South. The new factories often had chaplains, as did the military. The theological underpinnings of Korean Christianity had the regime's character; it infused Confucian ideals like hierarchy and conformity into rank-and-file structures of the church.

With the growth of the Reverend David Jo's brand of Korean Christianity, churches began to send missionaries to the United States. As recipients of USAID, Koreans felt the need to reciprocate; they would save white Americans to help America build a stronger

Christian nation—a campaign that ironically mirrored the missions of Horace Underwood and other missionaries who came to evangelize in Korea during the late nineteenth century. The University Bible Fellowship, established in 1951, became one of the largest organizations to send "tent-makers," or self-supporting missionaries, to American college campuses. The Korean missionaries did not speak English well, yet these highly educated professionals in their early thirties, taking advantage of the Hart-Celler Act, settled in large metropolitan cities like Chicago, Los Angeles, and New York to conduct their evangelism. The plan was to proselytize randomly among students whom they met on campus, to aggressively solicit meetings, and organize one-on-one Bible studies. The missionaries set quotas on the number of students they hoped to reach weekly. Given the enormous cultural and language barriers, rejection of their advances was common, but this only strengthened the resolve of Korean missionaries to work harder. One strategy to gain adherents was to open up their homes to students who needed help in math and science courses. This outreach expanded after the successful hosting of the 1988 Olympics, when the South Korean government eased restrictions on travel overseas. The engagement of missionaries with non-Korean organizations like Campus Crusade reflected a new mentalité that Koreans were no longer a people who depended on charity but instead had something unique to offer the world, especially their American patrons.

The Price of the Miracle on the Han River and the North's Isolation

Military and financial aid from the United States, and incorporation into Japan's economic networks as well as the product cycles of Japanese companies, bolstered South Korea's economic ascendancy. However, prosperity came at a high price, namely brutal repression of political dissent and exploitation of cheap labor. Korean women, who are often ignored in this narrative, played a significant role in the South's much-touted Miracle on the Han River industrialization program. Countless young women, many from the countryside, toiled for long hours while enduring extreme exploitation and sexual violence to produce cheap garments, shoes, wigs, processed food, electronics, and textiles in sweatshops and factories at places like the Guro Industrial Complex in Seoul. The roots of South Korea's democratic movement can find their origins in these factories, where female workers organized strikes to demand better working conditions and pay under Park's draconian martial law and government-controlled unions. Their protests, in turn, energized student groups to align with factory workers and participate in organizing more significant movements to overthrow the dictatorship. The first wave of men from lower classes and the countryside, who had fought in Vietnam or worked under miserable conditions in mines in Germany, returned home as another wave of male workers headed to the Middle East to work for conglomerates like Hyundai, which was financed by oil money to build infrastructure.

For the North, the impregnable self-sufficient ideal and *cheollima* work spirit, with its distribution system of foodstuffs and daily necessities and its planned economy, could not be sustained with the small amount of aid and subsidies coming from the Soviet Union and China. North Korea's economy declined as these traditional partners shifted to a market economy that was aligned more with the global economy. As North Korea's economy stagnated, it turned to Third World nations to procure hard currency by selling weapons and ammunition, and to offer instructors, often free of charge, to train foreign troops. The North would become increasingly isolated on the world stage as world events led to the fall of Communism in many countries (especially in the Eastern bloc) that had been natural allies in the past.

5   *Civilian Rule and the End of a Dynasty*

The 1990s marked a significant shift away from the Cold War in which South Korea had been embroiled since its birth as a modern state. It was also the first time that the nation elected a civilian president, ending military rule in the country. The South established diplomatic relations with China and Russia, opening its borders to ethnic Koreans to return to their homeland. The death of Kim Il-sung in the North was a watershed moment that gave birth to a new dynasty under his son Kim Jong-il. But in 1997, the North suffered a major famine that would result in widespread starvation and malnutrition, which forced it to implement economic reforms. The South also underwent a significant financial crisis that triggered massive layoffs and paralyzed its economy. These catastrophic events on the peninsula were reminders of years of deprivation after the Korean War, which remained part of the collective memory in both Koreas.

The 1990s: The Diaspora Returns Home

The year 1992 marked a historic milestone for South Korea: it was the year when diplomatic relations with China and Russia were

FIGURE 8. High-rise buildings (Pyeongyang).

established. The rapprochement with two Cold War neighbors paved the way for ethnic Koreans residing in Russia (*Goryeo saram*), the Sakhalin Islands, and China (*Joseonjok*) to return to their homelands. That year, the Los Angeles riots against Korean immigrant merchants, who endured six days of arson, looting, and civil unrest, were a sober reminder of the fragility of race relations in America, which Koreans had viewed as a land of promise.

A flurry of diplomatic activities signaled Korea's new place in the world. In June 1990, Roh Tae-woo met Mikhail Gorbachev in San Francisco, where the Soviet president articulated his desire to integrate the Soviet Far East and the Siberian region into the Asia-Pacific economy. This plan aligned with the Roh's Nordpolitik policy, which aimed to engage with Communist countries and bring North Korea out of isolation. Moreover, Roh hoped to pave the way for Korea's membership in the United Nations (which they secured in 1991) by courting the Russians, who possessed a veto in

FIGURE 9. High-rise buildings (Gangnam, Seoul).

the Security Council. One year later, on November 19, 1992, the South formalized relations with Russia by signing the Treaty of Basic Relations during Boris Yeltsin's visit to Seoul. This treaty supported bilateral ties between the two countries and established diplomatic relations between South Korea and Russia, dramatically altering the Asia-Pacific region. The rapprochement significantly lowered the possibility of direct Russian-American military confrontation. Three months earlier, the South had scored another diplomatic victory when it established diplomatic relations with the People's Republic of China, ending four decades of hostility after China supported North Korean troops during the Korean War. The joint statement called for an exchange of ambassadors and the normalization of relations, thus marking the end of the Cold War in East Asia.

The historic rapprochement between South Korea and its former enemies had a profound impact on its diasporic populations. The majority of ethnic Koreans known as *Joseonjok*

(*Chaoxianzu*) and Goryeo saram (*Koreiskii*) arrived in China and Russia, respectively, in the twentieth century during Japanese colonial rule. Some Joseonjok fled to Manchuria to join guerrilla groups whose aim was to overthrow the colonial government or organize a government in exile. The Japanese also forcibly drafted a large number of Koreans to work in their mines and factories in Manchuria during the Second Sino-Japanese War (1937–45). The Joseonjok often settled in the northeastern Chinese provinces of Jilin, Heilongjiang, and Liaoning. As a minority ethnic group in China, they were able to maintain their Korean identities in enclaves like the Yanbian Korean Autonomous Prefecture—one of five autonomous prefectures for minorities. By the end of the Pacific War, over two million Koreans lived in China. The normalization of relations between South Korea and China in the 1990s triggered the first wave of migration of Joseonjok to their homeland as migrant workers sought to pursue their Korean dream. This group included a large number of women who planned to marry Korean men, which corresponded with the South's goal of restoring ethnic homogeneity.

The other group, which referred to itself as the Goryeo saram, settled in today's post-Soviet states and comprised the largest diasporic Korean community. The name referred to *Goryeo* (and the modern exonym "Korea"), a kingdom established in 918 C.E., and *saram*, which means "people." During the colonial period, the Russian Far East and Siberia provided a sanctuary for Korean nationalists and Communists who were fleeing from Japanese authorities. Others were not so fortunate, when they involuntarily arrived in the Sakhalin Islands to serve as forced labor during World War II, which was meant to address workforce shortages in the coal mines. On April 1, 1993, the Supreme Soviet of the Russian

Federation declared that the political repression of Koreans in the Soviet Union and their forced deportation during the Great Terror under Stalin in 1937 had been illegal. The decree exonerated ethnic Koreans who had been accused of being Japanese spies. This allowed victims and their families to tell their own stories of Stalin's massive uprooting and deportation of roughly 180,000 Koreans from the Soviet Far East to the barren steppes of Central Asia. The exiles settled in Kazakhstan and Uzbekistan and established collective farms. Despite the process of Sovietization, the ethnic Koreans sought to maintain their culture. Of the approximately 500,000 ethnic Koreans in the former Soviet Union in 1992, the majority lived in the independent states of Central Asia. In general, neither the Joseonjok nor the Goryeo saram had any hope of returning to the homeland as long as the South had no diplomatic ties to China and the Soviet Union—circumstances that changed in the 1990s.

Meanwhile, the Korean diasporic community in the United States became concentrated mainly in Los Angeles, a top city of choice. Unfortunately, the community's sense of security was shattered on April 29, 1992, when a jury in a Los Angeles courtroom acquitted four police officers in the beating of Rodney King, an African American motorist whose video had sparked nationwide uproar over police brutality and racism. The police alleged that they had clocked King's Hyundai Excel by radar going over one hundred miles per hour (an almost impossible feat for a 1.5L engine hatchback), which they cited to justify their use of excessive force against King. Within hours of the verdict, the city was on fire, and it burned for days as protestors clashed with police while waves of angry mobs looted stores, stirring fear that the turmoil could spread to affluent areas like Beverly Hills. The riots exposed the social tensions between Blacks and Korean-owned businesses in low-income neighborhoods. Several weeks after King's violent beating, Soonja Du, a fifty-one-year-old Korean storeowner, fatally shot Latasha Harlins, a fifteen-year-old African American girl, for stealing a two-dollar bottle of orange juice. Du received a light sentence of probation. Du's Empire Liquor Mart had been losing money due to shoplifting by African Americans, who resented the owner for being openly contemptuous of them. The images of rioters looting and burning Du's store to the ground and of Korean shop owners brandishing firearms to protect their stores shocked Koreans back home. The weeklong violence resulted in fifty deaths, over one thousand injuries, and more than one billion dollars in damages. Korean-owned businesses suffered disproportionately; whole blocks of Koreatown ignited in flames, and Korean immigrants, who lacked any representation, felt abandoned by mainstream America. Many Korean Americans began to realize that economic success was not enough. They could no longer live in isolation but had to learn to be American and integrate into general society. Hence, after April 29, 1992, or *sa-i-gu* (4–2–9), Koreans living in the United States began to call themselves *jaemi hanin* (Korean Americans), rather than overseas Koreans, an important distinction, as Koreans began to see themselves as permanent residents of the United States rather than temporary sojourners.

Segyehwa: Civilian Rule and the Paradox of Globalization

On April 11, 1992, Seo Taiji and Boys debuted in Korea on MBC's (Munhwa Broadcasting Corporation's) talent show, performing their song "Nan Arayo" (I know) with energetic breakdance moves and synthesized accompaniments. While the trio, with their baggy jeans and baseball caps back-to-front, received the lowest rating from the jury, who found their music strange, their catchy song took Korean youth by storm, capturing the number-one spot for a record seventeen weeks. The success of Seo Taiji and Boys among teenagers shifted the focus of the Korean music industry and persuaded Yi Suman (who was heavily influenced by MTV while studying in California) to establish SM Entertainment (after his initials). He set out to create the first male idol quintet group, called H.O.T. (Hi-Five of Teenagers). Unable to form his band under Chun Doo-hwan's draconian censorship laws, Yi aspired to develop a rigorous in-house training system in his studio in Apgujeong, which included advice on etiquette and expert tips on how to deal with the media. Yi's studio was the forerunner of the ubiquitous star-making entertainment agencies scattered all over Gangnam today. In contrast to Seo Taiji's upbeat rap-rock song, H.O.T.'s "Candy" was far less edgy, yet the bubblegum-inspired pop song influenced the rise of many young boys' and girls' idol groups in the 1990s.

As the effects of globalization began to seep into Korean culture, the world of politics also began to shift. Kim Young-sam (1927–2015), a longtime opposition leader and a thorn in the side of dictators Park and Chun, garnered 42 percent of the popular vote in the 1993 election. He was the first civilian president in more than thirty years, formally marking the end of military rule. Elected on a campaign pledge to root out corruption, Kim first launched a series of investigations into the two previous military regimes for their roles in the 1979 coup d'état and the Gwangju uprising in May 1980. The Seoul District Court sentenced Chun Doo-hwan to death and Roh Tae-woo to twenty-two and a half years in prison; however, the Seoul Appeals Court reduced Chun's sentence to life imprisonment and Roh's to seventeen years. To fulfill his pledge of government transparency, Kim required all senior public officials and politicians to declare their assets (as well as those of their families), which led to the resignations of several generals and politicians and the creation of a real-name financial transactions system.

Although embarrassing scandals marred Kim Young-sam's presidency, it became best known for launching the *segyehwa* (globalization) initiative to open up trade and push for the financial liberalization of the South Korean economy. Kim's *segyehwa* policies aimed to transform the corporate cronyism and oligarchy in Korean politics (hallmarks of a developmentalist state) and promote Korea's position in the world as it emerged from three decades of authoritarian rule. Following the Asia-Pacific Economic Cooperation summit in Sydney in November 1994, Kim outlined his vision for deregulating the markets and decentralizing the role of the state, marking a neoliberal turn in Korean economics and politics. He persuaded the Organisation for Economic Co-operation and Development to admit a new democratic and prosperous South Korea as its member in October 1997.

Globalization demanded a reorganization of Korean state institutions and generated profound transformations in society. In 1994, the once mighty Economic Planning Board created under Park Chung-hee became integrated into a new Ministry of Finance and Economy, and into the Ministry of Trade and Industry. Kim argued that South Korea needed to prepare itself for global competition through autonomy and liberalization. For parents, the vague term *segyehwa* meant securing a competitive edge for their children through education. The interconnection between global and local contexts sparked an "English fever" (a term coined in the early 1990s) that pushed Korean families to send their children to the United States and Canada to receive an English-language education. The "goose father" was responsible for traveling a great distance to see his family. As passports became easier to obtain, the "early study abroad" trend became an essential educational invest-ment strategy for middle-class Korean families who aspired to raise their children as future global elites.

To his chagrin, Kim's efforts to implement a viable *segyehwa* policy collided with the global financial crisis of 1997 that sparked a series of corporate bankruptcies, beginning with Kia Motors. The crisis revealed deep structural problems in the South Korean econ-omy, especially unresolved tensions between the conglomerates, labor, and civil society. Foreign debts rose from $43.9 billion in 1994 to $158 billion in 1997; meanwhile, foreign reserves declined at an alarming rate. The reasons for the economic crisis in the South were manifold. First, businesses that had invested in Korea during its economic miracle had taken advantage of the dollar's weakness. However, when the United States began to strengthen its dollar (especially against the yen) in 1995, Korea suddenly faced a trade deficit, and its exports were no longer as profitable. Second, the conglomerates began to experience financial difficulties and accumulate enormous debts. Since the Park Chung-hee era, the Korean economy had relied on a close relationship between the state and industry; the country had backed the loans of the con-glomerates with its foreign currency reserves. Now the state was saddled with debt with a lowered credit rating from Moody's. When the Seoul stock exchange crashed, a staggering number of companies went bankrupt and laid off thousands of workers, who referred to the IMF as "I'M Fired." Finally, South Korea was not immune to the general Asian financial crisis and had to pay off short-term obligations with its foreign currency reserve, which dropped to dangerous levels.

Swallowing its pride, the South requested a bailout from the International Monetary Fund (IMF) to the tune of $55 billion. Under the terms, Kim pledged a sharp reduction in public spending, restrictions on the expansion of conglomerates, a commitment to an independent central bank, and open markets for foreign goods. It was hardly a win for Kim; the harsh terms raised the specter of Korean markets being flooded with American and Japanese products and unfair trade deficits. The business landscape changed dramatically with the takeover of many companies. For instance, in 1998, Hyundai Motor Company bought an insolvent Kia Motors, while General Motors purchased Daewoo Motors. Samsung Motors dissolved its $5 billion venture. Corporations that did survive encouraged the Korean public to donate their gold to rescue the country's economy in 1998. The national campaign inspired housewives to donate their rings, and athletes to give up their medals. All in all, the state collected three hundred kilograms of gold that year.

During the financial crisis, the South confronted a new threat to its identity. In the mid-1990s, Microsoft Corporation started to exert its dominance in the software markets. It covetously eyed the Hangul and Computer Company (later known as Haansoft), which appeared on the cusp of declaring bankruptcy because of slumping sales due to rampant software piracy and, more generally, the Asian financial crisis. On June 15, 1998, Haansoft and Microsoft Korea signed a memorandum of understanding that stipulated a buyout for $20 million and the discontinuation of its Korean word-processing software. To project a positive image, Microsoft announced a $77 million software donation to South Korean schools and institutions, in return for 19 percent of the company. The idea of a foreign company taking over the

Korean-language and word-processing market in South Korea touched a raw nerve. The backlash was immediate: a group of patriotic Korean investors and the media led a nationwide campaign to save the national language, offering Haansoft $10 million to keep the company in Korean hands rather than cede it to foreign ones. In 1998, Microsoft's $260 billion market valuation was estimated at almost the level of the entire South Korean economy ($317 billion).

Before Microsoft introduced the Korean-language version of MS Word during the 1990s, Hangul and Computer's word processor was installed in every company or government office. Before that time, the Korean language was excluded from most operating systems. A breakthrough occurred when Yi Changjin, a former mechanical engineer major from Seoul National University, displayed *hangeul* (Korean alphabet) in a word-processing program. He created the Hangul and Computer Company in October 1990 and called the Korean-language word-processing program "ARAEA Hangul." Sales reached roughly ten billion *won* (approximately five billion dollars) in 1993. Although Microsoft's subsidiary did well in selling its Windows operating system and popular programs like Microsoft Excel and PowerPoint, it did not do well in the language department. Koreans were unwilling to switch from ARAEA Hangul to Microsoft Word. Among many considerations, ARAEA Hangul could display over 11,000 combinations of the Korean language's phonetic characters, compared to Microsoft Word's 2,500. However, when Microsoft began to offer its Korean-language version for free, Korean users learned about the convenience of the Windows 95 operating system and started switching platforms. To compound matters, as Korean users were changing computers, which already had a preinstalled MS Word program, they no longer felt compelled to purchase ARAEA Hangul. Sagging sales then put the company in severe financial trouble.

On June 22, 1998, Yi Minhwa, a successful local businessman and founder of the Korea Venture Business Association, established the Committee to Save Hangeul Software to protect Haansoft from foreign involvement. Flanked by the local media and powerful civic groups, including the Hangeul Society—an organization that was established in 1912 under Japanese colonial rule to preserve and promote the indigenous script—the committee sought to brand Bill Gates as a colonizing force and called on college students to petition against this proposed takeover on popular online bulletin boards like Chollian and Hitel. On July 20, Haansoft announced its decision to decline Microsoft's offer and accept the proposal by Save Haansoft's Korean Software. It elected a new CEO, whose first act was rereleasing its word-processing program as Hangul 815, referring to August 15, the date when Korea was liberated from Japanese colonial rule.

As the Koreans fought for control over their language and economy, a golf player reminded them that the humiliation of "I'M Fired" could be transformed into "I'M Fighting." In 1998, twenty-year-old Bak Seri sank a birdie on the twentieth hole in a playoff to win the US Women's Open. She was the first Korean-born player to win the title—it was the third-most acclaimed moment in the sixty years of South Korean sports history (after the 1988 Seoul Olympics and the 2002 Korea-Japan World Cup). As one of the most gifted amateur golfers at Geumseong Girls' High School in Gongju City (South Chungcheong Province), Bak had moved to Seoul to train. In 1996, a year before she moved to the United States, she won six tournaments on the Korean LPGA circuit before earning a card to play in the majors in 1998. At the age of twenty-nine she was inducted into the World Golf Hall of Fame as the youngest entrant and recognized as a pioneer of the sport who had changed the face of women's golf. Bak retired in 2016, playing her last round at the US Women's Open at Corde Valle Golf Club in San Martin, California. She set off a golf boom in South Korea, inspiring countless young women to take up professional golf; by 2009, the number of women who played golf professionally had increased to forty-seven. As a result of Bak's success on the greens, the LPGA Tour turned into a revenue-generating event. "Seri's kids," like Sin Jiae, Choe Nayeon, and Bak Inbi, followed in her footsteps and started a golf revolution.

With the kind of optimism embodied by Bak Seri, South Korea weathered the Asian financial crisis and made a rapid economic recovery. In August 2001, it finished repaying its bailout loans of $19.4 billion three years ahead of schedule. The government introduced essential reforms such as higher regulations of loans and a limit on deposit insurance to encourage depositors to choose viable institutions. Most importantly, the crisis forced conglomerates to restructure their businesses to invest only in core industries, divesting from industries that did not fit their mission. By January 2003, South Korea's official foreign exchange reserves had expanded to $122 billion.

With the Century: Nuclear Weapons, Kim Il-sung's Death, and the End of a Dynasty

A few years before the South Korean financial crisis, North Korea also experienced a calamitous event: on July 8, 1994, Kim Il-sung unexpectedly died at the age of eighty-two after suffering from a heart attack. He had ruled the North for forty-eight years (twenty years longer than Joseph Stalin in the Soviet Union). The *suryeong* (supreme leader) had no peers, and the nation erected every monument and building in his honor. Kim had been scheduled to meet with South Korea's president, Kim Young-sam, in Pyeongyang on July 25, which would have been the first meeting between the two leaders since the division of the peninsula in 1948. Kim's death placed the armies of South Korea and the United States on high alert; the tensions on the border were exacerbated by Pyeongyang's ambition to obtain nuclear weapons. The DPRK desperately needed a reliable nuclear deterrent to ensure its national security against the threats of the United States and its allies and to maintain its place in world politics. The North's quest for nuclear technology also coincided with the decision by both superpowers to share atomic technology with countries aligned with their political interests; however, Kim faced serious hurdles because his relationship with the Soviet Union began to sour in the 1960s.

Kim Il-sung's sense of urgency to acquire nuclear weapons stemmed from his anxiety that the North was falling behind his neighboring countries. China, which had declared that nuclear energy was critical to the success of its First Five Year Plan, opened its first reactor in 1956 with the assistance of the Soviet Union. Closer to home, the North learned that under Dwight Eisenhower's Atoms for Peace campaign in 1953, the United States had shared science and technology with Taiwan and South Korea. The South had already arranged to obtain a nuclear reactor with the assistance of two American companies a couple of years after it signed a formal agreement with the United States in 1956, pledging to use atomic energy only for peaceful ventures. In this Cold War game, the North reached out to the Soviet Union, which offered technical assistance in building an experimental reactor under a joint agreement in 1959. A year earlier it had participated in the creation of the international Joint Institute for Nuclear Research in Dubno (Moscow district), which was designed to facilitate research and share information. The North's fears that the South had a technological advantage proved justified when Seoul announced the completion of an experimental reactor in 1960.

Despite its initial reassurances of support, the Soviet Union was ambivalent about the nuclear project in North Korea (especially in the context of the Sino-Soviet rivalry); its increasing reservations hampered the North's ability to achieve its nuclear ambitions. In the 1950s, Moscow and Beijing offered valuable training for North Korean scientists, and by the early 1960s the North had developed a small reactor at Yongbyeon, a heavily guarded military facility. Beneath the façade of cooperation, however, the Soviet Union was wary of potential Chinese nuclear capabilities, which threatened its political interests. In its effort to prevent Beijing from obtaining the technology to create an A-bomb—either from Soviet scientists or indirectly from its allies—the Soviet Union began to limit what it shared with Pyeongyang, which intensified its relationship with China in the 1960s. Although Soviet experts determined that uranium deposits in the North were not abundant (from their assessments of the mines), the Kremlin still worried about the potential resources that the Chinese could exploit.

Consequently, the Soviets devised a policy to share as little information as they could with the North about nuclear technology. They also suspected that they would have little control over North Korea's nuclear program, which did not enjoy a robust military capability at this time. At Khrushchev's insistence that the North sign the international Non-Proliferation Treaty, which was open for signatories in 1968, Foreign Minister Bak Seongcheol (1913–2008) refused, noting that it was unreasonable for countries that did not have a nuclear weapon to be signatories (by which he meant China but also hinted at his own country). Moreover, Bak protested that the United States, which already had a stockpile of nuclear weapons, blackmailed other countries with this knowledge as a way to "eternalize their rule."

The North was intensely aware of South Korea's nuclear leap forward. Under Park Chung-hee, the South began to harness nuclear power, not only for civilian use (in response to the oil crisis that quadrupled prices) but also for nuclear military capabilities. The Soviets continuously rejected requests by the North for assistance to build a nuclear power plant, not merely for military use but for energy purposes as well. It bears noting that the Soviet Union raised oil prices in the 1970s during the oil crisis, offering discounts to its Eastern bloc but not to the North, which desperately needed cheap energy for its economy. Kim adopted an increasingly belligerent tone after the Vietnam War, drawing attention to America's placement of nuclear technology in the South, and even threatened to liberate the South. The North also undertook a series of provocative actions, such as sending tanks to the DMZ in 1976 and threatening UN soldiers who tried to cut down a poplar tree that obstructed the view of a critical checkpoint (the tree-cutting incident). The North further sparked international outrage when it declared a fifty-mile military zone in the Sea of Japan and the Yellow Sea in advance of the Carter-Gromyko talks, so that the planned US troop withdrawal would be placed on the table. Both Moscow and Beijing had several concerns: the North's aggressive approach in its demand for nuclear technology, its refusal to be bound by international conventions, and finally the fear that if it attained atomic capability, the DPRK would draw its allies into an unpopular war. Frustrated in its efforts, the North tried to bypass the Soviets and obtain assistance from Eastern European countries, including East Germany, but it was to no avail.

In the 1980s, the North recognized that the era of Communist solidarity was over and decided to draw on its own research and efforts to construct a reactor. For a brief interlude starting in 1984, relations improved between the North and the Soviet Union. The Kremlin held negotiations with Pyeongyang about the construction of a nuclear plant and formalized an agreement after the North joined the Non-Proliferation Treaty in December 1985. However, the cooperation faltered when Moscow sent athletes to participate in the Seoul Olympics in 1988. Throughout the 1990s, the North continued to work diligently on its reactor, perhaps with the technological help of Pakistan.

Kim Il-sung died twelve years before the North conducted its first nuclear test in 2006. The announcement of his death was made just hours before the North was to hold talks with the United States in Geneva over its nuclear program on July 9, 1994; the North ultimately settled on the Agreed Framework with the Clinton administration to shut down the Yongbyeon complex and cease plutonium production in exchange for light-water reactors and aid from the United States. To satisfy the North Korean military and hardliners who opposed any capitulation to the United States, the new leader, Kim Jong-il, advanced a military-first policy, which became the driving force in the transition of power granting the Korean People's Army (KPA) the highest priority. By the time he took control of the country, Kim Jong-il had already served in almost all the critical positions, including General Secretary of the Central Committee of the Workers' Party of Korea, and Vice Chairman of the National Defense Commission in 1990. He was awarded the title "Marshal" when he was appointed the supreme commander of the KPA the following year. But before anything else, he needed to mourn the death of his father.

Kim Il-sung's death prompted a nationwide, ten-day mourning period, and after his funeral in Pyeongyang his body lay in state at the Geumsusan Memorial Palace embalmed in a glass coffin and shrouded with the flag of the Workers' Party of Korea. Residents of North Korea's capital wept hysterically as the hearse passed through the city to the mausoleum. The spectacle at the funeral attested to Kim's cult of personality as the father of the nation. The South banned its citizens from attending the funeral, but the North announced that it would welcome visits from Bak Bohi, an assistant to the Reverend Sun Myung Moon and the president of the Unification Church's daily *Segye ilbo* (World Times); Myungja Julie Moon, a Korean American journalist; and two pastors, identified as Kim Jinkyung and Hong Donggeun, all of whom attended the funeral. Kim's death stunned the capital. The only leader North Koreans had known since the birth of their nation was gone. Kim Jong-Il inherited his father's mantle to resume the high-stakes game of nuclear poker with the United States. He would also have to confront one of the worst famines of the twentieth century, which devastated his country.

In August 1995, North Korea submitted a formal request to the United Nations World Food Program (WFP) for humanitarian aid, out of desperation. Kim blamed massive floods and drought for the devastating famine that had led to widespread starvation, child malnutrition, and deaths. Several factors led to the unprecedented appeal for assistance. The famine was in part due to market reforms in the Soviet Union and China, which deprived the North of external trading partners and subsidies. Kim's inability to secure cheap imported fuel and increase fertilizer production contributed to a dramatic decline in harvests at the collective farms.

Moreover, widespread flooding decimated a significant portion of arable farmland and ruined the grain reserves that the state had stored underground. The floods also damaged the country's infrastructure, such as roads and hydropower plants, making it impossible to produce the energy necessary for food production. To compound matters, unseasonable cold weather had killed the saplings for the next planting. North Korea's mountainous terrain, which Kim Il-sung had relied on to protect people during the war, was hostile to farmers. There was only a small segment (18 percent) of arable land available during the short growing season. The country's food rationing system and an oversized army under Kim Jong-il's military-first policy could not weather the crisis; farmers hid their grain while local officials hoarded their resources. Breaking from the ideology of *juche,* Kim reluctantly opened the country to the world to solve the crisis at home.

But it was too late. Between 1995 and 1998, approximately two to three million North Koreans (10 percent of the population) died. By 1996, the North began to receive food aid from the United States through the WFP; shipments peaked in 1999 at nearly 600,000 tons, making the United States the most significant foreign aid donor to North Korea. The George W. Bush administration, however, significantly reduced its donations. Despite more than 3.5 metric tons of food donations sent from abroad, the food did not reach the most vulnerable populations. Soldiers and elites began hoarding aid food and supplies, selling them at outrageous prices. Undernourished mothers could not breast-feed their infants, and many of the elderly who were completely dependent on government rations through the Public Distribution System starved because they were unable to forage for famine food such as roots, weeds, and grass in the mountains. Women assumed the primary role in feeding their families; many resorted to operating illegal private fields and bribed officials to smuggle goods from China. At its peak in 1997, the famine led to a severe health crisis: acute malnutrition and loss of body mass (known as wasting) affected more than 15 percent of children under five years old and stunted growth in 66 percent of that age group. Koreans who had family members in China fared better than others: between 100,000 and 400,000 people engaged in border crossings to China and smuggling in a desperate search for food.

The North employed propaganda to fortify the people's resolve to survive without rebellion. The famine came to be known as "the arduous march [against imperialism]," invoking the memory of Kim Il-sung and his guerrillas who fought against the Japanese. The state banned direct use of words like famine, hunger, and death and stressed sacrifice (urging people to eat only twice a day) to rationalize its austerity policies. The North also resorted to judicial violence, criminalizing acts of hunger and survival: stealing food from the fields, border crossing to China to procure food, begging for food, and abandoning children. The famine gave birth to an entire population of homeless, migrant children known as *kkotjebi*. With its once heralded food rationing program in tatters, the North turned to the United Nations Development Program for help. The UNDP initiated the Agricultural Relief and Recovery Program to increase food production, which included rebuilding dams and dikes, introducing mechanized farm and irrigation equipment, and supplying high-quality fertilizer and seeds to farmers.

Confronting the Past, Dealing with the Present: The Ironies of Democracy

For the South, the 1990s was a period of reckoning when Koreans began to confront the collective trauma experienced during the dictatorial regimes of Park Chung-hee and Chun Doo-hwan. On January 10, 1995, SBS (Seoul Broadcasting System) aired the first of twenty-four episodes of *Sandglass,* a miniseries written by Song Ji-na and directed by Kim Jonghak. Merchants closed their stores early, and the streets were deserted when the show (one of the highest-rated Korean melodramas) began at 9:50 P.M. The show addressed the taboo subject of political repression through the tragic relationships of three friends who lived in the 1970s and 1980s. To convey a heightened sense of reality, the show included archival video footage of the Gwangju uprising in 1980 as well as vivid reenactments based on individual testimonies about the police violence. But it was the theme song, "Zhuravli" (Cranes), by the Russian Jewish "Frank Sinatra," Iosif Kobzon, that packed an emotional punch and gained widespread popularity in Korea. The lyrics, which mourned the Soviet soldiers whose deaths during World War II transformed them into cranes, resonated powerfully with Korean viewers.

The drama revolves around two unlikely childhood friends, who represent different political archetypes. Bak Taesu, raised in poverty by a mother who ran a brothel, is unable to enter military school because of his tainted political genealogy (his father was an alleged Communist sympathizer) and becomes a gangster. His best friend, Gang Useok, an intelligent young boy with firm moral convictions, grows up to be a lawyer. They both fall in love with Yun Hyerin, a dedicated political activist and the daughter of a wealthy casino magnate. Their lives diverge radically during the Gwangju Uprising, testing their friendships and loyalties. Yun, who joins the student protests against the dictatorship, is arrested and tortured by the police, while Taesu, an innocent bystander, witnesses the atrocities committed by paratroopers. Their friend Useok has become a soldier and must fire on civilians to protect the state. In the tragic end, Useok, now a prosecutor for the government, finds himself compelled to prosecute his best friend. The drama, which exposed the crimes of the state through the sandglass of time, had a profound impact on the Korean public. As viewers relived the horrific events and confronted the sins of their past—the massive injustices and human rights violations perpetrated under the military regimes—they longed for a brighter future. It was a dream their president promised to fulfill.

The Sunshine Policy: Kim Dae-jung, Korea's First Nobel Laureate

On February 25, 1998, South Korea inaugurated Kim Dae-jung (1924–2009), a lifetime opposition leader and the successor to Kim Young-sam, as its eighth president, just as the government signed off on the IMF bailout. He is remembered today as the first Korean to receive the Nobel Peace Prize, for his struggle for democracy and human rights in South Korea and peace and reconciliation with the North through his Sunshine Policy. However, Kim also played a significant role in creating a neoliberal state and society through reforms that would have a lasting impact on the South.

Kim was born in Sinan (South Jeolla Province) to a large family of middle-class farmers, one of seven children. His political biography was replete with near misses and persecution by the state.

During the Korean War, he managed to escape a death sentence after North Korean soldiers arrested him. Kim became active in the democracy movement in the 1950s and secured a seat in the National Assembly in 1961 (on his third attempt) only to have his election nullified when Park Chung-hee staged a military coup and dissolved parliament. Critical of Park, Kim made his first bid for the presidency in 1971, garnering more than 40 percent of the vote but losing the election to Park, who changed the Constitution to guarantee his position for life. After a traffic accident, which he believed to be an attempt on his life, Kim almost died in 1973 when KCIA agents kidnapped him from his Tokyo hotel room and dragged him to a ship, from which they planned to dump him into the sea. To his great fortune, US officials foiled the plan, but the Park regime placed Kim under house arrest, banning him from any involvement in politics. On Kim's release in 1979, after Park's assassination, Chun Doo-hwan charged him with treason and conspiracy for participating in the Gwangju Uprising and sentenced him to death. Another intervention by the United States allowed him to escape and live in exile in America until 1992, when Kim returned to make another bid on the presidency, which he lost to his friend Kim Young-sam. He spent several years as a visiting scholar at the University of Cambridge before returning home to run again for the 1997 election, which he finally won.

Kim introduced his Sunshine Policy under vastly improved political and economic conditions. South Korea had garnered an international reputation after the successful Seoul Olympics, where it showcased its economic achievements. The new policy also came six years after the collapse of Communism in the Soviet Union and, shortly thereafter, economic reforms in China, leaving the North bereft of its key supporters. The Sunshine Policy, which broke with outmoded Cold War models of containment, aimed to bring peace and reconciliation to the divided Korean peninsula. Taking inspiration from the Aesopian fable "Wind and Sunshine," the president resorted to traditional Korean ways of dealing with enemies, giving them gifts to prevent them from causing harm, or as one scholar put it, "engagement with security." Kim also looked to Germany's successful model of *Ostpolitik,* which normalized relations between East and West through mutual recognition and socioeconomic exchange and cooperation.

The Sunshine Policy, which acknowledged the tenacity of the North, rejected the assumption that the South would absorb the North when it collapsed. Instead of prioritizing unification, it emphasized more attainable goals like peaceful coexistence and reconciliation. Consequently, the plan stressed "joint development and prosperity," carefully distinguishing between economic and political cooperation. In other words, financial investments could be made without linkages to political events. For its part, the state focused on humanitarian aid; the South continued to assist in the famine despite the North's infiltration of Gangneung City by a submarine crew in September 1996. After events like this, hardline critics accused Kim of appeasement. The new policy also encouraged private businesses to engage with the North by easing border crossings and allowing greater investments. Hyundai's founder, Jeong Juyeong, exploited the new conditions to launch his Diamond Mountain Tourism Venture, one of the first inter-Korean projects for promoting tourism in North Korea. In the wake of the famine disaster, the DPRK welcomed this project because it promised to bring foreign investments and capital to its special zones. Jeong visited the North in June 1998 with gifts of five hundred head of cattle and fifty trucks, and a few months later the two partners signed an agreement that gave Hyundai exclusive rights for almost one billion dollars. On November 18, 1998, a deluxe cruise ship carrying some 1,400 South Koreans departed from the port town of Donghae to the Diamond Mountain—the first of many tourists to visit North Korea.

Hyundai's Diamond Mountain venture had mixed results. Kim's government touted it as a symbol of cooperation—a site for student exchanges, meetings, and so forth. But reciprocity from the North, though expected, was not always forthcoming. For instance, when Kim requested the establishment of a reunion center for divided families in exchange for fertilizer assistance, North Korea sarcastically rejected the talks as horse-trading and walked away from further negotiations. In all there were three formal reunions between divided families, until the shooting of a South Korean female tourist by a North Korean guard in 2008 ended the tour and family reunions. The Hyundai project and other Sunshine Policy projects drew criticism for their lack of transparency (such as bribes of the North) and collusion between the government and private businesses. Even when support was strong for the tourism project, only 370,000 people traveled to the Diamond Mountain, and ultimately the project suffered from an enormous deficit. Moreover, Kim's government paid cash remittances of $450 million to the North before the first historic inter-Korean summit in June 2000—better known as the cash-for-summit scandal. Critics of the Sunshine Policy also contended that despite any gains, the South had turned a blind eye to the repressive nature of the regime, basically giving it free rein without consequences.

While pundits agree that the Sunshine Policy brought more significant political contact between the two states, including several historic moments in inter-Korean relations and a Nobel Prize, they have not articulated its impact on individual lives, especially the diasporic population. The story of Muhammad Kkansu, a diasporic intellectual who was arrested in 1996 on charges of espionage and using a false identity, illustrates a slow shift in attitudes toward the North under the Sunshine Policy. Kkansu, who claimed to be an Arab of Filipino-Lebanese descent, was a prolific scholar of the Silk Road. He was conversant in twelve languages and was the sole expert in Arabic Studies in South Korea. Adopting the persona of a real aficionado of Korean culture, Kkansu regularly visited historical sites around the country and contributed his impressions as a foreigner to various popular magazines and newspapers. His performance was so credible that his graduate adviser and colleagues in the Department of History at Dankook University never even once suspected that he was not an Arab. Successfully evading suspicion for twelve years, Kkansu routinely faxed messages from various hotels in Seoul to a North Korean agent in Beijing. It was only through a simple twist of fate, when a lobby attendant at the Plaza Hotel in Seoul misidentified him as a wanted drug dealer after a botched fax at the hotel's business center, that he was arrested. The shocking revelation that Kkansu was not an Arab but a North Korean spy masquerading as a fifty-two-year-old academic took the country by surprise. Embarrassed over its failure to spot the fake identity and academic credentials, Dankook University immediately dismissed Kkansu and stripped him of his doctorate. The Ministry of Education quickly replaced an excerpt that he wrote for a middle-school textbook in 1991. For the authorities, this case represented a far more severe breach of security than the common stealing of identities of deceased or missing Japanese by North Korean operatives in neighboring Japan. In fact, this was the first spy case which involved an international network and the adoption of multiple nationalities by an individual who had infiltrated deeply into South Korean intellectual and social circles. Motivated by Cold War logics and reinforced by extensive coverage of other high-profile spy cases, the furor over Kkansu's elaborate scheme and ability to pass undetected generated widespread fear. The public expressed little interest in understanding the complex circumstances that gave rise to his life choices—the pressures that diasporic Koreans living in China, like Kkansu, were forced to experience in the postliberation era with the onset of the Cold War and national division.

Kim's Sunshine Policy, which created a less hostile stance vis-à-vis the North and an atmosphere of peace and reconciliation, allowed Kkansu to stave off execution or life imprisonment for espionage. On August 15, 2000, Kkansu was released after four years and a month in a solitary cell and subsequently given a presidential pardon with 3,586 other prisoners by Kim Dae-jung in 2003, and then naturalized as a South Korean in 2005. Changing his name to Jeong Su-il, he returned to a life of normalcy, which meant a return to his scholarship. Jeong published more than a dozen books on the Silk Road with reputable presses, as well as essential translations of works by Ibn Battuta and the Silla monk Hyecho. Like Eric Auerbach, who revived his career in the United States at Yale University, in 2008 Jeong established the Korean Institute of Civilizational Exchanges, where he continues to serve as the director at the age of eighty-five. Jeong's life exemplifies how historical circumstances forced many diasporic Korean populations to live parallel lives, at once demonstrating a sheer will and remarkable ability to survive under hostile conditions in a foreign land, and the ability to dissimulate by adopting an ambiguous identity. The Kkansu episode was also a sobering moment for Koreans who were caught unaware in the fantastic deception. It revealed the harmful results of ignorance about places like the Middle East, understood only through simplistic stereotypes and images. The fact that not one Korean saw through Kkansu's performance of Arab identity reveals the limits of a monolithic culture. While Kim's Sunshine Policy contributed to more engagement with and better awareness of North Koreans, social attitudes had not changed. There was still an ignorance about diasporic Koreans and foreigners (migrant workers, spouses, North Korean defectors, and ethnically diverse students from different countries), who began to arrive in the South in increasing numbers.

As the South experienced the crippling financial crisis of the late 1990s and the North struggled to feed its people during the famine, the two Koreas turned outward (one by choice, the other by necessity). For the South, normalization of relations with China and the Soviet Union brought not only economic benefits but also a solution to the low fertility rates in the countryside. Ethnic Koreans from China and Russia began to return to the homeland, triggering the first wave of international marriages, which now account for 13 percent of all marriages in South Korea. Kim's Sunshine Policy began to thaw relations with the North, allowing families who had been separated by the Korean War to reunite for the first time. Both the death of Kim Il-sung and the famine gave rise to a proliferation of grassroots markets in North Korea that helped people survive. The weakening of the North's traditional alliances and a devastating famine challenged its core *juche* ideology, forcing Kim Jong-il to turn to the world, even its twin nemesis, for assistance.

6 Kim-chic or the Axis of Evil?
Korea and the World

The separate trajectories of the two Koreas (especially in the 1980s and 1990s)—with the growing isolation of the North and rapid integration of South Korea into global markets—led to new respective reputations in the world. The South emerged as "Kim-chic," surpassing Japan to become Asia's preeminent trendsetter in fashion, music, television dramas, film, and other cultural production. The 2000s witnessed a remarkable transformation of South Korean society triggered by globalization and the digital revolution, prompting debates about taboo social subjects like homosexuality or confrontations about the changes of South Korea into a multiethnic and multicultural nation. The production and consumption of Korean popular culture after the Asian financial crisis reflected new dynamics and complexities of interregional circulation that challenged long-standing notions about the center (usually viewed as the West) and the periphery. Meanwhile, President George W. Bush's delineation of the axis of evil ironically sparked the world's fascination with North Korea and its reclusive yet enigmatic leader, Kim Jong-il, and his weapons of mass destruction. The North, which the West shunned as a pariah and dangerous nation, continued to draw inspiration from its revolutionary past as it attempted to find its new place in the global order.

Coming Out

The partial easing of censorship starting in the late 1980s facilitated the introduction of taboo sexual topics, such as premarital sex, rape, and sexual harassment, in Korean popular culture. These debates signaled that Korea was finally emerging from its long history of repression and authoritarian rule; however, homosexuality did not receive much if any attention until the 2000s when a television celebrity confessed his sexual orientation. In September 2000, Hong Seokcheon revealed that he was gay, and his promising career as a popular television personality came crashing down. Neither the South Korean Constitution nor its Civil Penal Code mentioned homosexuality; moreover, the term "coming out" was not part of the cultural lexicon. From 1994 to 2004, the World Values Survey found that 53 percent of Koreans felt that homosexuality was never justified. Hong's public declaration catapulted the issue of homosexuality into the limelight, igniting debates and constructing a new social discourse.

Hong Seokcheon (b. 1971) was born in Cheongyang County in South Chungcheong Province. He started his career as a male model and then switched to television to work as a reporter for the Live TV Information Center. When Hong came out, his career was on the rise. He appeared regularly in South Korea's version of *Sesame Street—PoPoPo—*and received rave reviews for the 1990s sitcom "Three Men, Three Women," in which he played an

FIGURE 10. North Korean boy practicing calligraphy.

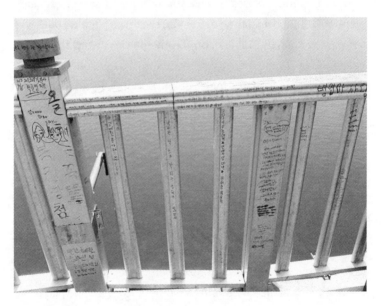

FIGURE 11. Suicide notes on the railings of the Mapo Bridge (Seoul).

effeminate fashion designer named Poison. When rumors began to circulate that Hong was gay, friends and people in the industry advised him not to discuss his sexuality if he wanted to maintain his career. But the anguish in hiding his true identity increasingly troubled Hong; unlike his gay friends in Amsterdam, New York, and San Francisco, he could not live a free and normal life. During a filming of a variety show, the comedian host asked in jest if he liked men. "Yes," Hong admitted. Although show producers edited his response, Hong did not deny his sexual identity when a journalist who had been at the show confronted him.

The reaction was immediate: in just one day Hong lost all of his television roles, his radio show, and advertisement contracts. Few producers were willing to test South Korea's attitudes toward homosexuality. Koreans were mostly ignorant about underground gay culture in their backyards. Until the 1990s, gay men met at designated theaters in Pagoda Park, Myeongdong, or in the narrow alleyways in the Nakwondong neighborhood, one of the larger red-light districts in Seoul and the primary cruising area for gays. Here they mingled with sex workers and gangsters to create their *ijok segye* (this side of the world) of gay saunas, *jjokbang* (small rooms to have sex), and gay bars. Gay organizations were still rare in the 1990s, but there were a few important ones. Korean gay men's Chingusai (Between Friends, 1994) and the lesbian group Girikkiri (Among Ourselves, 1994) allowed college students to form relationships with dignity. A more transnational gay quarter began to emerge in Itaewon, a neighborhood adjacent to the US military base in Yongsan where Korean gay men could meet foreigners and military personnel. The BBS (bulletin board system) operated by Chollian, Hitel, and Nownuri offered valuable information on HIV/AIDS and provided a venue for gay men to communicate openly with each other and create a community. This was the vibrant gay life in Seoul that most Koreans did not want to acknowledge, let alone the gay men and women who lived in their midst.

Even if he was the first openly gay celebrity, Hong was stunned by the severe social ostracism. His parents, who were bewildered by the news stories swirling around their son, begged him to change his mind. The very media industry that had pushed him to stardom now shunned him; death threats made Hong fear for his life. Pushed to the edge, he drank heavily and contemplated suicide. In retrospect, Hong explained that ignorance was to blame for the public response because many Koreans viewed homosexuality as a disease linked to AIDS or mental illness. The media used Hong's coming out as a springboard to discuss the social problem of gay Koreans who were forcibly admitted to mental institutions or who had committed suicide; soon, the discourse on homosexuality became framed as a human rights issue. When the National Human Rights Commission advised the government to draft a nondiscrimination bill in July 2007, the most vigorous opposition came from the conservative Christian community, which comprised one third of the Korean population and viewed homosexuality as an abomination (an attitude that has not changed even today). The policy of the military—specifically Article 92 of the Military Penal Code— still singles out same-sex acts as sexual harassment, and offenders are forced to serve a maximum of one year in prison.

Although Hong's very public coming out sparked a debate, it did not create higher tolerance and acceptance in society. Today many LGBT actors still hide behind masks at public rallies or news conferences. Hong, though, has thrived as a popular media personality featured in variety and reality shows in which he has even played an openly gay person. Still, his dream of an inclusive Korean society in which gays and lesbians live freely in mainstream culture has yet to be realized. Hong's story and discussions about homosexuality became eclipsed by the enormous successes of Korea's veritable heterosexual television dramas.

Winter Sonata's Yonsama and the Start of the Korean Wave

On January 14, 2002, four months before the much-anticipated 2002 Japan-Korea FIFA World Cup, the Korea Broadcast System aired the first episode of *Winter Sonata* directed by Yun Seokho. The drama not only earned good ratings at home but launched the Hallyu (Korean Wave) in Asia and worldwide. In early June, the Japanese consulate in Seoul forwarded a personal letter by a middle-aged Japanese woman to KBS praising the drama and emphasizing how much it had touched her life. Such enthusiasm from Japanese viewers impelled the Japanese broadcasting company, NHK, to air the show in Japan in 2004. The drama became so popular that its main actor, Bae Yongjun, rose to heartthrob status in East Asia as the Yonsama craze swept Japan (Yonsama is Bae's nickname, -*sama* being an honorific reserved for aristocrats). The show sparked new cultural practices, such as thousands of fans making pilgrimages to Nami Island in Chuncheon, Gangwon Province, one of the primary locations in the drama, to see a statue of the main characters at the spot where they first kissed. *Winter Sonata* represented an essential step for a Korean culture industry that recognized the potential for markets beyond its borders, and that began to develop an infrastructure to reach a broader, mainly East Asian audience. The show was not the first Korean cultural export to Japan, whose audiences were familiar with moderately popular films like *Swiri* (2000) and *JSA* (2001). However, *Winter Sonata*, first broadcast on satellite television, became a megahit through word of mouth by mostly female viewers, who created a modern fandom with all its unique identity-culture practices.

Winter Sonata's universal themes, like first love, resonated with many middle-aged Japanese women, who expressed nostalgia for youthful romances, sacrifice, and purity of love. Their emotional investment in the show transformed previous images and percep-tions of Korea, giving rise to the term "soap opera diplomacy." The wildly popular melodrama was the first contact point with contem-porary Korea for some who had imagined Koreans as a people from a distant past, still dressed in their traditional clothing; for others, it was a reminder of Japan's colonial legacy, which they needed to confront. The Japanese prime minister (Junichiro Koizumi) was forced to admit that Bae Yongjun was more popular than himself after three thousand middle-aged women gathered at Narita International Airport to greet the star. Yonsama was the second-biggest-selling brand in Japan in the first half of 2004, with DVD recorders being its main competitor.

Previously, cultural interaction between Korea and Japan had been unilateral: Koreans flocked to enjoy Japanese music and film, with an undeniable dedication to animation and fashion. All this now changed. According to the Korea International Trade Association, after the success of *Winter Sonata*, South Korea exported $490 million of cultural content to Japan in 2007 and increased this to $1.46 billion in 2013. The *Winter Sonata* craze also sparked a boom in enrollment in Korean-language classes such as Fuyusona (Winter Sonata) and generated more than $40 million in Japan from novels, travel guides, DVDs, and other merchandise.

Popular culture was a significant factor in reshaping Korean-Chinese relations as well. While the Korean Wave can be attributed to diplomatic normalization with China in 1992, it also opened the door to a flow of Korean pop music, dramas, and films to the Chinese market. All this became the springboard for the growing popularity of South Korean pop culture, starting with the boy group H.O.T. (High-Five of Teenagers), which had profited from the South Korean government's decision in the early 1990s to lift the ban on foreign travel for Koreans. Ironically, another factor in the rise of Korean pop culture was the Asian financial crisis in 1997. One of President Kim Dae-Jung's initiatives was to invest in information technology and popular culture, which he deemed the two main drivers of South Korea's economy. In his view, technology would create new industries, while popular culture would be the engine for generating content. By 2012, government funding constituted over 25 percent of all venture capital disbursed in Korea, and it allocated one third to the entertainment industry—music, movies, and dramas.

Let's Get Together Now: The 2002 Japan-Korea FIFA World Cup

The growing visibility of the South with cultural successes like *Winter Sonata* raised the stakes in the rivalry between the North and South. In the summer of 2002, FIFA ushered in the new millennium by staging the seventeenth World Cup, the most fabulous sporting event on the planet, held in Asia for the first time in its seventy-two-year history. In an unprecedented move, FIFA decided to allow South Korea and Japan to cohost the competition after a bitter bidding process, creating an unlikely, fragile alliance between two nations with a fraught history of colonialism.

As this was the first time the games took place in Asia, it reflected the global reach of soccer. To the world's astonishment, North Korea began to broadcast the games after refusing to participate or provide stadiums for a few games, as suggested by the South. The normally reticent regime even opened up its country to foreign journalists to attend several cultural and sporting events, including an extravagant Arirang Festival of mass gymnastics and artistic performance at the Rungrado May Day Stadium. The Western press speculated that the unauthorized broadcasts (which the German company KirchMedia denounced because the North failed to purchase broadcasting rights) were a signal that the North wanted to restart talks with the United States.

News that the South Korean team had advanced to the semifinals prompted near hysteria among the Red Devils, the official support club for the national team. The Red Devils phenomenon marked a decisive moment when a club deployed the digital revolution to create and mobilize a transnational sports fandom united by national pride. Transcending gender boundaries, the Red Devils transformed the game, not only with their massive female fan base (numbering over half to two-thirds of the spectators) but with the feminization of the game. Wearing their signature red (a color long associated with the Communist North) and devil headbands, the Red Devils led the exuberant cheering and swept the symbols of masculine violence (liquor, foul language, and fights) out of the stadium. The male bodies of the soccer players became the object of the female gaze, as suggested in the titles of journal articles such as "Kim Nam-il, Raw as Is!" in *Hangyoreh 21*.

Red Devils fans numbered approximately 80,000 before the opening games of the 2002 World Cup and skyrocketed to 200,000 after the first week of the tourney. More than 450,000 joined the

Internet-based soccer fan club and exchanged opinions about the matches through the Internet and instant messaging. The Internet generation had mobilized the entire nation and attracted global attention. This 2030 generation—people in their twenties and thirties who tended to be atomized and apathetic to social issues—were wired, making them a powerhouse in cyberspace.

The Red Devils redefined nationalism to include a renewed sense of pride after the humiliation of the Asian financial crisis in 1997. Infectious chants like "Daehan Minguk!" (Great Republic of Korea!), to the beat of a traditional drum, and songs like "Oh Pilseung Korea" (Victorious Korea) provided a venue for more Koreans—especially women—to participate in patriotic display, which had been dominated by men before these games. The World Cup also provided an opportunity to showcase Korea's successful recovery and reentry on the global stage, making the country a tourist destination, much like *Winter Sonata* had done. The victories of the Taeguk warriors also sparked passionate patriotism among diasporic Korean communities around the world, from Los Angeles to Toronto to London, allowing Koreans everywhere to experience a new type of belonging to the homeland. The digital mobilization of the Red Devils did not happen in a vacuum; it built on the innovative digital infrastructure that Korea had started to develop in the 1990s.

From Digital Immigrants to Digital Natives:
The PC-Bang and the Digital Revolution

On March 20, 1994, Brian (Minho) Jeong opened the BNC (Business Network Club), one of the first Internet cafés in South Korea, which offered basic office equipment such as a copier, a fax machine, and a PC with a dial-up modem and voice-mail system. Like a hotel business room, the BNC provided coffee, snacks, a language interpreter, and secretarial services. In June of that year, Jeong offered similar services to foreigners in Itaewon near the Hamilton Hotel and opened several more BNCs for college students near Hongik University. While Jeong's business venture failed, it was a precursor to the PC-bang (PC rooms), which first appeared in 1996 and then took off in 1998 following Blizzard Entertainment's real-time strategy PC-game *StarCraft*. Until then, the South Korean government did not regard computer gaming as a legitimate leisure activity or as an industry to be nurtured, but rather something that was off the beaten path of mainstream culture. South Korea now touts itself as the most wired nation on the planet, with over 95 percent of its households having high-speed or broadband access. In part, the gaming industry (worth billions of dollars) was a driver of digital speed, Internet accessibility, and the creation of a new youth culture obsessed with video gaming.

The government crackdown on Korea's only telecommunications company, the monopoly Korea Telecom, allowed competitors like Hanaro Telecom to start a broadband service using an asymmetric digital subscriber line (ADSL). This allowed the PC-bangs (which number more than 23,000 today) to offer faster connections, permitting players to indulge in multiplayer computer games for an hourly fee of five hundred to one thousand *won* (less than a dollar). *StarCraft* became the catalyst for improving broadband services as players blamed poor connection speed for their defeats. The success of *Lineage*—a popular MMORPG (massively multiplayer online role-playing game) by NCSoft—also helped create more demand for high-speed connections. PC-bangs started offering snacks and beverages to their patrons (similar to

Jeong's first Internet cafés) and lowered hourly fees if patrons played longer. By 2005, the Korean online game market was worth $1.4 billion, accounting for 56 percent of the entire Asia Pacific market share.

StarCraft was initially published by LG Soft, a division of LG Electronics, in 1997. As a result of the Asian financial crisis, the company had to follow the IMF mandate to downsize. Kim Yeongman, a managerial staff member at LG Soft, decided to establish a start-up company based on *StarCraft,* and secured the copyright for the game. Kim's HanbitSoft started distributing free copies of the game to the PC-bangs, which had begun to bloom like mushrooms. The national economic crisis of 1997 was a catalyst for creating the high-speed infrastructure and for relaxing governmental regulations for the Internet and communications industry. A new generation of gamers—comprised mainly of unemployed college graduates and workers whose companies had to lay off a large percentage of their force—spent many hours playing *StarCraft* in these PC-bangs. From its launch in 1998 to 2002, South Koreans purchased approximately 3.5 million copies of *StarCraft,* which accounted for more than half of the worldwide sales. The game also gave rise to a new youth culture and a rapidly growing pastime in eSports, a professional gaming league sponsored by major corporations and televised on two cable television channels, five Internet protocol (IP) television sites, and two web portals. These are remarkable statistics given that Korea was a latecomer to the Internet revolution, with broadband services first being introduced only in 1998.

Many Korean digital and gaming venture companies started their operations in the aftermath of the financial crisis in 1997, as the government nurtured commercial Internet services and created competition by eliminating monopolies. Local portal sites started to emerge in the late 1990s, replacing the old text-based bulletin board system (BBS) service. Daum Communication launched its e-mail service before Yahoo or Hotmail could capture the local markets, while Cyworld, South Korea's version of MySpace or Facebook, began to offer communication services for personal networks in 2001. Likewise, Naver Intellectual created the most local popular search engine for disseminating knowledge, making it very difficult for Google to penetrate the South Korean market; and An Cheolsu's antivirus company provided its version of cyber-security. Although government-led initiatives played a key role in reconfiguring the media landscape, the explosive growth of broadband services would not have been possible without the active participation and acceptance of this new technology by Korean society, which is well known for its impulsiveness and keen consciousness of the need to not be left behind by others. South Koreans today are no longer digital immigrants but natives. The entire country has embraced the information and communication technology of local companies like Samsung, LG, SK, and KT, which have continued to strive for better technologies and services.

Triumph of the Will: The Arirang Mass Games of North Korea

The North had entered the new millennium reeling from the collapse of the Soviet Union (which was one of its key trading partners and sources of aid), from natural disasters, and famine. Its population still suffered from food insecurity and scarcity of energy. The year 2000 marked the height of international food assistance during a period of high unemployment and shortage of food supplies. The failure of the Public Distribution system (which included all means of production, even agriculture) and general weaknesses of the Socialist planned economy led to a series of reforms in July 2002. The state experimented with monetization strategies such as paying market prices to farmers—that is, pricing goods to reflect the actual cost of production; the aim was to incentivize farmers to produce more food. The state also eliminated subsidies for food, transportation, electricity, and housing, but not for social services like education and healthcare. The reforms also decentralized industrial enterprises to make them more autonomous and profitable, but the state still maintained central control of the overall economy.

To help its people survive the transition to a cash-based economy, Pyeongyang raised wages and also officially recognized the small-scale private markets known as *jangmadang* (ground markets) that had emerged during the famine years. Initially, these illicit markets consisted of goods spread out on tarps on the dirty ground, often in the outskirts of a city or in dark alleyways. Starving children looked for opportunities to steal food—even a few kernels of corn—from these markets during the "arduous march." To maintain some semblance of control over the black market, the government began to regulate prices and collect rent for stalls, which were primarily run by married women. The *jangmadang,* which some have likened to a farmers' market, offered not only agricultural produce but also essential consumer goods smuggled in from China, like rice cookers, cell phones, Russian vodka, and cosmetics. Scholars have argued that the *jangmadang* best reflects the real prices and market conditions in North Korea. For instance, the artificially low price of rice increased 309 percent after 2002, while corn rose 587 percent. Runaway inflation hampered ordinary people's purchasing power, and crippling sanctions limited more considerable expansion of trade, but the *jangmadang* marked a new shift, not only in the economy but in the culture of North Korea as new products and ideas began to seep in through the borders.

While the North implemented painful economic reforms, it looked to sports and culture to showcase its unique strengths. During the 2002 Japan-Korea FIFA World Cup, the North had captured the global stage, reminding the peninsula of its common historical roots and culture. From early August to September 2002, North Korea held its first Arirang Festival, a grand mass gymnastics and artistic performance, at the 150,000-capacity Rungrado May Day Stadium in Pyeongyang to celebrate the ninetieth anniversary of the birth of Kim Il-sung. While it could not rival the World Cup in terms of popularity, the celebrations featured over 100,000 participants in an extravaganza of gymnastics and other dramatic performances, capturing the Guinness world record as the grandest event of its kind. Based on a popular folk story about a young couple torn apart by an evil landlord, the festival captured through emotional performances the tragic division of the Korean peninsula after the bloody civil war, and the longing for reunification. Some twenty thousand schoolchildren, who made up an entire side of the stadium, flipped through 150 pages of colored cards in unison, creating a continuous human mosaic of slogans and images, like pixels on a large computer screen. Waves of children flooded the arena waving Kimilsungias (blue orchids) and Kimjongilias (vermillion-colored begonias), named after Kim Il-sung and Kim Jong-il, and performed elegant dances, while thousands of gymnasts performed highly complex choreographed routines to beautiful music. Soldiers wielded bayonets displaying their martial arts skills, showcasing the nation's strength and the triumphant history of revolutionary struggle under the great leader. The mass games had their roots in Kim Il-sung's Flower Gymnastics during the period of his anti-Japanese activities, which drew inspiration from the gymnastics educator Friedrich Ludwig Jahn (1778–1852), who devised the *Massenturnen* method to train children in mass games. It became the signature mark of large nationalist movements such as the Czech Sokol (falcon) movement in Prague in 1862, and later the rallies of the Third Reich and Communist regimes of the Eastern bloc.

Despite its reclusiveness, the North had employed sports in the past as a way to showcase the prowess of its athletes, a symbol of its successful *juche* ideology. The Arirang pageantry was both a domestic celebration, broadcast across the country, and a presentation to the world to exhibit its history in breathtaking form, from the struggles of its people under Japanese colonialism, to its resiliency during the war, to its utopian future. Although some have viewed the mass games as pure propaganda, they functioned to communicate crucial foreign policy issues; they critiqued the forced division of the country (the separation of star-crossed lovers in Arirang) and expressed longing for reunification—the latter theme becoming more prominent over the years. The beautiful aesthetics and innocence of the children masked the North's militarism and belligerent political stance in the world. The mass games launched the beginning of foreign spectatorship, as starting in 2002 the North allowed a small delegation from abroad (such as Russia, China, Cuba, and even Mexico) to attend. By 2005, South Koreans received permission to participate in the mass games (albeit temporarily), which opened the gates for several thousand tourists from many countries in subsequent years. The 2002 games did not herald the entry of North Korea into a globalized world but rather demonstrated its shrewd employment of a globalized stage to articulate its vision for a reunified Korea. It was a message that fell on deaf ears in the United States.

The Axis of Evil: North Korea's Image Problem

On January 29, 2002, in his State of the Union address, President George W. Bush singled out Iran, Iraq, and North Korea as rogue states that comprised "the axis of evil," whose nefarious aspirations to seek weapons of mass destruction could threaten world peace. Bush's new hardline policy effectively put an end to the Agreed Framework, an engagement strategy brokered during Bill Clinton's administration with the DPRK. The axis of evil trope not only shaped US policy but also sparked a cottage industry of American films, books, and video games such as *Apocalypse, Crysis, Homefront,* and *Red Dawn,* in which North Koreans replaced the Soviets and Chinese as the evil nemesis of the good America. As the axis of evil metaphor gained currency, Bush's administration sought to rally the American people to his war on terror campaign.

From the crude impersonations in sitcoms to comedy shows like *Saturday Night Live,* Kim's North Korea would also become fodder for video games and B-rated action films. *Newsweek* magazine conferred to Kim Jong-il the title "Dr. Evil," the fictional character played by Mike Myers in the popular *Austin Powers* films, who routinely plots schemes to terrorize the world with his sidekick Mini-Me, a cloned dwarf of himself, and Number 2, his crony who wears an eye patch and runs the evil Virtucon Industries. Kim Jong-il's wedge-shaped pompadour and oversized sunglasses made him a target and a huge source of entertainment. The North Korean propaganda outlets that glorified the great leader also offered writers more fuel to fan the flames. In 2004, *Team America: World Police* created a parody of Kim as an evil dictator who feeds a UN weapons inspector to his sharks. The North Korean News Agency accused the makers of the James Bond film *Die Another Day* of lowdown, dirty slander. In this movie, James Bond (Pierce Brosnan) is captured by North Korean agents and must serve a lengthy prison sentence but is then mysteriously released and pursues Zao, a North Korean terrorist (played by the Korean American actor Rick Yune) across the globe. Three years later, Vin Diesel, who rose to stardom with *Fast and Furious,* starred in a comedy film as a US Navy Seal who must protect five children from a pair of undercover North Korean agents. When MGM decided to remake *Red Dawn,* a patriotic Cold War film released in 1984 that did well at the box office, the studio wanted to maintain the basic story line of a group of farm kids in the heartland of America who repel a Soviet invasion, but it needed a new villain as the Cold War had ended in 1991. When the producers decided to replace the Russians with the Chinese as the aggressors, it caused significant concern among potential distributors, who feared that an adverse reaction might affect Sino-American relations and have long-term implications for the film industry, as China represented an important market. The filmmakers settled on North Korean villains without fear of economic retribution.

North Koreans also started to appear as evil villains in firstperson shooting games such as *Ghost Recon 2, Homefront,* and *Crysis.* Developed by the German developer Crytek and published by Electronic Arts, the protagonists in *Crysis* face off against hostile North Korean troops who hold an archaeologist team hostage on

Lingshan Island in the South China Sea, demanding that they unlock the source of power contained in the Alien Mountain. In the game, Kim Jong-il dies in 2011 and is succeeded by Kim Jongchul (in real life the elder brother of Kim Jong-un), who develops the economy and makes North Korea one of the wealthiest and most technologically advanced nations in the world thanks to its military power and nuclear capabilities. The United States responds by deploying a team led by Lieutenant Jake Dunn (codename Nomad) to fight against the North Koreans. The game continues with a fight against the Ceph, an extraterrestrial species that have been dormant on the island until they start to battle with the Americans and North Koreans over a nuclear container. The game not only reinforced the image of North Korea as an enemy but brazenly challenged the legitimacy of Kim Jong-il's leadership.

From the *South Park* cartoon series to *MADtv, The Simpsons, Family Guy, The Daily Show,* and *30 Rock,* where the Korean American comedian Margaret Cho lampoons Kim Jong-il, the mysterious dictator from the North began to appear frequently in late-night shows in the 2000s as he became part of American popular lore. This is somewhat ironic since Kim's favorite pastime was watching films; he was a cineaste who allegedly owned twenty thousand DVDs and even confided with former US secretary of state Madeline Albright that he had watched Steven Spielberg's *Amistad* and found it moving. *Die Another Day* provoked the North's wrath because it presented the North Korean leader as a puerile child and buffoon. Hollywood relied on an old caricature of Asian men, disregarding the political correctness that had prompted the industry to be more careful with stereotyping. This simplistic portrayal further deepened the clichés of Kim as a harmless idiot, overshadowing the human rights abuses in the North and the fragile geopolitics of a region threatened by nuclear war. Meanwhile, as the North dealt with its image problem abroad, the South had to deal with the suicide of its president and with political intrigue.

Stone Bean vs. The Bulldozer: ROK Politics

On May 23, 2009, Roh Moo-hyun (1946–2009), the ninth president of South Korea, jumped to his death from a forty-five-meter cliff behind his home in Bonghwa village, penning a suicide note on his computer that apologized for burdening the nation with the corruption probes against him. Roh's successor, Lee Myung-bak, had dogged him every step of his presidency to undo his accomplishments—from inter-Korean reconciliation efforts to ending regionalism and protecting minorities. Lee had worked to tarnish his rival's reputation, empowering a group of prosecutors and the conservative media to turn on him and his family, which pushed Roh to the edge.

While both men hailed from humble families, Roh's political career as a human rights lawyer had a profound impact on his presidency. During the December 2002 presidential election, netizen groups created an online support club, Nosamo (People Who Love Roh Moo-hyun), which aided his success in the presidential election. Roh gained extensive public support with voluntary fundraising and campaigning by citizens during his campaign. When candidate Jeong Mongjun withdrew his support for Roh on the night before the election, *ohmynews,* an Internet newspaper, broke the story. In response, 570,000 people accessed this article and redistributed it using bulletin boards and cell phones to urge people to vote. Roh's surprising win empowered the so-called 386

Generation, who were active participants of student protests against the authoritarian regimes and advocates for a more conciliatory position vis-à-vis North Korea. His supporters were also inspired by his commitment to overcome regional enmity, a long and deep rivalry between the southwest (Honam) and the southeast (Yeongnam) provinces stemming from uneven economic development. The latter had prospered as a major industrial center under President Park Chung-hee, while the former stagnated.

The transition of power to Roh went smoothly with the full support of the previous president, Kim Dae-jung. Roh's nickname, Stone Bean, suited the small but tough man who had been too poor to attend college. In 1960, Roh participated in a boycott against writing mandatory essays that required students to praise the dictator, Syngman Rhee. He worked odd jobs while studying to pass the bar examination (South Korea does not require examinees to have graduated from a university or law school) and later succeeded as a judge and a human rights lawyer who would defend student activists from the authoritarian state. In 1988, he grilled members of the junta involved in the massacre of civilians in Gwangju. Then, in 2002, he defeated Yi Hoechang with the narrowest margin of victory to become the ninth president of South Korea.

Roh continued Kim's Sunshine Policy even in the face of criticism from the United States and conservative groups. Despite the North's brazen provocations, such as detonating a nuclear device and firing a Taepodong-2 missile in 2006, Roh brought the two Koreas back to the table to agree on a range of economic cooperation projects in a second summit with Kim Jong-il in 2007. The North agreed to continue discussions about reconciliation and forging closer economic ties. Despite Roh's achievements, which included making South Korea the world's tenth-largest economy (with a nominal GDP that exceeded $20,000), he nonetheless faced an impeachment bill in 2004. Opposition parties accused him of economic mismanagement and election law violations; these unsubstantiated accusations tarnished Roh's image even after the Constitutional Court found no evidence for the allegations and put him back in power.

Roh's successor, Lee Myung-bak, who had charged the president with corruption and nepotism, embodied these very vices and diverted the country from the path of political reform. Back in December 1978, Lee Myung-bak, then CEO of Hyundai Engineering and Construction, had helped to build the Somang Presbyterian Church with his small Bible study group, many of whom lived in the Hyundai Apartment units in Apgujeong-dong. Drawing out a deferred payment plan, Lee offered to build the church, promising to keep the overall construction costs to a minimum. After Lee became an assemblyman in 1992, he volunteered for three years as a traffic attendant for the six o'clock morning service at the church as a way to meet the sixty thousand members of the church and become an elder. As president of Korea, Lee inundated his administration with his personal connections, so that the acronym SKY, for Seoul National University, Korea University, and Yonsei University—the three most prestigious universities in South Korea—came to be satirically associated with his administration as Somang (his Presbyterian church), Korea University, and the Yeongnam region. Lee shamelessly appointed professors from his alma mater to crucial positions and offered posts to individuals with ties to his hometown in Yeongnam district. Political allegiances since Park Chung-hee had been drawn along regional lines. The Yeongnam region was home to the country's staunchest conservative leaders, while progressive candidates dominated the western areas like Honam (the rice bowl region). Lee's penchant for an administration "close to home" led to rampant nepotism and cronyism in government, which his predecessor Roh Moo-hyun had attempted to eliminate.

Lee's successes were linked to his urban development projects. When he won the mayoral election in Seoul in 2002, he initiated a project known as Greening. This included the restoration of the Cheonggye Stream—a waterway he had paved over with an elevated highway in 1968 while working at Hyundai Engineering and Construction. Lee's new urban renewal project, which replaced the industrial infrastructure with an entirely new landscape, cost the Seoul Metropolitan Government over $900 million and required more than 120,000 tons of water to be pumped in daily from the Han River and other sources. Lee also approved the construction of Seoul Forest Park, the renovation of a grassy field in front of Seoul City Hall where residents of Seoul could assemble for various events. His administration also added rapid-transit buses to the city's transportation system, allowing companies to share the profits from all routes while solving the traffic gridlock in Seoul. These controversial gentrification projects around Seoul, including the building of five "new-towns" about twenty kilometers outside of Seoul to create better living conditions for low-income residents, catapulted him to victory in the next presidential election. All these megaprojects earned Lee the famous nickname The Bulldozer.

One of Lee's trademark campaign pledges was his so-called 747 promise, named after the Boeing aircraft. He promised 7 percent annual economic growth, increasing the per capita income to $40,000, and claimed that the South Korean economy would become the world's seventh largest within a decade. Despite all the talk, South Korea's economy saw an average increase of 2.9 percent during Lee's administration. Moreover, Lee got caught up in controversies about food safety, described below, which diminished his credibility as a leader.

Let Them Eat Royal Cuisine: *Hansik*, Nation Branding, and Mad Cow Disease

On April 27, 2008, just a few months after Lee Myung-bak took office, *PD Notebook,* an investigative journalism program, aired an exposé titled, "Is American Beef Really Safe from Mad Cow Disease?" which set off massive antigovernment protests. The protestors questioned Lee's motives in reversing the ban on US beef imports after the detection of bovine spongiform encephalopathy (BSE) and cases of mad cow disease had been confirmed in the United States in 2003.

On June 1, 2008, police barricaded the streets near the Blue House with police buses and shipping containers as tens of thousands of protestors joined the demonstration. A teenage schoolgirl holding a lit candle became the symbol of the anti-US beef protests. Nightly candlelight vigils occurred to protest the resumed imports. Through vast networks of texting and instant messaging, protestors articulated their grievances and distributed anti-2MB pamphlets (2MB referred to Lee Myung-bak's purported brain capacity: two megabytes). At protests, people wore cow costumes (presumably representing mad cows) and masks from the movie *V for Vendetta.* Another rally on June 10 drew a crowd of over eighty thousand as protestors, raising their candles to the sky, called for renegotiation of the Free Trade Agreement (FTA) with the United

States. This prompted a mass resignation by Lee Myung-bak's cabinet, including his prime minister.

The television program cited the research of a Hallym University professor who mistakenly claimed that Koreans were twice as susceptible to contracting BSE from eating US-imported beef because of a gene found uniquely in 94 percent of Koreans. Unsubstantiated rumors continued to proliferate online, generating alarm about the safety of diapers, instant noodles, cosmetics, and other products that might have been tainted by mad cow disease. When the Ministry of Agriculture received a complaint, the government directed the prosecutor's office to investigate the misrepresentations made by the *PD Notebook* program and its instigation of civil unrest. In June 2009, the state indicted four producers and one writer; however, unrelenting demonstrations compelled Lee's government to negotiate an amendment to the FTA deal with the United States to limit shipments of beef from younger cattle, which were less susceptible to mad cow disease. The mad cow fiasco led to a dramatic drop in Lee's approval numbers, which fell below 20 percent.

Lee had better luck with *makgeolli,* for which he became Korea's pitchman. Long regarded as a poor man's alcohol, this unrefined, milky-colored, pungent, and slightly carbonated fermented rice drink was notorious for causing significant headaches, chronic belching, and nasty hangovers. Still cheaper than a bottle of water, *makgeolli* quickly became a lucrative industry (worth $240 million in 2008, and roughly $300 million in 2009). According to the Korean Customs Services, exports (mostly to Japan) soared annually. In 2009, the Samsung Economic Research Institute declared *makgeolli* South Korea's product of the year, outranking other favorites like the LED television, Yuna Kim, and the Wonder Girls, and touted it as South Korea's next big cultural export.

The rebranding of *makgeolli* was part of Lee Myung-bak's ambitious program to globalize Korean cuisine (*hansik*). Identifying five dishes on par with sushi and pasta, it launched a $77 million gastro-diplomacy initiative to globalize Korean food overseas, aiming to quadruple the number of Korean restaurants abroad and increase food exports by registering *gochujang* (red pepper paste), *doenjang* (soybean paste), and *insam* (ginseng) with Codex Alimentarius, a collection of internationally recognized standards relating to foods, food production, and food safety. The government spent tens of millions of dollars over the years to promote Korean foods identified as *hansik,* paying TV broadcasters to air documentaries, and magazines to feature various Korean dishes. State agencies also offered cooking classes at overseas cultural centers and provided financial aid and other support to Korean restaurants to develop dishes and upgrade services.

Although Japan imported *makgeolli* in small amounts in the early 1990s for its *zainichi* (foreigner residing in Japan) Korean population, exports started to increase significantly with the viral popularity of the first Korean Wave in 2004 as Korean culture enthusiasts in Japan began to make frequent trips to Korea. Unlike the 1970s, when the majority of Japanese tourists were middle-aged men looking for cheap sex, this new wave of tourists, comprised mainly of middle-aged women obsessed with Yonsama, started to show interest in all things Korean. This meant consuming a lot of Korean food and *makgeolli* in touristy areas like Myeongdong and Sincheon. As more Japanese women tourists raved about the low alcohol content of this traditional drink and as the demand in Japan increased, major convenient stores such as 7-Eleven and Carrefour as well as *izakaya* pubs started selling *makgeolli* to their customers.

According to the Korea Agro Trade Center in Tokyo, in 2009 Korea exported 6,157 tons of *makgeolli* to Japan, a 26 percent increase from the previous year. Sold in one-liter bottles at 630 yen, advertisers focused on its female clientele, marketing *makgeolli* as a wellness drink. Health enthusiasts jumped on the bandwagon, swearing that several swigs a day of this ambrosia could miraculously increase one's longevity, relieve stress, lower cholesterol, assist digestion, improve blood circulation, get rid of liver spots, reduce blood pressure, invigorate metabolism, relieve fatigue, boost one's immune system, relieve constipation, prevent cervical cancer, cure menopausal disorder, and provide the body with ten amino acids. For example, in May 2009, Kooksoondang, one of the largest exporters of *makgeolli,* sold more than thirty thousand bottles of Yonsama Makgeolli in less than a week at Goshire, Yonsama's restaurant chain in Japan. Given the proximity of Japan and Korea, Kooksoondang was able to export raw *makgeolli* (unpasteurized), giving consumers the original flavor of rice.

With the sudden rise of *makgeolli* in Japan, SBS produced a five-part documentary series in 2009 about the popularity of *makgeolli* in Japan, rekindling interest and even national longing for this traditional beverage. Choe Bul-am, an actor and senior, urged his generation to reminisce with nostalgia about the good old days of their youth, drinking *makgeolli.* Reminiscing over his mother's famous tavern in Myeongdong, Choe praised the thirst-quenching quality and refreshing aftertaste of *makgeolli,* debunking its hackneyed reputation as a cheap drink. To quench this sudden longing for *makgeolli,* distributers started hawking frozen bottles along mountain trails (sold as *hasanju*—alcohol for coming down the mountain), golf courses, and the new bike trails along the Han River.

To appeal to the palate of a younger clientele, advertisers took a page from their Japanese counterparts, marketing *makgeolli* as both a wellness product and an urban chic cocktail served with exotic ingredients like pine nuts, saffron, lotus leaf, and yuzu. In response to the sudden *makgeolli* craze at home, the South Korean government pledged financial support to nurture this fledging national industry. Much like the IT industry, which received significant subsidies from the government after the financial crisis in 1997, *makgeolli* breweries started to receive similar preferential treatment; in 2009, the government promised $133 million in subsidies and tax breaks for the next five years. Government agencies like the South Korean Ministry of Food, Agriculture, Forestry, and Fisheries (MOFAFF) also sponsored a variety of events, such as the Makgeolli Transformer Exhibition on September 3, 2009, which featured locally brewed *makgeolli* from all seven provinces to educate local consumers and prospective foreign importers. To appeal to the patriotic drinker, the government pledged to develop fifteen new strains of local rice and restore historic malts and recipes, which had disappeared during the colonial period. It also promised to patent new fermenting techniques through a government-sponsored laboratory (Korea Culture Institute), systematize the processing of local yeast, and establish a licensing system like the Blue Master program in Germany. It created a new labeling system for *makgeolli* akin to the French AOC (Appellation d'Origine Contrôlée) for all local wines based on the place of origin of their ingredients—a tall order for the state in such a short time. To stir national sentiments, local brewers with financial backing from the state launched the Makgeolli Nouveau in November 2009 to go head-to-head in competition with the annual release of the French Beaujolais Nouveau.

In response to the waning of the first Korean Wave, the Korean government launched a series of new programs, such as the Han-Style initiative in 2007, to boost its lagging tourism industry. To capitalize on the success of *Winter Sonata* and *Daejanggeum* (Jewel in the Palace) tour packages, the Korea Tourism Organization launched several campaigns promoting "authentic" Korean food and drinks to lure tourists mainly from Japan. Professional sommeliers, trained and licensed to pair Korean dishes with *makgeolli*, became ubiquitous in tourist areas, especially at designated Korean-style restaurants. Despite the craze and government-led initiative, cultural critics were skeptical, arguing that this was simply a fad waiting to fizzle. On the one hand, promoting *makgeolli* as a "national product" into the global market was successful because it symbolized the triumph of neoliberalism and the cultural reconversion of a crude product into a cross-class and transnational commodity. But despite calls from critics at home and abroad to allow receiving countries to adapt Korean food and drinks to fit into local contexts (which had allowed General Tsao's chicken, the California sushi roll, fortune cookies, and chop suey to succeed in the United States), government agencies like the Presidential Council on National Competitiveness and MOFAFF disagreed. They planned to invest millions of dollars in rebranding *makgeolli* as both a unique part of Korea's distinct cultural tradition and a globally viable public brand, which would in turn boost Korea's poor national brand index rankings. This strategy turned out to be a dismal failure. The excessive costs, poor marketing, lack of synergy at home and abroad, as well as larger problems with South Korea's nation-branding initiatives made it impossible to sustain the campaign.

Lee's schemes—from creating *makgeolli* as the drink of Korea to his multibillion-dollar plan to refurbish South Korea's four major rivers, despite protests from environmentalists—revealed the limits of the bulldozer approach. The failures of Lee's government to address deep inequalities and social problems in the new South became apparent not only in the food industry but also in the government's relation to the most marginalized groups in Korea.

Marginal in a Prosperous Nation

In 1992, Chandra Kumari Gurung, a Nepali woman in her midthirties, went to South Korea to work as a "foreign trainee." Gurung, like other migrant workers from Nepal, worked long hours for minimum wages under hazardous conditions as an "apprentice," laboring in menial factory jobs that most Koreans now shunned. In 1993, Gurung suddenly disappeared, and her Nepali friends had no clues to her whereabouts. When she lost her wallet and could not pay for her meal, Gurung panicked because she could not articulate to the restaurant owner what had happened. She would spend the next six years and four months at a women's shelter as a "mentally deficient vagrant" before being transferred to a psychiatric hospital after experts diagnosed her with schizophrenia. Despite numerous attempts by Gurung to explain that she was from Nepal, the police and social services assumed that she was a mentally ill Korean woman from the countryside. Soon after her release, the NGO Nature Trail helped to track her down, and Yi Suktae, a Korean lawyer, assisted Gurung in filing a lawsuit against Cheongnyangni Mental Hospital for her forced incarceration. In April 2000, the South Korean government offered an official apology, and Gurung finally returned to Nepal on June 14, 2000. A Seoul court awarded her a paltry sum of $23,500 several months later for her suffering.

For most migrant workers, Gurung's ordeal did not come as a shock. The absence of laws protecting foreign workers compelled them to work longer hours to pay off debts, along with interest, to the brokers who brought them to Korea. The majority of unskilled laborers hired to work in factories lacked any knowledge of the hazardous chemicals and had not received proper training on how to run the factory machines. All this contributed to occupational accidents and diseases and made foreign workers vulnerable to exploitation by employers who knew that they were powerless to complain to the authorities.

In the early 1990s, South Korea established the Industrial Training System, in which temporary foreign workers fell under the category of trainees (apprentices) rather than legal laborers. The rise of undocumented workers increased under this system, prompting the government to create the Employment Permit System (EPS) and the Non-professional Employment (E-9) visa, which allowed companies with severe labor shortages to employ foreign workers legally. The majority of these new positions were primarily "3-D" (dirty, dangerous, demanding) jobs designed to support the Korean workforce. The EPS included a bilateral arrangement with sixteen countries promoting cross-border labor migration in Asia; it led to the rise of foreign migrant workers in Korea and contributed to the creation of more than 180 NGOs and support groups. The increase in marriages between migrants and Koreans in the rural areas contributed to the first wave of multicultural families as 238,000 international marriages were registered from 2006 to 2012; Vietnamese women comprised the largest group followed by the Joseonjok (ethnic Chinese Korean). While international matchmaking agencies have thrived in South Korea for more than a decade, brokering thousands of cross-border marriages for bachelors in the rural areas, many female marriage migrants still struggle with age difference, loneliness, depression, as well as language and cultural barriers, which are primarily to blame for the prevalence of domestic violence and divorce.

The Forsaken: Mixed-Race Children and Orphans

In 2006, when Hines Ward (b. 1976) became the first biracial Korean to win the Super Bowl most valuable player award as a member of the Pittsburgh Steelers, he found himself cast in the media spotlight in South Korea. Once a social pariah, Ward returned to his birthplace of Seoul with his mother, welcomed with open arms by Koreans. Donating one million dollars to create the Hines Ward Helping Hands Foundation to support biracial and multiracial children in Korea, Ward opened up public debates about the stigmatization of racial difference and social discrimination in society. The story of mixed-race children in Korea as well as the return of hundreds of diasporic Korean adoptees from fifteen countries (such as Belgium, Denmark, France, Sweden, and the United States) in search of their birth families, led to soul-searching and critiques about the practice of international adoption and the plight of single mothers who lacked adequate social support and welfare.

On February 5, 2006, Hines Ward was named the most valuable player in Super Bowl XL after catching a forty-three-yard pass from wide receiver Antwann Randle El for a touchdown to drive the Pittsburgh Steelers in a decisive 21–10 victory over the Seattle Seahawks. Overnight, the biracial Korean wide receiver went from being a social pariah to a national hero in South Korea. As cameras zoomed in on the tattoo of his name etched on his arm in *hangeul*, the public was surprised to learn that he was the mixed-race son of a GI and a Korean woman. Most South Koreans had never heard of Hines Ward nor even cared for American football. Ward's mother, Kim Young Hee, who had worked at a nightclub as a waitress, met his father while he was stationed in South Korea. After they got married, they moved to the United States when Ward was a toddler but divorced shortly thereafter. The US court granted Ward's father custody because his mother spoke very little English, but the boy ran away at the age of seven to live with his mother, who worked three jobs to raise him. Stigmatized as a "Yankee whore," Kim realized that she could never raise her son in her homeland. At her own mother's funeral in 1998, her friends and family members had ostracized her, even spitting on her for marrying a Black man. It was no easier for mother and son in the Korean American community, where they failed to find acceptance.

Given the past rejection, Ward struggled with his newfound popularity. When Korean companies offered lucrative endorsements for Ward's visit to Seoul, he decided to use his celebrity status to address prejudices against mixed-race children in Korea. Donating one million dollars to launch the Hines Ward Helping Hands Foundation, Ward reached out to some 35,000 mixed-race children, including a new group of *Kosian* (children of mixed Korean parents and other Asian parents), who suffered from severe bullying and discrimination. In response to his campaign to raise awareness, South Korean newspaper editorials began to call for higher tolerance and compassion for this marginalized group of children.

In South Korea it was common for family members to shun or expel their daughters from the household if they had a mixed-race child. Kim Insun (b. 1957), better known as Insooni, was one of the few biracial African Americans to become a successful singer. Like

Ward, she was born to a South Korean mother and an African American father who served in the military, and she had to constantly hide what she called her "nappy hair" with a hat during performances to conceal her Black identity. When she was twenty years old, Insooni got her break when a producer heard her debut as a member of the female trio the Hui Sisters. However, due to her inability to pass, the television industry banned her from shows and denied her the right to participate in international singing competitions as a representative of Korea, thereby revealing the deeply embedded prejudices of Korean society.

By the early 2000s, several generations of Korean adoptees came of age, and a growing number began to return to their birth country. Critical of the adoption system, they aimed to change the perception of orphans, widows, single mothers, and adoption practices. Together, the returning Koreans created the organization Adoptee Solidarity Korea, which called for an end to international adoption of South Korean orphans. They pressured the Korean government to focus instead on promoting sex education, monitoring orphanages and foster care, increasing domestic adoption, and expanding services for single mothers. They also established transnational organizations such as GOA'L (Global Overseas Adoptees' Link) and spaces like the guesthouse KoRoot, which offered a home for adoptees visiting Korea. In 2004, the Seoul Metropolitan City officially recognized GOA'L as an NGO, and it has been receiving state subsidies since 2006; it even opened its first overseas branch office in Santa Barbara, California, to help American adoptees navigate the emotionally fraught journey of the return "home."

Since the mid-1950s, more than 200,000 Korean children have been adopted by families in Western nations. Returning to their homeland to attempt to reunite with birth families has become common with roughly three thousand visiting Korea every year, some on government-sponsored heritage tours or through other agencies. In 1999, members of GOA'L lobbied with other adoptees and local civic groups to make adoptees eligible for the F-4 visa (people of Korean heritage) under the Overseas Koreans Act. This visa would facilitate a more straightforward return to Korea, granting them long-term residency rights and the ability to work freely with Korean nationals in their search for their biological parents. On April 24, 2010, the National Assembly passed the Nationality Law Revision allowing adoptees to regain their Korean citizenship without having to surrender their current citizenship. This was a critical amendment, as before this, adoptees lost their Korean citizenship immediately after being adopted and leaving the country. On April 18, 2011, thirteen adoptees from Canada, France, Germany, the Netherlands, Switzerland, and the United States posed in front of cameras at the Ministry of Justice when they became the first international adoptees to be granted Korean citizenship. In her memoir *Fugitive Visions,* Jane Jeong Trenka (b. 1972) offers a very candid view of life as an adoptee struggling with her identity in the United States. Writing in an ethnographic style, Trenka also provides a glimpse into the collective experiences of returning adoptees who choose to live in Korea. She explores the feelings of homesickness and longing for the homeland in America, and of isolation in Korea due to language barriers and an inability to fit into a homogenous society (while at the same time feeling a sense of identity and belongingness).

The struggles of multiracial children and adoptees to find their place in Korean society are deeply embedded in the history of South Korea as a direct product of the Pax Americana and Korean nationalism. The return of Korea's stepchildren has exposed the ugly realities of prejudice against multiracial children and the social stigma faced by their mothers, which still exist behind the South's façade of progress and prosperity.

Education Fever: The *Hagwon* and Competition for Success in the ROK

The emergence of South Korea as a global economic power generated new anxieties about how to stay ahead of the race. Prosperous South Koreans now looked for new ways to give their children a competitive edge to succeed in a global economy. Private education (*gwaoe*), banned by President Chun Doo-hwan from 1980 to 1990 to "promote equality," promised to be the route to success. Today the for-profit *hagwon*s, or private cram schools, have increased across the country, offering to help students prepare for their critical high school and university entrance examinations. For some children, the *hagwon* is also a space where one can socialize with friends, which is essential given the demanding pressures of school. By 2010, the number of *hagwon* had increased to seventy thousand nationwide and led to an inflation of real estate prices in neighborhoods that boasted the best schools.

The intertwined history of elite education and real estate is best illustrated in the case of Gangnam. In the 1970s, the Seoul government forced some of the top primary and middle schools to relocate to Gangnam as part of the gentrification project, and soon these institutions became associated with a successful entry into elite high schools and universities. Today a higher than average concentration of *hagwon*s are located in the Daechi-dong neighborhood in Gangnam district, which is called the "Mecca of private education." Real estate values have skyrocketed, increasing the prices of apartments like Eunma or Useong 300 percent despite their appearing like dilapidated tenements. Most of the buildings are five or six stories and are plastered with signboards advertising special cram schools for math, English, and other subjects. The *hagwon*s in Daechi-dong send the most students by percentage to South Korea's so-called SKY universities—Seoul National University, Korea University, and Yonsei University—as well as Ivy League universities in the United States. The neighborhood is always crowded with parents, students, and yellow *hagwon* school buses that queue along the crammed streets to pick up students.

On average, South Korean parents spend more than fifteen billion dollars on private education annually, more than three times the average for other OECD nations. In 2010, 74 percent of all students engaged in some private afterschool instruction, or "shadow education," at an average cost of $2,600 per student for the year. In 2008, the state imposed a curfew of 10 P.M. on *hagwon*s in Seoul, even rewarding citizens for turning in violators in order to level the field. Despite these legal measures, parents prefer to spend more money, sending their children to small, expensive private *hagwon*s instead of the larger ones. Admission at a top *hagwon* is competitive and based on a student's test scores. Students from the top *hagwon*s consistently outperform their counterparts in almost every country in reading and math, which prompted then-president Barack Obama to speak glowingly of South Korean parents who invest in their children's education, while he lamented how far American students had fallen behind. Without this education obsession, South Korea perhaps would not be where it is today; however, this intense focus has exacted a heavy price from the Korean people and particularly their children. The one-size-fits-all government-led, uniform curricula and relentless focus on education have resulted in formidable exam performers, who are accustomed to a rigid, hierarchical system; this has also stifled creativity and innovation. The single greatest motivation to study at an elite *hagwon* is to gain admission to a SKY university. The end-all university entrance exam is so critical to students' futures that parents invest heavily in private education. On the day of the entrance exam, parents crowd churches and temples to pray for their children's success; planes are grounded to reduce noise levels; and offices and the stock market open later in the day so students can get to designated exam sites on time. Not surprisingly, students experience extraordinary levels of pressure in this stressful environment. South Korean students are the unhappiest among OECD countries and have one of the highest student suicide rates. Test results and university acceptance statistics reveal that investing in an elite *hagwon* can have a positive impact (although it is not the sole factor). In 2000, for instance, among the 713 Seoul high school students who enrolled in Seoul National University, 292 (41 percent) were from the three Gangnam districts, the majority from the top *hagwon* in Daechi-dong. These statistics have not changed in 2019.

The competitive Korean educational system has led to the emergence of a new type of "managerial mother." As early as 1964, mothers became engaged in educational politics: when a school entrance exam question inadvertently included two right answers about the ingredients in taffy, outraged mothers began to cook taffy outside the Ministry of Education using the alternative ingredient to express their anger over the blunder. Eventually, pressure from the mothers won the resignation of both the vice education minister and the superintendent of Seoul, and several dozen students received retroactive admission offers. Today mothers often gather in cafés in Daechi-dong to discuss tips or even to hire a manager so that their child can enroll in a prestigious *hagwon*—a phenomenon captured in the recent hit JTBC drama series *Sky Castle* (2018). Mothers (even those with high levels of education) often relinquish their careers to become a full-time parent and academic manager, dedicating their lives to the success of their children and meanwhile earning the nickname Gangnam ajummas (middle-aged woman). A more unsavory term applied to women is the Daechi-dong mother or Gangnam's equivalent of the Tiger Mom in the United States. Naturally, critics have decried the existence of the *hagwon* for creating greater inequality between the poor and the wealthy in South Korea.

Another form of cultural capital in Korea's quest for global influence is the knowledge of English, which has been linked to success in the job market. Prospective employers routinely require applicants to take the TOEFL (Test of English as a Foreign Language) or the TOEIC (Test of English for International Communication) to demonstrate proficiency in the language. In 1997, the Ministry of Education introduced the English language in elementary schools, but parents began to invest privately in their children's English education. According to a report by the Samsung Economic Research Institute in 2008, Koreans spent about fifteen trillion *won* ($15.8 billion) on English learning per year. In addition, more than forty thousand schoolchildren and their mothers moved to English-speaking countries like Australia, Canada, India, Malaysia, New Zealand, the Philippines, Singapore, and the United States while the fathers remained at home. Driven by a desire to give their children an edge by becoming fluent in English, these "wild geese" families have upended traditional migration patterns at high financial, social, and psychological costs. Geese families who travel to the West have faced unexpected emotional hardships. Korean students, who represent the third-largest group of international students in the United States, suffer as invisible outsiders who struggle with different cultural values and second-language anxiety, especially at the beginning of their studies abroad. Studies have found that they are less likely to seek help for mental health issues such as depression and anxiety due to social stigma and cultural discomfort about asking for help. Couples who live separately also report insecurity in their relationships but justify their decisions in the framework of sacrificing their happiness for the sake of their children.

The Republic of Fakes? The Sin Jeong-a and Hwang Useok Scandals

Korea's obsession with educational credentials and the pressure to succeed led to two major controversies that rocked the academic world. In 2007, Sin Jeong-a (b. 1972) created a national scandal shortly after her appointment as one of the directors of the 2008 Gwangju Biennale when Dongguk University charged her with fabricating a doctoral degree from Yale University. The press depicted her as a seductress who used her powerful lover, Byeon Yanggyun (the onetime presidential secretary to Roh Moo-hyun and a Yale alumnus), to obtain government money to help her rise to fame. Meanwhile, and much like Sin who was at the pinnacle of her career and stood as the poster girl of modern Korea, Hwang Useok, a professor of theriogenology and biotechnology at Seoul National University, also became embroiled in a global scandal. His infamous fabrication of a series of experiments on stem-cell research appeared in high-profile journals such as *Science* in 2004 and 2005. Once called the Pride of Korea, Hwang was charged with embezzlement and violation of bioethics laws and was fired by the university.

These two sensational cases reveal not only the intense pressures on academics to produce world-class research but also the problem of plagiarism and counterfeiting in South Korea. South Korea has had a long history of producing fake goods, from phony Pierre Cardin suits in Myeongdong in the 1970s to counterfeit Nike and Adidas products in the 1980s. Counterfeit producers in places like Dongdaemun thrived until quite recently as the government began to crack down on violations of intellectual property rights, in turn pushing piracy abroad to places like China and Vietnam, where Korean counterfeiters continue to ply their trade in one of the largest counterfeit markets in the world. To many academics, the fraud seemed credible in the "Republic of Forgery." They could point to the multiple pending IP and copyright disputes, especially Samsung's ongoing patent lawsuits (despite signing on to numerous international IP treaties) and the ruling by a US court in August 2012 that Samsung had copied Apple's designs. In a very competitive academic job market with only a handful of positions available at the elite schools, plagiarism and falsification have been rampant and more sophisticated, as illustrated in the cases of Sin Jeong-a and Hwang Useok.

Sin had already been in the media spotlight. In 1995, when she was twenty-three years old, Sin claimed to be one of two survivors rescued from under the rubble of the Sampung Department Store after being trapped for eight hours—it was one of the deadliest building collapses before the World Trade Center attack in New York City in 2001. The disaster in Seoul killed 502 people and injured 937 people. Just like the teenage con artist Frank W. Abagnale in the 2002 biographical crime film *Catch Me If You Can* starring Leonardo DiCaprio, Sin's skills at hobnobbing with fine-art dealers and patrons and her claims to two degrees from the University of Kansas and Yale University secured her a job at the Kumho Museum in Seoul in 1997. When she applied for an assistant professorship at Dongguk University, Sin submitted "Guillaume Apollinaire: Catalyst for Primitivism, for Picabia, and Duchamp," which later turned out to be a carbon copy of Ekaterini Samaltanou-Tsiakma's doctoral dissertation, submitted to the University of Virginia in 1981. By 2002, Sin was the chief curator of Sungkok Art Museum, one of the best in Seoul to feature exhibitions of contemporary artworks. Behind the scenes, Dongguk University art faculty became suspicious about Sin's academic credentials from Yale. When Yale University officials announced that Sin's diploma was a forgery, to their astonishment Dongguk filed a fifty-million-dollar lawsuit in 2008 against the Ivy League school, submitting a fax sent by a Yale officer confirming Sin's degree (which turned out to be an administrative error). Investigations revealed that Sin had scaled the heights of the academic and art world with only a high school degree, exposing a corrupt system of nepotism in the highest circle. Racy photographs of her lover—a close aide to President Roh Moo-hyun—revealed the connections that had catapulted Sin to such prestigious positions. Sin received a light sentence of eighteen months in jail for forging her credentials and for embezzling money from the Sungkok Art Museum.

Sin's downfall was matched by another professor, Hwang Useok (b. 1953), whose reputation as the Pride of Korea was ruined after the journal *Nature* charged Hwang of fabricating evidence that he had successfully created human embryonic stem cells through cloning—results that he published in the prestigious journal *Science* in 2004 and 2005. In contrast to Sin, Hwang's credentials were real, but he brazenly flaunted all laws of bioethics to conduct his research. Hwang earned his master's degrees in veterinary medicine and a doctorate in theriogenology at Seoul National University. After a brief stint at Hokkaido University, he joined the faculty at his alma mater in 1986. Hwang's meteoric rise to fame began in 1999 when he claimed that he had cloned a cow—a stupendous feat—though without any valid data. In May 2004, Hwang announced that his team of scientists had made a significant breakthrough in biotechnology when they created eleven human embryonic stem cells using 185 eggs; this was the basis of his article in *Science,* which led to numerous grants from the Ministry of Science and Technology and other agencies. Hwang soon became the head of a new World Stem Cell Hub at Seoul National University Hospital and achieved the status of a national hero. The ability to extract stem cells from a cloned human embryo was revolutionary and promised new treatments for spinal cord injuries and Alzheimer's disease. Hwang dazzled the world when he introduced the world to Snuppy, the first cloned Afghan hound in 2005, which earned the dog the Invention of the Year title by *Time* magazine.

On June 1, 2005, Ryu Yongjun, a researcher in one of Hwang's laboratories, e-mailed the Korean television network MBC (Munhwa Broadcasting Corporation) concerning fraud, while *PD Sucheop* (Reporter's Notebook), an investigative journalism show, aired two programs that probed Hwang's research projects. Allegations surfaced that Hwang not only fabricated evidence but coerced female members of his research team to donate their eggs. Hwang's collaborator, Gerald Schatten from the University of Pittsburgh, requested that *Science* remove his name from their article, which he claimed was inaccurate and unethical. The scandal took a dramatic turn when Hwang's associate, No Seung-il, reported to media outlets that nine of the eleven lines were flawed because of contamination and the switching of some stem-cell lines. An independent panel found that Hwang had intentionally fabricated the results published in *Science*; there were no patient-matched embryonic stem cells in existence. The board charged Hwang of deception and violation of ethical standards, destroying the credibility of the Korean scientific community.

Despite Hwang's admission of ethical violations, hundreds of South Korean women offered to donate their eggs for stem-cell research in a show of support. His supporters even created a website, taking egg-donation pledges online, which reached 725 in early December 2005. To them, Hwang was the Albert Einstein of South Korea, who deserved the stamp released in his honor in 2005, featuring the silhouette of a man standing up out of a wheelchair. To salvage its reputation, Seoul National University fired Hwang for his violations of bioethics in 2006. The Seoul Central Court then sentenced him to a two-year suspended jail time for embezzling research funds and illegally purchasing human eggs, barring him from any further stem-cell research. Today, despite his tarnished reputation in the scientific community, Hwang continues to clone animals in his laboratory, Sooam Biotech, which has partnered up with different companies in China and the United States to clone cattle and dead pets.

Strangers Forever? North Korean Defectors, Refugees, or People of a New Land?

On January 9, 2005, the Ministry of Unification in South Korea announced that the term *saetomin* (people of a new land) would replace *talbukja* (people who fled the North) as the official term to refer to North Korean refugees—thereby angering the North Korean state. Since 1953, more than 27,000 North Koreans have defected to South Korea. New Malden, a tiny London suburb, has one of the highest concentrations of North Korean defectors, the vast majority being women, among its twenty thousand Korean residents. Their tales of escaping the North, the challenges of seeking political asylum in the United Kingdom and other European nations, and the reasons for not wanting to settle in South Korea as ordinary migrants reveal the precariousness of being a North Korean today.

Between 1961 and 1993, the South Korean government treated defectors as national heroes. A special law, which provided all defectors a financial package based on a defector's political and "intelligence value," and mandated their protection, remained in effect until 1993. With the fall of the Iron Curtain, the South Korean government altered its policies vis-à-vis defectors, which affected, too, the way South Koreans view them today. Triggered by catastrophic famines in the North, the first large wave of defectors fled to third countries (especially in Southeast Asia) via China in the mid-1990s; yet they had little choice but to settle in South Korea. The refugee option was limited: if they crossed into China in search of food, they could not claim asylum because they were unable to document "persecution" as mandated by the UNHCR (United Nations High Commissioner for Refugees). The process to enter the South was equally complicated, as North Korean refugees faced interrogations by the National Intelligence Service and the National Police Agency before being sent to Hanawon, an enclosed government resettlement facility. Here they enrolled in a settlement support program for three months of indoctrination before the state deemed them fit to be integrated into the local community, with various government subsidies from employment assistance to housing and medical benefits.

By 2015, there were some thirty thousand North Koreans in the South, many of whom had defected following the famine. Despite all the fanfare behind the propaganda from South Korean loudspeakers promising a free and prosperous life, many found it challenging to survive in the capitalist South. Although they shared a common ancestry, decades of historical hostility and radically different patterns of socialization created cultural and social barriers that alienated the two peoples. South Koreans rarely trusted the newcomers, whom they viewed through their antagonism toward the DPRK. Such distrust pressured defectors to request exemptions from compulsory military service (as permitted by Article 64 of the Military Service Act), which contributed to feelings of marginalization in their new home. To allay suspicions, defectors felt compelled to conceal their identity by feigning a South Korean accent and performing the speech, gestures, and mannerisms of their new compatriots. The newcomers also found themselves boxed into low-income neighborhoods despite the generous housing assistance and welfare benefits they received. Unskilled North Korean women who were unemployed before they left their homes confronted the most significant challenges in finding employment. With few opportunities for economic success or social mobility in South Korea, some defectors resorted to secondary migration, relying on brokers to seek new opportunities in Europe or the United States, which have rejected them. This left them vulnerable to extortion and sexual violence. Moreover, since the South Korean government immediately recognized North Korean defectors as citizens after their naturalization at the Hanawon center, they could not claim refugee status. As a result, they were treated by potential host countries like any other migrant and deprived of benefits and legal representation.

One exception was the United Kingdom, which accepted North Koreans as refugees starting in 2004; however, in 2008 the UK Border Agency announced it would deport any North Korean defector who had already been granted asylum in the South over concerns of a wave of Chinese immigrants attempting to pose as North Korean defectors. Today there are roughly seven hundred North Korean defectors among the twenty thousand Koreans who have made New Malden their home. During the 1970s, as the number of South Korean companies began to expand globally, Korean businesses and students were drawn to New Malden for its cheap housing prices and relative proximity to London. During the 1980s, a vibrant Koreatown began to emerge as the population grew significantly. Many North Koreans who ended up in New Malden were double defectors—moving first to the South and then to the United Kingdom, a country that traditionally had neutral relations with North Korea. New Malden was attractive to them because it boasted over twenty Korean restaurants, a Korean supermarket, a Korean-language church, property agents, taxi companies, cafés, a *noraebang* (karaoke), a bakery, and a Korean newspaper. While many of the signboards in both English and Korean suggested a peaceful coexistence, old tensions and discomfort simmered beneath the surface between North and South Koreans. The latter came to England for work or to enhance their education, while the former are all refugees.

The population of defectors in New Malden did not hail from North Korea's elite, like Thae Yong-ho (Tae Yeongho), North Korea's former deputy ambassador to the United Kingdom, who defected with his family in 2016 to South Korea. Instead, they were former soldiers or workers who had to make heart-wrenching do-or-die decisions to defect and suffered from the trauma of leaving loved ones behind. Preferring to settle alongside other Koreans, defectors had little incentive to learn English and integrate with other ethnic groups. Ironically, without the economic assistance of South Korean companies and small businesses, the North Koreans could hardly have survived, let alone build a community of their own. Many have worked in establishments owned by South Koreans, especially in menial jobs such as waiters or as factory workers. Today these refugees congregate at the Korean Nationality Residents Association, one of two North Korean groups that provide support, run a Korean-language school, and host cultural events.

While New Malden might offer a glimpse of what a united Korea might look like in the distant future, it also reveals deep divisions—from political and cultural differences to the trauma experienced by defectors—that require healing, reconciliation, and trust. The harrowing life story of Choe Junghwa (b. 1966) reveals the complexity of each defector's individual experience. The devastating famines that killed more than three million of his compatriots motivated Choe to flee his homeland. Forced to witness the death from starvation of three of his brothers, Choe hustled goods in the black market, saving enough money to pay a Chinese broker to smuggle his wife and son out of the North. Although he chose to migrate to Great Britain because he had read about the Industrial Revolution as a child, the realities of life in New Malden failed to match his expectations. He struggled to learn the English language and adjust to a country that had various ethnic groups. Opportunities for upward social mobility seemed elusive as he worked at a Korea Food warehouse like many of his compatriots, who ironically found it more comfortable working for South

Koreans than employers of other nationalities. Still haunted by his past, Choe followed the sparse news about North Korea, which focused almost exclusively on its military posturing and its threats against the West.

Bury the Enemy or Brinkmanship? Nuclear Testing and Long-Range Rockets

On October 9, 2006, the DPRK detonated a nuclear device registering 3.6 on the Richter scale in tunnels dug into a remote mountainous site called Punggye-ri in North Hamgyeong Province. This event prompted swift international condemnation. The UN Security Council urged the DPRK to commit to the denuclearization of the Korean peninsula rather than threaten peace and stability in Asia and the world. The North Korean Foreign Ministry announced the detonation as a historical event and a great leap forward in developing a self-reliant defense capability. North Korea was now the ninth country to have nuclear weapons, joining an exclusive club of nations. During the first round of the six-party talks on North Korea's nuclear weapons program in 2004 (which involved China, Japan, Russia, South Korea, and the United States), there were hopes that the North would denuclearize in exchange for energy and other aid. The failure of the talks reminded the world that the North's nuclear ambitions were serious. On a diplomatic front, the talks showcased the North's ability to use its capability to gain financial guarantees from the West, which pundits called the practice of "nuclear brinkmanship."

The clandestine nuclear weapons development program in the North began in the early 1980s when it constructed a plutonium-producing reactor in Yongbyeon. In 1994, during the Clinton administration, the North signed the Agreed Framework with the United States to freeze the reactor program in exchange for fuel and the construction of two modern nuclear power plants fueled by light-water reactors. However, in 2002 the North started to pursue uranium enrichment and plutonium technologies, citing American belligerence by the George W. Bush administration and reneging on the principles outlined in the Agreed Framework. This resulted in the expulsion of inspectors attached to the International Atomic Energy Agency, and the North started to reroute fuel rods for plutonium production. In 2003, the North withdrew from the Nuclear Non-Proliferation Treaty after the United States failed to deliver the light-water reactors and other items that were stipulated in their earlier agreement.

To fund both their nuclear and their missile technology programs, the North Koreans earned hard cash abroad by supplying roughly 40 percent of the world's theater missile system, which includes launch platforms, missile stocks, and infrastructure. North Korea's earlier ballistic missile ambitions faced several failures in the late 1970s as it tried to replicate Soviet and Chinese short-range missiles. Using its connections with Egypt, the North was able to procure Soviet-built Scud-B missiles, allowing its engineers to design replicas such as the Hwaseong-5, a short-range ballistic missile that could be developed further to deliver a nuclear head. It is through the indirect technical assistance of China, Pakistan, and Russia that the North Koreans succeeded in building their nuclear program. The North claimed that it required this technology, not only to protect its independence but also to bargain for its security. And while it navigated the politics of nuclear disarmament, the North also conducted cultural diplomacy to showcase the new image it had fashioned for itself.

We Bring the Musicians: The New York
Philharmonic and Symphonic Diplomacy

On February 26, 2008, the New York Philharmonic Orchestra played an entire concert in the East Pyeongyang Grand Theater, which was aired on North Korean State Television and broadcast live internationally on CNN in Canada and the United States and on MBC in South Korea. Given the recently stalled nuclear talks, the North's offer of unprecedented access to the country to some three hundred foreign reporters who covered this historic event was a significant gesture. By granting Internet access and unrestricted international phone calls, the North made a symbolic connection with the global networks of the world.

On August 13, 2007, the New York Philharmonic announced that it had received an invitation to perform in North Korea through a representative from the Ministry of Culture. A couple of months later, a group of officials representing the orchestra traveled to Pyeongyang to tour three concert halls, which included two of the most renowned theaters: the Moranbong and the East Pyeongyang Grand. The parties negotiated the logistics of the concert, including opportunities to meet with local musicians, rights for broadcasting, and other logistics to ensure that the concert would be a success. In December, Zarin Mehta, president and executive director of the New York Philharmonic, and Bak Gilyeon, North Korea's ambassador to the United Nations, held a joint press conference announcing the acceptance of the invitation and billing the event as "a manifestation of the power of music to unite people, and an opportunity to bring about mutual respect through culture and softening relations."

Individuals became personally invested in this historic cultural exchange. Yoko Nagae Ceschina, a Japanese philanthropist living in Italy, offered a generous donation, while Bak Samgu, the chairman of the Kumho Group, provided an Asiana Airlines Boeing 747 to fly the orchestra to Pyeongyang. To make the most of the cultural exchange, conductor Lorin Maazel arranged for North Korean musicians to participate in master classes with members of the Philharmonic. Supporters of the event praised it as a meaningful step toward peace, while detractors viewed the concert as a publicity stunt by the North to lend legitimacy to its regime by serenading Kim Jong-il. In 1956, the Boston Symphony was the first American orchestra to play in the Soviet Union, and the Philadelphia Orchestra performed in China in 1973, but this was the first time that a large American orchestra and its staff (130 members) set foot in Pyeongyang. Aficionados of classical music scoured over the selection of pieces for hidden meanings. In a country that banned jazz-style music, George Gershwin's *An American in Paris* seemed subversive while Dvořák's Ninth Symphony, "From the New World," inspired by Native American and African American spiritual music, highlighted the diversity of America. Given the North's engagement with the Black Panthers in the 1970s, North Korean officials may have listened to the piece ironically as a symbol of American oppression of the disenfranchised. The evening's concert ended with the popular Korean folk song "Arirang," reminding Koreans about their divided land. While Kim Jong-il was conspicuously absent, Yang Hyeongseop, the president of the Presidium of the Supreme People's Assembly, attended the concert, providing an official face to the event. Whatever the intent, for one evening the New York Philharmonic Orchestra played in the halls of

Pyeongyang, raising hopes and longings for peace, reconciliation, and healing.

Revealing Is Healing: The Truth and Reconciliation Commission

All the beautiful music streaming from the North could not heal the violent scars left by the brutal repression of dissent in the South from its birth. Between late October 1948 and July 1949 in Gurye County (South Jeolla Province), where three regiments of the South Korean army were stationed, the constabulary forces indiscriminately tortured and massacred numerous civilians shortly after the Yeosu-Suncheon rebellion in October 1948, when two thousand soldiers mutinied against Rhee's anti-Communist government to protest the bloody crackdown on an uprising in Jeju Island, which had opposed separate elections in the South without the North. Members of the Korean Youth Association in Gurye also participated in the systematic mass killings of civilians, instigating incidents and offering false testimonies against civilians for allegedly abetting local Communists. Through onsite examinations and field surveys, a group of archaeologists began exhumations on June 18, 2007, unearthing some seventy civilians detained by the Gurye Police Station, who were executed in the front yard without due process and buried around Bongseong Mountain.

Since the creation of the Truth and Reconciliation Commission in South Africa to come to terms with the legacy of apartheid and colonialism, South Korea established its own in 2000 to confront the ghosts of its past. After the first Truth Commission (Presidential Commission on Suspicious Deaths between 1975 and 1987) under President Kim Dae-Jung completed its work in 2004, the National

Assembly demanded a more comprehensive report by an independent commission to examine Korea's modern history, which included Japanese colonialism, national division, three long decades of dictatorship, and the history of Koreans abroad, as well as other traumatic episodes in Korea's modern history that were swept under the carpet by the Cold War and dictatorships. On December 1, 2005, the South Korean Assembly enacted a law to establish an independent Truth and Reconciliation Commission (TRC), whose scope extended to political killings, torture, forced disappearances, fabricated trials and executions, and other human rights abuses committed by the state.

With the participation of one female and fourteen male investigators who relied on a staff of 240 members and an annual budget of nineteen million dollars, the commission began to investigate various atrocities committed from 1910 to 1993, relying on petitions filed by civilians. The final report provided information on civilian massacres and human rights abuses, which had once been considered taboo topics and a violation of the National Security Law. The investigation led to the publication of four volumes and two electronic files, which were made available to the public in December 2010. In the case of the Gurye massacres mentioned above, the commission advised the South Korean government to offer an official apology to the bereaved families of the victims, restore the honor of the dead by revising historical records on the basis of its findings, and employ the study to educate the public.

Putting a face on the suffering were individual narratives like the story of Seo Changdeok (b. 1948), a fisherman who was abducted in 1967 for six days by North Koreans. He endured unspeakable torture for thirty-three days at the hands of Rhee's security forces and was forced to make false confessions about being a North Korean spy. Another story involved Im Seongguk (1950–85), whom the security forces tortured for twenty-eight hours in Gwangju, causing him to die from wounds caused by electrocution. The commission's report contained shocking accounts of civil rights violations by the KCIA, falsified espionage charges against individuals using the National Security Law and the Anti-Communist Law, and horrific civilian massacres during the Korean War by right-wing vigilante groups and the ROK military. To establish the truth behind events of the past, the commission urged various governmental authorities implicated in these atrocities to declassify documents. This included the nation's police forces, the Ministry of Defense, and the National Intelligence Service—all of whom the commission requested to cooperate with investigators as they identified burial sites through corroborating evidence of witnesses. Through the truth-finding commissions, researchers conducted meetings and seminars with various governmental organizations, sharing their discoveries while working closely with local organizations to conduct interviews and exhumations in consultation with bereaved family members.

When the conservative Grand National Party took control of the National Assembly in February 2008 under President Lee Myung-bak, many of the members on the commission began to feel pressure to discontinue their work as it faced significant budget cuts and restrictions on their investigations. Progressives clashed with conservatives when Sin Jiho, a lawmaker from the Grand National Party, proposed a draft bill to merge multiple truth-finding commissions as battles erupted over the content of the texts. When the government dissolved the TRC in June 2010, the commission had investigated thousands of incidents of extrajudicial killings, mass executions, and torture. What made the commission's report so essential and historic was that it focused primarily on the stories of the victims and in a very Confucian way attempted to rectify past wrongs by restoring the dignity of those who were accused rather than indicting those who committed atrocities.

7   *Korea in the World*

The 2010s marked an increasing global fascination with everything Korean—K-pop, Samsung phones, cosmetic surgery, and food, as well as Google Maps images and Instagram photos of the DPRK. Rising from its humble origins, the South now represented global engagement, demonstrating its leadership by hosting the G-20 summit and Winter Olympic Games in 2018. Following Kim Jong-il's death in 2011, the world watched with bated breath as his youngest, Swiss-educated son, Kim Jong-un, took the reins as the supreme leader. The young Kim inherited an economy in shambles after a devastating famine, decades of mismanagement, and sanctions from the West. He also took control over a massive arsenal of nuclear weapons and a history of military provocations. Despite their differences, the two Koreas shared some common problems: one of the highest suicide rates in the world, low birth rates, gender inequality, and human rights violations as outlined by Amnesty International.

The Next Shining Sun: The End of a Dynasty and the Beginning of the Next Dynastic Cycle

On December 19, 2011, the North Korean State Television News reported that Kim Jong-il had died two days earlier of a massive

FIGURE 12. #MeToo movement in Seoul.

heart attack while traveling on his favorite armored train. South Korea's military clambered into high alert as questions swirled around the survival of the regime. Hours after the shocking announcement, the Workers' Party called on the country to unite under the leadership of our comrade Kim Jong-un, the youngest son of Kim Jong-il, who became the third generation of his family to lead the country on his appointment as the supreme leader of the DPRK. The fresh "cherub" face—one that uncannily resembled that of his grandfather Kim Il-sung—stoked new hopes for a thaw or at least Chinese-style reforms in the North.

The second child of Kim Jong-il (1941–2011) and Go Yeonghui (1952–2004), Kim Jong-un (b. 1983) was the first North Korean leader to be born after the founding of the nation. On January 15,

FIGURE 13. PC-Bang (video game arcade) in Seoul.

2009, the elder Kim appointed Kim Jong-un to be his successor. To legitimize the dynastic succession and protect his son's rise to power, Kim elevated him to a four-star general and head of the Central Committee of the Korean Workers' Party in 2010. By creating a rivalry in the regime's elite power base, Kim made it possible for his youngest son to exploit competition to consolidate power. Some viewed Kim Jong-un's appearance at prominent events such as the sixty-fifth anniversary of the Workers' Party and the inspection of military facilities as the grooming of a new leader. His father, Kim Jong-il, had deliberately passed over his elder son, Kim Jong-chul (b. 1981), a musician more suited for a quiet life than his blood brother who took over the reins. Their sister Kim Yojong would play an essential role in the Workers' Party Political Bureau and more recently in global politics as the face of North Korea (such as at the Seoul Winter Olympics and at summits with South Korea's president, Moon Jae-in).

To consolidate his power, Kim resorted to time-honed tactics of the regime, purging high-ranking party and military officials (beginning with the chief of the army, Ri Yongho) who posed a potential threat to the new regime. The world was shocked, however, when the young leader ordered the execution of close family members, an unprecedented display of ruthlessness even for the North. In December 2013, the South Korean National Intelligence Service reported that the North had employed an antiaircraft gun in the grisly execution of Kim's uncle Jang Songtaek for plotting a coup against his nephew—the same method used to execute Hyeon Yongcheol, a general who allegedly fell asleep during a meeting. Jang, who was widely considered the second-most powerful official in Kim's inner circle, had been a strong advocate of economic reform and had close ties with China. In another shocking incident, Kim's half-brother, Kim Jong-nam (son of the actress Song Hyerim)—once a favorite of the party elites to succeed his father—was assassinated in broad daylight at a check-in counter at Kuala Lumpur International Airport (Malaysia) in 2017 when two women rubbed the lethal chemical agent VX on his face, killing him within minutes. Longtime North Korean observers noted that eliminating enemies or those who threatened the regime was one traditional way to tighten control over any form of dissent and remain in power for a long time, which Kim Jong-un intended to do.

Who Is Kim Jong-un? Ask The Worm and the Japanese Chef!

Kim Jong-un remains an elusive figure despite occasional appearances in the media. According to the North Korean state, Kim obtained two degrees—one in physics at Kim Il-sung University, and another as an army officer at the Kim Il-sung Military University—but neither has been confirmed let alone provides any more insight into his persona. What is certain is that Kim Jong-un, his siblings, and their mother lived in Switzerland for several years. Records indicate that between 1998 and 2000 Kim Jong-un attended the Liebefeld Steinhölzli state school in Köniz. He studied in special foreign-language classes under the alias of Bak Un and was registered as the son of an employee of the North Korean embassy in Bern. Some of the more personal observations come from defectors and Kim's circle of quirky international acquaintances—from the flamboyant NBA star Dennis Rodman to Kim's father's longtime personal sushi chef, Kenji Fujimoto.

On February 26, 2013, Dennis Rodman (b. 1961), nicknamed The Worm for his fierce defensive and rebounding abilities and one of Kim's favorite basketball players (in addition to Michael Jordan of the Chicago Bulls), stunned the world by making an unexpected trip to Pyeongyang. He was the first American to meet with Kim Jong-un since he assumed control over the country after his father's death. Rodman participated in several more trips, including one that he organized with several former NBA veterans to host an exhibition basketball game. Rodman's unofficial "hoops diplomacy" revealed some intriguing clues about the new leader and a glimpse into the inner world of North Korean politics and society. The US State Department announced that Rodman's visits to the North (five in total) represented a private mission rather than an official visit. Calling Kim Jong-un "a friend for life" and an "awesome kid," Rodman, who sat courtside with Kim and even attended a private dinner, urged President Barack Obama to engage with the leader of the North, observing that both men shared a mutual love of basketball. Rodman suggested that Kim desired to engage with the South, a meaningful gesture since there was no peace treaty after the truce that ended the Korean War of 1950–53. Although human rights groups and members of the US Congress criticized Rodman for his close personal relationship with Kim, no one could deny that the former basketball player had opened up a channel to the North. During his second trip in September 2013, Rodman announced the birth of Kim Ju-ae, the daughter of Kim Jong-un, to the world. Later, he offered Kim a copy of Donald Trump's book *The Art of the Deal,* which introduced Kim to America's future president.

Kenji Fujimoto (b. 1947) was one of the few non-Koreans to have ever associated with Kim Jong-un while serving the elder Kim, as his personal sushi chef and court jester. In 1982, Fujimoto responded to an advertisement seeking a sushi chef for a one-year contract to teach young chefs in Pyeongyang. After laboring to instruct young apprentices on the fine art of making sushi, Fujimoto was invited to make sushi for Kim Jong-il. Content with his cooking skills, Kim made Fujimoto his closest confidant; the two went on leisure trips together—shooting, riding, and jet skiing. Fujimoto traveled around the world in search of expensive spirits, Chinese melons, Czech beer, Uzbek caviar, Thai papayas, and Danish pork for Kim's table. According to Fujimoto, Kim sometimes asked him to watch the children, whom he introduced to Japanese video games, remote-control cars, and VHS tapes of the Bulls playoff games, featuring Michael Jordan and Dennis Rodman. Fujimoto claims that young Kim Jong-un was obsessed with sports, especially basketball, golf, roller-blading, snowboarding, and skiing. He disclosed mundane but essential details about the children, such as Kim Jong-un's birth date, January 8, 1983. Fujimoto was not free to leave the North indefinitely; promising to bring Kim Jong-il a sea urchin dish from Hokkaido (which he had seen in an episode of *Iron Chef,* a famous Japanese cooking show) in March 2001, he then defected to Japan via China and went into hiding. In an ironic twist, on July 21, 2012, after receiving a personal invitation from Kim Jong-un, Fujimoto decided to take up the generous offer to fly to Pyeongyang, where he later opened his sushi restaurant. While it is unclear why Fujimoto accepted Kim's offer to return to North Korea, it may have been because his wife and children still lived in Pyeongyang and he wanted to reunite with them.

The insights by Rodman and Fujimoto revealed a new leader who was more engaged with the outside world than his father but also committed to the future of his country through serious economic reforms as well as nuclear buildup to provide the North with a military deterrent—what Kim called the "parallel development line." Having declared victory on the nuclear front with successful test-fires of intermediate-range and intercontinental ballistic rockets, and an atomic detonation test, Kim announced his new "strategic line" at the Central Committee of the Workers' Party of Korea in April 2018, instructing party members to channel all efforts to improving the economy. As part of the nuclear club, Kim could now stand tall alongside his adversaries and use his arsenal to seek concessions that would foster North Korea's economy, such as the removal of international sanctions, economic aid from South Korea, and normalization of relations with the United States and Japan.

Precarity in the North: North Korean Workers for Hire

Kim's most significant challenge to his economic and military ambitions has been the crippling international sanctions of the past two decades, which have left the country with few legitimate sources of foreign currency. As a result, the North Korean state has been actively sending workers overseas to procure hard currency for the regime, which has had a profound impact on the domestic and international policies of the North. Today some 65,000 North Koreans are working abroad in 3-D jobs (dirty, dangerous, demanding) in places like China, Russia, Mongolia, Southeast Asia, and the Middle East as hired laborers in factories, forestry, mines, construction, and restaurants—often under miserable conditions.

As the North Korean economy began its nosedive in the 1990s, the government established restaurants and other establishments from Beijing to Phnom Penh, dispatching young women, mostly from elite families, on three-year assignments to work as waitresses and entertainers. The state carefully vetted the workers to ensure that they were loyal to the regime. As a result, when twelve women and their manager fled the restaurant in Ningbo, China, in April 2016, their defection shocked the North Korean state (more than the South). Their bold decision to defect, risking the lives of their families back at home, triggered temporary closures of many of these restaurants. In contrast to the higher socioeconomic background of the female workers, the North exported many more male laborers. Some 60,000 to 65,000 workers have traveled to Siberia, the Middle East, Africa, and Eastern Europe to work, sending back annual remittances estimated at $150 to $230 million. While many men have worked in lumber projects in the Far East, the boom in the construction business in the Middle East has created a high demand for cheap labor. Roughly one hundred trading companies have been overseeing these North Korean workers. For instance, Qatar has hired approximately three thousand North Korean laborers to build the 86,000-seat stadium in Lusail City, which will host the 2022 World Cup finals.

Despite remitting most of their money back to the government, these workers' paltry monthly salaries still exceed what North Korean workers can earn at home. They are fed well, and their accommodations are much better than back home. For some, this kind of overseas experience is a way of learning about the outside world. Despite the lures of living in a capitalist society, the vast majority of workers are married and have families back home, making it very difficult for them to defect. Communication between family members has been changing (though ever so slowly) with the North's entry into the digital age.

Intranet or Internet? North Korea Enters the Digital Age

On January 7, 2013, Google's executive chairman, Eric Schmidt, visited North Korea with former New Mexico governor Bill Richardson on a so-called fact-finding private mission. Despite objections by the State Department over the timing of the visit, coming less than a month after Pyeongyang launched a long-range rocket (which the United States interpreted as a belligerent act), the two men and a group of US business executives forged ahead.

They visited the Korea Computer Center, the most prominent IT hub in Pyeongyang, and met with North Korean scientists, engineers, and government officials to discuss the digital revolution in the world's last "closed country." Given the reality of sanctions that were still in place and the tensions between the United States and North Korea over the detained Korean American Kenneth Bae in Pyeongyang, such talks about improving North Korea's information technology did not seem to make sense at this time. This also marked a critical moment when Americans realized that the North was not cut off from the digital world—and the profound implications of that knowledge.

While Google Earth and Instagram have offered never-before-seen images of North Korea to the world, taken by tourists and satellite images, the North remains a secretive country. Its computers operate on the Gwangmyeong (walled garden), a national intranet service, or private network, that is not linked to the global Internet and is only accessible to a small percentage of the population. What Schmidt wanted to ascertain was how the regime utilized the Internet and to compare that with China, which has set strict regulations on Google and its other products. The discoveries were quite revealing: the country's 3G network operated through an Egyptian company called Orascom with a tiny pool of IP (Internet Protocol) addresses, which follow a set of rules that computers use to route data on the Internet. The Pyeongyang University of Science and Technology had registered only one IP address on the global Internet out of 1,024 in use for the entire country. Anyone with access to the Internet worked under tight supervision. A tour of Kim Il Sung University in Pyeongyang also provided Schmidt and his team a glimpse of the computer science department where students showcased their web-surfing skills, reminding the world that a powerful cyber army operated one of the world's most sophisticated hacking operations.

In contrast to the South, one of the world's most wired nations with almost its entire population on smartphones, the North only began to circulate mobile phones among the elites in 2002. By 2012, the number of subscribers to Koryolink—a joint venture between Orascom, Korea Post, and the Telecommunications Corporation—had increased to more than one million users; by 2015, there were more than three million users in a country of some twenty-five million. With an increasing number of cross-border traders and smugglers, North Koreans have been able to access different content from China, mostly through USB drives. Many defectors in South Korea can now communicate with their families back in the North by delivering contraband mobile phones to them through brokers. While Schmidt did not raise these issues, he observed that North Korea was undergoing its digital revolution with a new generation of literate computer majors linked to e-libraries and an operating system called Red Star along with its web portal, Naenara (Our Country). While Schmidt and his team acknowledged that the training of such cadres in programming could produce a generation of computer hackers, their goal was to communicate the value of having access to technology, which would not only help computerize factories but also potentially develop a positive image of the North abroad.

During a meeting between Kim Jong-il and then US secretary of state Madeleine Albright, Kim asked for her e-mail address, which shocked observers at the time. Yet North Korean IT firms had been developing software for banks in the Middle East, applications for cell phone makers, and even video games for Japanese and South Korean companies for some time. While sanctions prohibit the sale of US products like iPhones to the North, North Korean programmers have been working with European entrepreneurs to create IT venture companies like Nosotek to develop platforms for computer games and other programs. As Schmidt and his team observed, despite the dearth of computer labs and IT centers, a generation of young North Koreans was learning how to program; the most talented are being sent to India and China to hone their skills. In the annual mass games, propaganda posters now hail CNC (computer numerical control), or the use of computers rather than humans to control machine tools, as key to the North's future, as competition at the top universities to study computer languages and programs like Linux is fierce. In many respects, these students are no different from college students in South Korea or the United States. They play video games, listen to online music, and read e-books offered through their library.

For the rest of the world, Google's open and free access policy has generated an interest in learning more about the mysterious and reclusive North Korea. Using satellite images, Google Maps now offers to the world a detailed view of the North—from roads to subway stops, landmarks, electricity networks, and even Kim Jong-il's mausoleum. More problematic for Kim Jong-un are the detailed images of gulags that have been inserted by volunteer cartographers who have drawn on crowdsourcing to compile publicly available materials like satellite images to map out camps like Hwaseong (a penal labor colony alleged to house ten thousand political prisoners), the nuclear facility in Yongbyeon, and the Vinalon Complex. Schmidt's open access has empowered a group of amateur sleuths around the world, who have been enabled by the collaborative power of the Internet to uncover state secrets such as the North's labor camps and nuclear test sites, using Google Map Maker.

"Gangnam Style": Korea's First Viral Video

In the South, digital technology and social media—from smartphones to YouTube—facilitated the rise of a new Hallyu, or Korean Wave, that swept over the world. An unexpected global phenomenon occurred in July 2012 when Psy, a controversial Korean musician, released his eighteenth single titled "Gangnam Style." By September, the Guinness World Records declared the quirky yet catchy "Gangnam Style" the most liked video on YouTube with five million daily views, eventually reaching the one billion mark. The song topped the iTunes charts in thirty-one countries and won the best video at the MTV Europe Music Awards. Psy's signature horse gallop prompted parodies and reaction videos from celebrities like Britney Spears, Katy Perry, Robin Williams, Tom Cruise, Joseph Gordon-Levitt, even London's mayor Boris Johnson and US president Barack Obama, who hailed its popularity. Unbeknownst to most fans even in Korea, the seven-year-old boy (Hwang Min-u) featured in the video with Psy would later be identified as a biracial Vietnamese Korean who had appeared in several variety and talent shows.

Psy, whose given name is Bak Jaesang (b. 1977), grew up in an affluent family in the Gangnam District in one of the snobbiest neighborhoods, Apgujeong, sometimes called the Beverly Hills of Seoul, with its own Rodeo Drive. His father ran a successful business manufacturing equipment for semiconductors and wanted him to take over the company. Family pressure forced Psy to major in business administration at Boston University, but he soon dropped out and enrolled at the Berklee College of Music. After attending several classes, Bak gave up his college career and returned to Seoul to pursue a career as a singer. In January 2001 his first album, *Psy from the Psycho World,* got slapped with a fine because of its vulgar contents, while his second album, *Sa 2,* triggered even more controversy when civic groups accused him of promoting sexual content and sequestered his music to the adults-only section. Like all Korean men his age, Bak faced mandatory military service but received an exemption because his work at a software development company was allegedly of national importance. That front soon proved to be a sham, and when the army discovered that Psy was performing at concerts and appearing on local television, it drafted him to serve in the Fifty-Second Army Infantry Division as a private first class for eighteen months.

Rotund like Kim Jong-il and quirky like his doppelganger, Austin Powers, Bak did not move up the controlled K-pop star system, nor did he lip-sync like many of the big idol groups at the time. He wrote his music, choreographed his own dances, and was notorious for holding wild concerts. Before his claim to fame, Psy was a regular on the domestic charts; although he faced bans for his obscene lyrics, his albums did well. They were promoted by YG Entertainment, a label run by Yang Hyeonseok, who was a former member of the popular group Seo Taiji Boys. "Gangnam Style" critiqued the façade of modern Korean culture through a contrived K-pop performance. Psy's parody of the wealthy elite exposed the superficiality of Gangnam. Trotting around on his fake horse, surrounded by name brands, cosmetic surgery, and K-pop music, Psy showed that underneath all the glitz, it was just a performance, nothing more than child's play. The music video juxtaposed a fancy beach, a high-end club, and a sauna at a five-star hotel with a children's sandbox, a bus full of seniors going on a group tour to the countryside, and a seedy sauna with a bunch of gangsters. His depiction of *doenjangnyeo* (soybean paste women), who crimped on cheap cups of ramen noodles for lunch to splurge on a six-dollar cup of java at Starbucks, mocked the empty pursuit of status symbols.

Psy's "horse dance" became a part of pop-music history just like the Macarena dance or Michael Jackson's moonwalk. At its height, "Gangnam Style" was the favorite song to play at sporting events all over the United States and on variety shows like *The Ellen DeGeneres Show, Today, Saturday Night Live,* and *MTV Live*. While other K-pop labels had attempted US crossovers, investing millions of dollars on artists like the Wonder Girls, G-Dragon, Rain, and CL to produce English-language songs, Psy broke barriers because his song was in Korean and aired all over the world. He paved the way for BTS, South Korea's biggest boy band with a fan base that spans the globe, to stick to original Korean lyrics without having to pander to English-speaking audiences.

In contrast to the first Korean Wave, which featured television dramas like *Winter Sonata* and some video games, the cultural exports of the second wave, starting in 2008, include popular K-pop music, animation (such as webtoons, discussed below), and online games like *Lineage* and *PUBG* (Playerunknown's Battlegrounds). Worth billions of dollars, these cultural commodities reach a global audience through digital technology and strategic coordination of entertainers, corporate enterprises, and the government, which views the Korean Wave as an integral part of the national economy. As recent scholars have observed, the Korean Wave represents South Korea's new soft power on the global stage and its ability to focus the spotlight on itself. Just as *Winter Sonata* generated fascination with all things Korean, so too did "Gangnam Style" spark interest in Korean culture, tourism, food, and beauty, the latter promoting neoliberal values of choice, self-help, and empowerment.

K-Beauty: The Cosmetic Surgery Capital of the World

For all its horseplay, "Gangnam Style" was a critique of Koreans' obsession with plastic surgery, makeup, and skincare, better known today as K-beauty, a billion-dollar industry that has captured the global markets. Debates about Korean beauty standards were already prevalent in a society inspired by movies like Kim Yonghwa's *200 Pounds Beauty* (2006), an adaptation of Yumiko Suzuki's hit manga (comic), *Kanna's Big Success!* The film was an instant hit at the box office, selling more than six million tickets nationwide and grossing over $42 million; it was nominated for several domestic film awards. The story line follows the life of Hanna (Kim Ajung), who stands behind a curtain providing the vocals for a famous singer, Ami, whose voice does not match her beauty. As a ghost singer, Hanna lives a mundane existence, stigmatized because of her obese body (169 centimeters, 95 kilograms). Her sexy voice allows her to work anonymously as a phone-sex operator, concealing her figure and inviting men on the other end of the line to use their imagination. During her ghost singing, Hanna develops a huge crush on the director, Sangjun, whose father owns the entertainment company that has hired Ami to sing. Hanna's friends, who know her real worth, persuade her to have plastic surgery to align her grotesque body with her smooth, silky voice. Following the procedure, Hanna is reborn as Jenny, a singer whose debut song, "Maria," is an instant hit. At the time, popular opinion was split. Some critics argued that the film glorified plastic surgery as the only path to success for women lacking ideal bodies, while others praised it for raising awareness about the intense social pressures for women to undergo the knife in order to gain acceptance.

South Korea has gained a reputation as the plastic surgery mecca of the world, making Gangnam one of the most popular destinations in Asia with reportedly over five hundred aesthetic centers. Some clinics occupy as many as sixteen floors and boast signboards that read "Before and After," "Rebirth," and "Reborn." Today South Koreans have the most plastic surgeries per capita on earth. Procedures include not only the popular double eyelid surgery, but rhinoplasty, V-line surgery (jaw-slimming), facial contouring, shaved cheekbones, high-bridged noses, botox infusion, *aegyo sal* (injecting fat under the eyes), dimple creation, and calf reduction. The procedures are so common that several presidents, including Park Geun-hye and Roh Moo-hyun, also went under the knife while they were in office.

"Lookism," which promotes discrimination in the workplace, forces Koreans to micromanage their physical appearance starting at a young age. A typical high school graduation gift for a Korean teenager today is either a nose job or double eyelid surgery to ensure desirability on the marriage and job markets. Photographs are required on almost every document—from college to job applications and resumes—institutionalizing the pernicious impact of lookism at the very onset of adulthood. In a fiercely competitive society, both men and women feel empowered to transform their appearances, all the more so when advertisers cast investments in "body works" as the path to success. In reality, these neoliberal beauty regimes control consumers under the guise of free choice and self-management.

The slim K-pop idol appearance was not always the beauty norm in Korea. During the Joseon period (1392–1910), a rigid patriarchal system along with Confucian ideals enforced a strong, dominant masculinity and submissive femininity. A study of paintings during the Joseon dynasty suggests that among the elites, a round forehead indicated an economically savvy and virtuous housewife, while a thin crescent-moon–shaped eyebrow signified a wise woman. The ideal woman was to have thick shoulders, a deep navel, buxom belly, and flat hips. In contrast to elite women, who veiled themselves during the day, women from the lower classes were less modest, exposing their breasts, for example, to nurse in public places. The most controversial reform for men near the end of the Joseon dynasty was the Short Hair Act (1896), which mandated that elite men (*yangban*) cut off their topknot, a sign of class and manhood. The hair reform represented a heresy against the body, prompting cries of outrage and resistance. During Japanese colonial rule, the "New Woman" began to bob her hair, wear one-piece skirts, and use makeup—the Western style of the 1920s. In contrast to the traditional woman (the wise mother, good wife), the New Woman challenged social mores by publicly asserting her sexuality, intelligence, and individualism, incurring the wrath of Korean nationalists for indulging her vanity without considering her family or her colonized nation.

Plastic surgery in South Korea had its roots in the Korean War when Dr. David Ralph Millard, a plastic surgeon for the US Army, provided free double eye procedures alongside reconstructive surgeries for injuries. Millard's development of the blepharoplasty technique interested sex workers around military bases, who sought to appeal to American soldiers by altering their faces to have more westernized features. Plastic surgery created a new racialized hierarchy through body works that celebrated white (Caucasian) features. Celebrities in the 1970s further popularized the double eyelid surgery in a culture where mono-lids were deemed unattractive by the new beauty standards and aesthetics of the day.

In the past decade, the masculine ideal has transformed significantly to blur gender lines, drawing on historical images and contemporary aesthetics. The original *hwarang,* or flower boy, from elite Buddhist families belonged to a cultural-military corps during the Silla dynasty (57 B.C.E. to 935 C.E.). He was famed for his military prowess and physical beauty, which was enhanced with cosmetics and beautiful clothing. The contemporary flower boys, who first appeared in the drama *Boys over Flower* (2009), did not display the virile or warrior-like image idolized by previous generations but instead popularized the androgynous look. To attain these elegant facial features required grooming: hair color, cosmetics, even careful skincare. By 2011, South Korean men spent a remarkable $495.4 million on skincare products, or roughly 21 percent of global sales, as the rise of the flower-boy ideal gained prominence in popular culture and the fashion industry over the past decade. Another immensely popular drama, *Descendants of the Sun* (2016), was a trendsetter for the new male image of the "spornosexual" male, a term defined by Mark Simpson to describe the cultural phenomena of buffness and gym culture. Today there is a fine blending of the two ideals: a flawless androgynous face with a buff body complete with abs, biceps, and other muscles. The new man embodies physical fitness, which falls into the rationale of neoliberalism that produces individualized selves through diet, fitness, body management, and cosmetic surgery, fostering self-development or what Koreans would call well-being. These kinds of lifestyle changes have affected how both men and women now think about their bodies and themselves.

The intense focus on body works has elicited criticism both at home and abroad. Korean feminist organizations, like Womenlink, have conducted Love Your Body campaigns to raise awareness about the obstacles of lookism to promote gender equality. Ironically, such campaigns have inadvertently developed a neoliberal agenda of self-management. In the United States, the discourses adopt explicit racial tones, assailing Korean women for "trying to be white" and for the uniformity of their appearance. When Oprah Winfrey explored the lives of thirty-year-old women in her "Around the World with Oprah" in 2004, she pointed out to Lisa Ling that Korean plastic surgery was incomprehensible to her, because the women "still look Korean." Postcolonial feminist scholars point out that this discourse portrays Korean women as ignorant and as objects of control (in their desire to look white), in contrast to Western women who have agency over their bodies. Moreover, one scholar points out that the critiques reveal more about anxieties over whiteness and the rise of Korea as a global power than they do about the actual motivations of Korean women.

Despite criticisms at home and abroad, South Korea has capitalized on the Korean Wave and taken the global cosmetic surgery market by storm. Medical tourism, which the government targeted as a significant area of growth, has witnessed a boom by attracting tourists from Asia who want to look like beautiful K-pop stars. The South Korean government has eased hospital regulations and assisted in simplifying the visa process for overseas patients, who are mainly from the Middle East, China, Southeast Asia, and Russia. In a recent report on medical tourism by South Korea's Ministry of Health and Welfare, the state projects to host close to a million medical tourists by 2022. The replication of K-pop faces around the world is an eerie consequence of marketing Korean beauty through body works.

K-Coffee

K-culture would not be complete without its coffee. Coffee consumption began to take off in South Korea after Starbucks entered the market in 1999. It opened its first café near Ewha Womans [*sic*] University and introduced Koreans to Americano, a dilution of espresso with hot water. The history of coffee in Korea can be traced back to Emperor Gojong (1852–1919), the first monarch in Korea to become a coffee aficionado, when Antoinette Sontag, the sister-in-law of the Russian ambassador, shared the addictive drink with him during his asylum at the Russian legation in 1896 in the aftermath of the First Sino-Japanese War. In the 1950s, American GIs introduced Koreans to cheap instant coffee, and the *dabang* (coffee salons) culture, which had first appeared in Myeongdong (Honmachi) during the colonial period, took off again in certain districts in Seoul, from Jongno to Chungmuro and Daehangno. These cafés, which featured attractive female servers, became a gathering spot for businesspeople, students, and artists and later turned into popular dating sites. By 1959, there were more than three thousand coffee salons all over Korea, a third of them in Seoul, and by 1976 Dongsuh Foods had cornered the instant coffee market with its mix sticks of coffee, sugar, and powdered cream, making South Korea the largest consumer of instant coffee in the world by the 1980s.

Through a joint venture partnership with Shinsegae, a South Korean department store franchise that has been involved in marketing and product development, South Korea now holds the distinction of having the most number of Starbucks locations in a single city (Seoul). Multinational brands such as California's The Coffee Bean & Tea Leaf and Italy's Pascucci have followed Starbucks' lead, expanding their operations throughout the peninsula, as have local groups like E-mart and smaller home-grown chains that have joined the coffee craze. According to the latest surveys, South Koreans consume more coffee than their staples, rice and *kimchi*.

Pathways for Peace: The United Nations and the World Bank under Two Global Leaders

Korea aspired to be a leader in global culture but also to be the face of global politics. On January 1, 2007, Ban Ki-moon (b. 1944) was elected as the eighth Secretary-General of the United Nations and reelected in 2011 to serve a second term. A few years later, Jim Yong Kim (b. 1959), a Korean American physician, anthropologist, and the former president of Dartmouth College, replaced Robert Zoellick in 2012 to become the president of the World Bank. The life stories of two powerful men in the world and their worldview as ethnic Koreans reveal how their backgrounds shaped their visions for a new world order.

Ban Ki-Moon was born on June 13, 1944, in the small farming village of Haengchi in North Chungcheong Province. When Ban was six, his family sought refuge in a remote mountainside during the Korea War. As a young student, Ban excelled in the English language, and in 1962 he won an essay contest sponsored by the Red Cross, earning him a trip to the United States where he met US president John F. Kennedy, which further cemented his aspiration to become a diplomat. His elite education—an undergraduate degree in international relations from Seoul National University (1970) and a master's degree in public administration from the John F. Kennedy School of Government at Harvard University (1985)—prepared him for his long diplomatic career as ambassador to Austria and Slovenia, from 1998. As the foreign minister of South Korea under President Roh Moo-hyun, Ban played a vital role in the six-party talks to defuse the nuclear crisis in the North before announcing his candidacy for the position of UN Secretary-General.

On his confirmation, Ban found himself mired in a series of crises in an increasingly polarized world—from the North Korean and Iranian nuclear threats to the humanitarian crisis in the region of Darfur, Sudan. His second term was marred by his inability to engage quickly in significant hotspots around the world, such as the bloody civil war in Syria, the Arab Spring movement, and Russia's annexation of the Crimea in 2014. Critics argued that Ban erred too often on the side of diplomacy rather than asserting himself more forcefully against powerful member states, as his predecessor Kofi Annan had done. Although not personally responsible, Ban took the blame for organizational failures such as sexual abuse by UN peacekeepers in the Central African Republic; he organized rigorous independent panels to investigate and report (the study was led by Canadian Supreme Court Justice Marie Deschamps). In his defense, Ban maintained that an organization with 193 member states—each with the ability to obstruct a policy or plan—slowed down the United Nations' responses to crises. He was often frustrated by the intractability of the Security Council and stubborn obstacles posed by the General Assembly.

Although Ban acknowledged the structural problems and the personal challenges, he took pride in his progressive social policies. His commitment to ending poverty led to the ambitious Sustainable Development Goals, while his advocacy for women's rights made emergency contraception available for women raped in conflict zones. During his tenure, the number of women in the United Nations in senior management positions increased by more than 40 percent—more than under any other secretary-general. Ban made it his top priority to appoint Michelle Bachelet (the former president of Chile) as under-secretary-general of the newly created UN Entity for Gender Equality and Empowerment of Women, which sought to create an environment in which "every women and girl could exercise her human rights." He was also an open supporter of LGBTQ rights, insisting on benefits for same-sex spouses of his UN employees despite opposition from some countries in the General Assembly. In 2008, Ban characterized climate change as "the defining challenge of our era" and strongly supported the Paris Agreement as a Peace Pact with the Planet. Near the end of his tenure, Ban became increasingly vocal in his criticism of human rights abuses in various countries, including Myanmar, Israel, and Saudi Arabia, and called for safeguarding vulnerable populations.

Unlike Ban, who received criticism for his lack of fluency in English, Jim Yong Kim, who was appointed by Barack Obama to head the World Bank in 2012, had grown up in America, where his family moved when he was five years old. He was a trailblazer on many levels, as his impressive resume indicated: he had been the chair of the Department of Global Health and Social Medicine at Harvard Medical School before serving as the president of Dartmouth College—much to the astonishment of the Asian American community. As a global health leader, he founded Partners in Health with his colleagues to provide community-based healthcare to the poor in Haiti, Peru, Mexico, and other countries and led the "3x5 initiative" of the World Health Organization to treat and eliminate HIV/AIDS globally. However, critics questioned Kim's experience and educational qualifications—which did not include business or finance—to be the president of the World Bank.

Drawing on his experience in global healthcare, Kim proved to be an inspired choice. Under his leadership, the World Bank made several profound changes. It engaged in fighting corruption through its Department of Institutional Integrity, which listed 202 phone numbers to report fraud and corruption, thereby allowing the World Bank to prosecute and blacklist corrupt firms. In line with Kim's primary expertise, the World Bank invested in public health through combating malaria and tuberculosis and promoting water and sanitation projects. Like Ban Ki-Moon, Kim's commitment to the environment led the World Bank to defund ecologically pernicious projects and fund clean-air and fuel-efficiency projects. Kim envisioned that the World Bank and its 189 member countries would work to end extreme poverty by 2030—through reliable data to help make decisions; cutting-edge research (e.g., using demography to create projections about aggregate global populations); educating professionals in developing countries; and strongly emphasizing including civil society organizations in the World Bank as staffers and partners to ensure local participation and involvement. Kim's sudden resignation on February 1, 2019, took the world by surprise, and many lamented the exit of a visionary leader. The engagement of ethnic Koreans like Ban and Kim to fight for social justice issues within institutions like the United Nations and the World Bank raised the profile of South Korea; but it also meant that the country (now considered a subempire by some) would come under greater scrutiny for its treatment of vulnerable populations, especially non-ethnic Koreans who had migrated to Korea for marriage or labor.

Reimagining the Nation and Nationalism: Multiculturalism in South Korea?

On April 11, 2012, Jasmine Bacurnay Lee (b. 1977) made history when she won a seat as a member of the Saenuri Party in South Korea's National Assembly, becoming the first non-ethnic Korean to serve as a lawmaker. Anti-immigrant nationalists immediately called for her expulsion from the position, likening her presence to poisonous weeds that corrupted the body polity and pure Korean bloodlines. "A foreigner has no place in our politics," her detractors heckled. Such xenophobic rhetoric was what prompted Jasmine Lee to run in the first place: to represent migrants like herself who were marginalized in Korean society. The state showcased Lee's election as a success of its multicultural governance—a concept that it had co-opted from civic groups. However, critics argued that the state's multiculturalism (*damunhwa*) aimed to regulate diverse ethnic populations through its neoliberal policies, which benefited the country. As a symbol of multiculturalism, Lee provoked anxieties about the very identity of Korea—its myths as a "one blood" nation and monoculture.

Jasmine Bacurnay y Villanueva, born in the Philippines, never expected to become a Korean citizen. She met Lee Dongho (a second officer of a Korean freighter) at her parents' store when she was a student at the Ateno de Davao University and married him in 1994. Almost a decade before multicultural programs came in vogue, Jasmine Lee had difficulties finding an affordable place to study Korean, let alone other support groups to help her adapt to her new home. As the only non-Korean in their neighborhood, Lee worried about how her two multiethnic children would be treated at school; to avoid stigmatizing them, she deliberately missed parent-teacher conferences. In a *Huffington Post* interview, Lee affirmed that she learned everything about Korean society from her husband, with whom she went for drinks almost every night and sang at the karaoke bar. When Lee's husband died tragically of a heart attack while rescuing their daughter from a stream in Gangwon Province in 2010, the Korean media portrayed her as a grief-stricken widow, the ideal assimilated migrant wife.

In the mid-2000s, when multiculturalism became widespread in public discourse, Lee became a television personality, appearing in shows like *Love in Asia* to dispel the stereotype of migrant wives as prostitutes. In one episode of the show, her son Seung-geun asserted that he aspired to be the "second Obama," reflecting Lee's vision for the future of multiracial children in Korea. Lee also appeared in a minor role as a Vietnamese bride in the feature film *Secret Reunion* (2010) and then played a Filipina who abandons her infant son in *Punch* (2011), which drew more than five million viewers. In the film, the son, Wandeuk, grows up with his hunchback father without any knowledge about his migrant mother. When his father and uncle are away in search of work, Wandeuk learns from his high school teacher, who also works as a minister with undocumented migrants, that his mother worked in Seongnam. Although the film does not focus centrally on Jasmine Lee's character, her role nonetheless helped to raise awareness about migrant wives and the false assumptions about them as uneducated opportunists, who were undeserving of their privileges in Korean society. Lee has noted that while Koreans had been more welcoming when there were fewer immigrant families, the increase in their numbers has caused a backlash, making them easy scapegoats for Korea's problems.

The state's adoption of multiculturalism coincided with a sharp rise of foreign residents and a demographic crisis. According to the

Korean Statistical Information Service, they numbered 536,627 (1.1 percent of the population) in 2006 and 1,741,919 (almost 3.4 percent of the population) in 2015. In 2007, the Committee on Foreign Policy viewed the immigrant wives and their mixed-race children as part of the solution to the problem of decreased fertility and an aging population. The state's neoliberal vision found expression in two legal measures—the Better Treatment of Foreign Residents in Korea (2007), and Multicultural Family Support Act (2008)—which sought to improve the quality of life of multicultural families and protect them from discrimination. By definition, a multicultural family was made up of a Korean national by birth and a foreign-born migrant. The media upheld Lee as the ideal migrant hero because she had not only successfully assimilated into Korean society (speaking fluent Korean) but also become self-reliant. Lee noted that multicultural programs in South Korea tended to racialize and objectify migrants under the guise of support; for instance, her family was singled out to receive free rice from the community center, even though they hardly needed food assistance. Her children received special exemptions from certain activities at school although they were Korean citizens. NGOs also criticized the programs for imposing Korean patriarchal values on migrant women and not recognizing genuine multiculturalism.

Government multiculturalism did not extend to marginal groups like migrant workers (who were not married to Koreans), refugees, or ethnic Koreans from China. The neoliberal restructuring of the Korean economy and integration into the global market led to an influx of migrant workers. Once a migrant-source country that sent miners, nurses, and workers abroad, Korea now relied on migrant workers who performed the so-called 3-D jobs. Initially, low-skilled, single men migrated to South Korea, but in the 1990s women also began to arrive as workers in the service industries (like the restaurant business). The rise of migrant communities changed the landscape of Korea. In the neighborhood of Wongok-dong in Ansan City (Gyeonggi Province, roughly 40 kilometers south of Seoul), dozens of shops and restaurants catered to factory workers from Southeast Asia. In Itaewon in the Yongsan district, migrant workers from the Middle East and Africa created their enclaves, where they could attend the largest mosque in Seoul and shop for halal food. The neighborhoods of Garibong-dong in Guro District and Daerimdong in Yeongdeungpo District in Seoul have among the higher concentrations of ethnic Chinese workers who work in the factories.

Until the mid-2000s, the notorious Industrial Trainee System (ITS) oversaw migrant labor, which gave local small businesses and industries extraordinary control over the workers, leading to deplorable working conditions and meager wages. Critics even likened the ITS to modern slavery. Under Roh Moo-hyun's administration, the government promoted the Employment Permit System in 2003, a fairer and transparent framework that offered migrant workers the same rights as Korean workers by alleviating the working hours and including benefits. This system regulated legal migration, enforcing harsh regulations for undocumented workers, who were vulnerable to arrest and deportation.

In 1994, the South Korean government began accepting applications from refugees to settle in the country. It had expected North Koreans, not some five hundred Yemenis who fled their homes to avoid the civil war in 2018 and landed on Jeju Island (a point of entry that did not require a visa because the government saw it as a way to promote tourism). Rumors that the refugees were radical Muslims who were responsible for the disappearance of women from the island led to mass protests and petitions to reject their application. Under international pressure, the South Korean government allowed the Yemeni refugees to stay temporarily on humanitarian grounds. The Yemenis did not match the state's multicultural vision and provoked the ire of the majority of South Koreans. Jeju's borders were no longer open to individuals from several Muslim countries (Yemen, Pakistan, and Somalia) without visas.

Ethnically Korean: The Joseonjok in Korea, the Chaoxianzu in China

Since Korea and China established diplomatic relations in 1992, the largest group of immigrants in South Korea are ethnic Korean Chinese (called Joseonjok in the South) who were lured by economic prospects in the South to follow their "Korean dream." Workers could earn higher wages, sometimes four to six times what they made in China. Moreover, as a minority group in China, the Joseonjok (who generally had high levels of education) worried about rising tensions with the Han Chinese and longed nostalgically for their homeland. By 2016, the Korean Immigration Service reported that some 800,000 Korean Chinese were living in the South. Paradoxically, their common bloodlines, family ties, and language did not ease the road to citizenship; in fact, the Joseonjok confronted many more obstacles to legalized residency and work than Korean Americans or adoptees who needed to demonstrate their heritage to obtain the coveted F-4 visa. Citing market concerns, the state relegated the Joseonjok (who were still Chinese citizens) to the status of temporary migrant workers, restricting the number of H-2 entry visas granted to them. Feeling betrayed and unwelcomed, the Joseonjok migrant workers also felt disillusioned by workplace discrimination—their inability to rise above low-paid, low-skill jobs, in contrast to the privileges enjoyed by the Korean Americans. All the fascination about the two million ethnic Koreans living in China quickly dissipated among the South Koreans, harboring negative stereotypes of the Joseonjok, who developed their enclaves and mobilized politically to assert their rights. The media often sensationalized crimes by Joseonjok, like the "Suwon Murder Case," the gruesome rape, murder, and mutilation of a twenty-eight-year-old woman by O Wonchun in April 2012. The image of the Joseonjok as hardened criminals engaged in the drug trade and human and organ trafficking was central to Na Hongjin's thriller *The Yellow Sea* (2010). The shocking violence and "rivers of blood" (to quote a *New York Times* review) sparked outrage among members of the ethnic Korean Chinese community, who decried the crass stereotyping for commercial gain. The cold reception by Korean society has led to feelings of nostalgia among the Joseonjok for their old homes in China, although most do not plan to return.

Some Joseonjok have preferred to remain in China, where they have succeeded in finding a niche for themselves. For example, Jin Xing (Kim Seong), one of the first of few transgender women to be officially recognized as a woman by the Chinese government, is known popularly as "Jin Xing, the transsexual star of dance." Jin was born on August 13, 1967, in Shenyang, Liaoning, to ethnic Korean parents. Her father was already a second-generation Korean, while her mother was a refugee who arrived in the 1950s. Like fellow *Chaoxianzu* ("ethnic Korean" in Chinese), she studied in a local Korean elementary school in Shenyang, a provincial northeast city in China. Jin's life changed in 1987 when she was selected for an intensive modern dance program, which included master dance classes (sponsored by the American Dance Festival) led by pioneers of contemporary dance Martha Graham and José Limon, who would be her future mentors. Jin's brilliant performance of a Central Asian ethnic dance won her a scholarship to study in New York, where she struggled with gender dysphoria. Following years of performances in America and Europe, Jin decided to return home in 1994. Her decision to undergo sex reassignment surgery in China was shaped by her sense that she belonged there, that China offered a safe, protective space for her transition to being a woman. The avant-garde art scene in Beijing provided the ideal platform for Jin to work through her feelings in public before the surgery; at the "About AIDS" experimental theater show, she found a sympathetic audience with whom she discussed her dreams of being a woman. To make it official, her father, an officer in the Chinese military, helped Jin obtain a new identity card with her self-identified gender. Jin adopted three children and married a German businessman based in Shanghai. Despite being an ethnic Korean, Jin has emphasized her Chinese nationality as a primary aspect of her identity. The only time she mentions her Korean roots is when she credits the "Korean rhythmic movements" of her dance to her mother's friends or when she recalls the racial discrimination she felt as a child. As a national celebrity who owns her own dance company and has appeared on popular television shows such as *So You Think You Can Dance,* Jin has not felt a need to immigrate to Korea—a place that has become a site of great interest for Chinese society.

In 2014, South Korea became the third-most popular destination for mainland Chinese tourists after Hong Kong and Macau, tallying over six million visitors a year. The influx of Chinese tourists can be attributed to the government of Jeju Island's no-visa policy and the offer of permanent-resident status to Chinese who purchase a single property valued at 500 million South Korean *won* or more. This status makes them eligible for the same medical and educational benefits as ordinary South Koreans—a very enticing incentive for the wealthy. While Chinese investments in real estate have certainly contributed to the economy of Jeju Island, the residents are angered by the environmental destruction that has come with overdevelopment, as well as the rising property prices. To cater to Chinese consumer appetites and buying power, the Myeongdong neighborhood in Seoul has been transformed into a mecca for cosmetics and other goods. Chinese-language advertisements and clerks now dot the landscape, and rental prices in this part of central Seoul have skyrocketed. Merchants in Myeongdong and elsewhere suffered for more than a year after China decided to suspend group packages to South Korea; countless businesses lost millions of dollars after South Korea agreed to deploy the US-made antimissile system known as THAAD (Terminal High Altitude Area Defense), which the Chinese have deemed as a threat to their national security.

After the 1992 normalization of diplomatic relations between China and South Korea, South Koreans began to move to China as employees of Chinese corporations, creating expatriate communities in Beijing, Dalian, Shanghai, and Qingdao. To ensure that their children received an excellent education, seven Korean international schools—all recognized by the Korean government— were established in Yanbian, Beijing, Shanghai, Tianjin, Yantai, Qingdao, and Dalian between 1997 and 2003. These schools became an attractive option for parents who wanted their children to avoid the competitive examination system at home. Moreover, the cheap tuition and English and Chinese languages offered at the schools, and the low cost of living compared to Seoul, were pull factors for Korean migration to mainland China. Today China is also home to many North Korean refugees, party officials, traders, government-contracted waitresses, and contract workers—the city of Dandong, in particular, as North Korea's gateway to the world. From Dandong's main thoroughfare, the North Korean city of Sinuiju is visible on the other side of the Yalu Aprok River. Almost 70 percent of all trade in and out of North Korea occurs between these two cities, with more than twenty thousand North Koreans working legally in Dandong, employed mainly in garment industries, machinery, and fisheries. An indication of this hybrid site are the many signboards in Chinese and Korean. Whenever the North Koreans detonate a bomb or fire a missile, strict UN sanctions have a rippling effect on the livelihood of citizens in Dandong.

In the age of globalization, the new K-subempire attracted immigrants for the purposes of marriage and work while its own citizens traveled to countries like China to work in corporations. Border crossings in both directions challenged the identity of the once monoethnic nation as individuals, civic groups, and the state competed to define citizenship, rights, and privileges, leading to new racial and class hierarchies in Korean society.

From "Selfless Daughter" to the First Elected Female President: The Rise and Fall of Park Geun-hye

When Park Geun-hye (b. 1952) was elected as South Korea's first female president in a male-dominated political world on February 25, 2012, it appeared that South Korea had finally achieved a new level of democracy; however, Park's reliance on hardline conservatives who reflected the dictatorial rule of her father, Park Chung-hee, her refusal to take responsibility for the tragic Sewol ferry disaster that killed some three hundred people (mainly high school students), and corruption on the Choe Sunsil scandal all led to her downfall, impeachment, and imprisonment. Her retreat from hard-won democratic processes (e.g., freedom of speech) recalled her father's authoritarian rule and was a sober reminder that despite its meteoric economic rise, South Korea's democratic institutions remained fragile and vulnerable.

Park, the daughter of South Korea's longest-ruling dictator, entered the realm of politics at the age of twenty-two, assuming the role of First Lady after her mother's assassination in 1974. In 1998, she was elected to the National Assembly and served as the leader of the ruling party on two occasions before becoming the president of South Korea, earning the monikers "selfless daughter" among her ardent supporters and the unapproachable "Ice Princess" among her critics. Among conservatives who were nostalgic for her father's developmentalist dictatorship, Park represented the heir who would continue her father's legacy, especially given her campaign promises of economic planning and reform. Her supporters admired her resilience after she was slashed on her face by an assailant just as she was about to deliver a speech to support then mayoral candidate O Sehun. On the other hand, others found her too scripted, unable to communicate, earning her the name "Marie Antoinette" (transliterated in Korean as *mal e an tong hanae*).

Park's inability to communicate sympathy for families who lost children on the Sewol ferry, which sank on April 16, 2014—she cited the responsibility of transportation systems, not her government— prompted angry calls for her impeachment. Onboard the ferry were 475 passengers, 339 of them high school sophomores and teachers from Danwon High School who were on a fieldtrip to Jeju Island. The ferry, which made an "unreasonable sudden turn" causing it to start capsizing, sent out its first distress signal at 9 A.M.; by 10:23 A.M., it had submerged entirely, killing 304 people, including 261 students and teachers. The captain of the ferry advised passengers to remain in their cabins before he fled the scene, and the coast guard dispatched to the scene did not conduct a systematic rescue attempt, neglecting passengers in their cabins. Children sent text messages and videos to their parents with desperate pleas for help and final goodbyes when help did not materialize. Investigations revealed that the coast guard had been more concerned about legal accountability and following a chain of command than about the lives of the passengers. They only picked up the fleeing crew.

To make matters worse, the government announced that all the children were safe on the basis of false information. Parents waited by the shore for news about their children—a mother shouting at the divers that her heart was "turning to ashes." When the final numbers of the dead were reported, families, wild with grief, could hardly process the news. They hung yellow ribbons and pictures of their children in front of the presidential Blue House, holding candlelight vigils and demanding answers and accountability, which failed to come. The Sewol ferry accident was declared one of the most traumatic in contemporary Korean history.

Relations with the North were also at their lowest point under Park, as her conservative administration took a hardline position after a series of missile tests in 2016 when Kim Jong-un sought to accelerate his nuclear program. During her presidency, the North Korean state media frequently disparaged Park, using violent and misogynistic language, labeling her as a "crafty prostitute," a "cold-blooded animal," and a "comfort woman of the United States." The North would go as far as imposing a death penalty on her over an alleged plot by Seoul's intelligence services to assassinate Kim Jong-un, further exacerbating tensions between the two states.

In late October 2016, another scandal broke that sealed President Park Geun-hye's fate. The avalanche of events was triggered by a protest at a private women's college, Ewha University, where students rejected expansion plans to create the Future Life University, which would offer a degree in beauty and hygiene. When the university president called in police to suppress the protests, students learned that she had tight connections with the Blue House. In this context, they also began to scrutinize the special treatment of a fellow student, Jeong Yura, the daughter of Choe Sunsil, who always skipped classes but received high grades. Complaints about preferential treatment of students exposed the secret world of money, influence, and power. The news media discovered that Choe had used her connection to the Blue House to extract billions of dollars from the major conglomerates, such as Samsung and Hyundai, to support two foundations. The ties between the two women went back to when Choe's father, a religious cult leader, mentored Park following the assassination of her mother. According to reports, Choe, who was not elected to any government position, influenced state policies, raising questions about influence peddling and corruption. Vigils and daily protests calling for Park's impeachment lasted for six weeks as anger about her negligence during the Sewol ferry tragedy grew. The corruption scandal intensified the public's grievances against wealth inequalities and the ability of individuals to benefit themselves and their families through government and corporate connections. On

FIGURE 14. Protest against Park Geun-hye and Sewol ferry disaster.

December 9, the South Korean National Assembly voted unanimously for impeachment and temporary removal from office, which the Constitutional Court of Korea validated on March 10, 2017. Park became the first sitting president to be removed from office, prompting a new presidential election on May 9, 2017, when Moon Jae-in became the twelfth president of South Korea. In the end, Park's attempts to support the Ministry of Gender Equality and the expansion of other programs for women (although she failed to appoint more women to political offices) were overshadowed by her failures. Before she left office, her approval ratings had dropped to a meager 4 percent.

The special treatment of privileged students like Choe Sunsil's daughter at Ewha University, and fundraising for organizations based on connections to the Blue House, raised the ire of ordinary Koreans who struggled to get ahead in a very competitive nation.

FIGURE 15. Inscriptions on the Juche Tower (Pyeongyang).

Indeed, the pressures to succeed were taking their toll on mental health even among high-achieving and prosperous Koreans.

Mental Health at Home and Abroad

Shocks rippled through the K-pop world when the news broke that Kim Jonghyun, the lead singer of the popular and influential five-member boy band SHINee, had committed suicide in his private hotel room on December 18, 2017. He was only twenty-seven years old. In his farewell letter to a close friend, Jang Huiyeon (Nine9 of the band Cloud9), Kim admitted that he could no longer battle the depression that had finally consumed him. Scouts from SM Entertainment had discovered Kim when he was only fifteen years old and playing with a band in high school; in 2008, he formed a popular boy band under the same label. "The princes of K-pop" sold hundreds of thousands of albums and singles, becoming one of the most successful idol groups in South Korea. Kim was not the first K-pop star to kill himself; nineteen-year-old Korean American Charles Park (known as Seo Jiwon in Korea) was one of the early stars to take his life. Female artists and actresses, such as the beloved Choe Jinsil (known as "the nation's actress"), disillusioned by the stress and vicious online culture, were not immune to the pressure to be the best in an industry some have likened to *The Hunger Games*. High-profile suicides, including that of the embattled former South Korean president Roh Moo-hyun in 2009, captured national headlines, raising questions about a suicide epidemic as a public health issue.

Fears in the media were not unfounded. In 2013, South Korea had the highest suicide rate among thirty OECD countries, averaging 43 deaths per 100,000 (15,000 deaths a year) and outpacing Hungary and Japan. It ranked first in the rate of female suicides, with 11.1 per 100,000, more than double the OECD average of 5.4. The neoliberal reforms imposed by the International Monetary Fund in 1997 that dismantled social safety nets, along with the breakdown of traditional family support systems, had a devastating effect, especially on the elderly. Due to the absence of a national pension system (which only began in 1988) and a shortage of social services, nearly half of the country's elderly population now lived below the poverty line, leading some to kill themselves so as not to be a financial burden on their families. The K-youth culture also alienated the elderly, who lamented the decline of traditional values and loss of connection to the new generation.

The societal expectation of upward social mobility—from university to employment (preferably in a wealthy *jaebeol,* or conglomerate)—has created intense pressures, which start in adolescence and can lead to emotional and mental distress. South Korean high school students today spend an average of sixteen hours a day studying for tests that are graded on a curve—all in an intense competition to gain admission at one of the top three (SKY) universities in South Korea. In this "winner takes all" *Battle Royale* system, life is like a game of survival. The goal is to obtain a stable job at a top company rather than follow one's passions. Some young Koreans refer to themselves as belonging to the *sampo* generation—a portmanteau for *sam* (three) and *po* (*pogi,* or giving up)—in which they must give up three major life events, such as marriage or children, to succeed. Those who lack socioeconomic power comprise the *opo* and the *chilpo,* where they must give up five and seven things, respectively. For the most desperate, the *ilpo* generation, this means sacrificing everything that has value in order to survive, which is almost like giving up one's life. The young, who call themselves the *n-Po* generation (the give up generation), distinguish between the "dirt spoon" class who come from nonprivileged backgrounds, and the "golden spoon" class who hail from wealthy households. The former pejoratively call Korea "Hell Joseon," comparing the current hellish conditions for the young to the oppressive caste system of slaves and landowners during the Joseon dynasty. This kind of pessimistic outlook on life among the youth has contributed to high levels of depression and high suicidal rates.

After university, employment comes with its own set of concerns. The emergence of contingent workers in the 1990s meant the absence of job security and well-paying jobs. South Korea's university graduates live precarious lives, in perpetual fear of being trapped in low-wage jobs that will lead to downward social mobility. The term "880,000-*won* Generation," coined by U Seokhun, an economics professor, represents what a temporary staff or contract worker earns per month in net pay. A growing number of highly educated Koreans with degrees are unemployed or work in jobs below their skill level. As a result, college students have spent more time enhancing their *spec* (résumé) by delaying graduation, taking more courses, and earning certificates that promise to lead to high-paying jobs—and attracting a desirable candidate for marriage. But the dream of full-time employment is elusive, as most Koreans will work long hours in small to medium-sized businesses for notoriously low pay because companies now prefer contract or part-time employees. To add to their humiliation, contingent workers have become more dependent on parental support into their thirties, earning the nickname Kangaroo Tribe for nesting in their parents' pouches.

Those who experience mental health issues refuse to seek professional help for fear that their medical records will become public, thus jeopardizing their employment opportunities. Anxieties about privacy also make it difficult for Koreans to establish trust with their healthcare providers. Revelations about mental health issues can also harm an individual's chances on the marriage market, as well as those of other family members. According to the Health and Welfare Ministry, about 90 percent of suicide victims suffered from a diagnosable psychiatric illness, but only 15 percent of them received proper treatment, reflecting the strict taboo around the topic. Although Koreans were prone to ignore problems around mental health, an event in the United States gave them a wake-up call.

On April 16, 2007, Cho Seung-hui killed thirty-two people and wounded seventeen others at Virginia Polytechnic Institute and State University in Blacksburg, Virginia, before turning the gun on himself. Koreans were shocked to learn that the gunman responsible for the horrific mass shooting was an ethnic Korean who had a record of mental illness. Although Cho spent most of his life in America, his actions induced a collective sense of regret and guilt in Korea. The Korean ambassador to the United States, Yi Taesik, fasted for thirty-two days to express his sorrow; he also sought to allay fears by protecting the rights of Koreans who planned to visit or study in the United States. Similarly, President Roh Moo-hyun sent messages of condolences to the United States but convened his cabinet to debate measures to address political fallout from the massacre rather than hold a serious discussion about Cho, his struggles with mental health, and his violent suicide.

Koreans who felt ashamed about Cho's actions had to reckon with violence in their own backyard and the suicides of their very young, who were caught up in the cruel system of competition. The mentality of "winner takes all," based on the neoliberal logic that individuals are responsible for their success or failure, led to extreme bullying and hazing among school-age children. Students identified the loser—someone who was different due to class, physical appearance, ability, and so forth—and engaged in acts of severe ostracism and violence. Perpetrators primarily targeted children with disabilities and those from mixed-race backgrounds for bullying. According to testimonies of victims, bullying could take several forms, from social exclusion to branding with cigarette burns to cyberbullying. A study by the Chicago Policy Review reported that suicide was the most common cause of death among the young between the ages of fifteen and twenty-four. One horrifying case involved Im Seungmin, a thirteen-year-old who jumped to his death from his seventh-floor apartment window in 2012 because he could no longer endure the beatings, burnings with lighters, and chokings with an electric wire. He did not tell his parents about the bullying, which was not surprising, as boys were less likely to report such incidents. Im's shocking suicide sparked debates about how to prevent bullying in Korea's intensely competitive environment.

Korea rolled out its first suicide prevention initiative in 2004 (for which the state did not allocate any special funds) and then created a national mental health system through the Mental Health Welfare Center. The Seoul Suicide Prevention Center, established the following year, set up a phone hotline that appeared to be effective in providing support for the elderly population. Suicide rates began to decline for women as well as men in their twenties and seventies and over, which some attributed to the second national suicide prevention initiative of 2009 that had access to more considerable resources. But suicides continued to increase among men between the ages of thirty and forty-nine, reflecting continued stress about employment and economic success.

Birth Strike: The Ticking Time Bomb and an Aging Population

The high rate of suicide among South Koreans added fuel to national anxieties about the demographic crisis characterized by extremely low birth rates and an aging population. In December 2016, South Korea's Ministry of the Interior was forced to close its pink birth map, which documented the number of women of childbearing age. Color-coded in dark pink for districts with larger concentrations of potential mothers, and pink for fewer numbers, the map created outrage among women who decried the government's treatment of their bodies as mere reproductive tools to raise the birth rate. Demographers concur that South Korea has the lowest birth rates in the world; in the third quarter of 2018, the birth rate dropped to 0.95, making South Korea the only country in the OECD with a rate below 1.30. This is a staggering decrease from 6.16 children per woman in 1960. The alarming trend is well below the birth replacement level (which requires at least 2.1 births per woman) and has prompted a group of demographers to predict that by 2750 South Koreans will go extinct. To compound matters, South Korea is home to the fastest-aging society among OECD nations, with a population of elderly people that is disproportionate to young people. One scholar has estimated that today 100 working Koreans support 37 citizens who are receiving social benefits—what is called the dependency ratio. Without more births, this ratio will tilt and place a heavy burden on young people in the future.

Despite government investment of some eighty trillion *won* ($70 billion), including subsidies for families with children under five to address the low birth rate over the past ten years, it has not succeeded in turning the tide, for several reasons. First, a decrease in the number of Korean marriages as individuals choose to remain single has been an essential factor. Some defer marriage until later in life or choose to stay single because of hostile workplace policies, such as a reluctance to employ mothers or even pay for maternity leave, although the law mandates it. Low birth rates also result from married couples who have fewer children. Parents cite long hours at work, expensive daycare costs, and the extraordinary expenses of raising a child to adulthood (such as cram schools) as obstacles to having more children; instead, they focus all their energies onto one child. The implications of the low birth rates are far-reaching; not only will South Korea have difficulty supporting its aging population, but its economic growth rate is bound to decline. Institutions such as schools are already shuttering their doors due to the small number of children.

Some have looked to the North to solve the South's demographic problems. As North Korea is one of the few remaining closed countries, the few official statistics on its population come from two censuses conducted in 1993 and 2008. They showed that marriage was virtually universal in North Korea. In 2014, the United Nations reported that North Korea also experienced a fall in its total fertility rate to 2.0, while its birth rate was 1.9—not too far above the South. The World Health Organization noted that the North also had a suicide problem: in 2012, 9,790 suicides occurred in North Korea, a country with a population of 22.5 million. North Korean defectors have revealed that the North treats suicide as an act of treason against the state rather than one stemming from mental illness. According to North Korean testimonies, patients with chronic mental illnesses have been hospitalized in state-run facilities called Number 49 hospitals, which are located in remote areas. As a rule, the North Korean press tends to cover up the high suicide rates to showcase the superiority of the social system, under which suicides are allegedly nonexistent. Migrants from the North suffer from depression, anxiety, and trauma triggered by their fears of capture, the guilt of leaving behind family members, or torture at the hands of northern officials. What is similar between the North and South is the severe social ostracism, shame, and fear that induce families to conceal the mentally ill behind closed doors, and an unwillingness to obtain help from mental health professionals.

High levels of suicides, extremely low birth rates, and an aging population are a recipe for a time bomb that threatens the very existence of the Korean nation. As shown earlier, the demographic crisis has opened the doors for Koreans to consider immigration and the acceptance of multicultural families. That road has been rocky, as social attitudes are slow to change.

Misaeng (Incomplete Life)

South Korea's demographic crisis is not the only news hitting the headlines. Koreans misbehaving constitute a category of their own. On December 5, 2014, Heather Hyun-a Jo, vice president of Korean Air, assaulted a male flight attendant to express her dissatisfaction with the way he had served the nuts (in a humble bag instead of on a proper plate). She demanded that the pilots return to the airport gate at John F. Kennedy International Airport in New York City to drop off the humiliated attendant. Jo's father—the chairman of Korean Air—was forced to issue an apology after the "nutrage" video went viral. An investigation revealed that Jo had attacked another flight attendant in 2013 for improperly cooking her ramen noodles—an incident the airline covered up by ordering its employees to remove all records of Jo's outburst and requiring the two victims to downplay the attack. For Koreans watching the video, Jo's behavior was nothing extraordinary; instead, it was emblematic of the arrogance of the powerful families of conglomerates and their abuse of power in the workplace.

On the basis of witness testimonies, the Seoul District Court charged Jo with changing the flight plan at JFK International Airport (an offense that carried a penalty of up to ten years in prison) rather than committing violence against her employees. However, the Seoul High Court overturned her conviction and reduced her sentence to ten months, which she could serve after a two-year probation. She was released immediately. The civil lawsuits filed by the flight attendant and cabin crew chief had to be dropped; they were no match for the most powerful law firms that represented Jo. Moreover, it was difficult for an American court to prosecute a party in Korea.

South Korea's record on social progress—that is, its ability to meet basic human needs—despite being the world's eleventh-largest economy, is embarrassingly weak; for instance, only 10.4 percent of its GDP goes toward social programs, and there is no social safety net. In fact, according to the Korea Labor Institute (2011), vulnerable populations like the elderly live in poverty (48.6%). The South's taxation system privileges economic elites, resulting in a gaping hole between the poor and the rich. The quality of life, even with the possession of smartphones and other digital technologies, is stressful—as reflected in the average sleep time (7 hours, 49 minutes), one of the lowest in the world.

Despite the country's quantum leap into the twenty-first century through innovation and technology, South Korean attitudes toward gender equality have been slow to change, even with the creation of a Ministry of Gender Equality and Family. Male power remains entrenched in Confucian values and traditions, allowing husbands to "discipline" their wives with impunity behind closed doors. Violence against Korean women—sexual assault, domestic violence, and homicides—remains a taboo topic, and reporting (especially among male victims) is extremely low. Korean women make up the majority of victims of violent crimes; according to the Korean Women's Development Institute, the number of sexual violence cases reached thirty thousand in 2014. Until the mid-1990s, rape victims had to demonstrate that they had attempted to protect their chastity, under Penal Code 32 (Crime against Chastity). The court ruled on their innocence, accessing their prior sexual history, their behavior according to gender norms, and their attempts to resist assault. Opposition to the scrutiny of rape survivors rather than perpetrators galvanized the Women's Movement, which pressured the government to pass the Act on Punishment of Sexual Violence Crimes and Protection of Victims in 1994. But institutions that were intended to protect individuals have been slow to change; in fact, studies have shown that rape myths still influence Korean police, who are responsible for investigating the crimes. The recent #MeToo movement has revealed the high levels of sexual violence and the tremendous social pressure on women to remain silent.

In July 2018, the Korean Institute for Gender Equality Promotion and Education released a report that observed an uptick in misogynistic content, comments, and bullying on online sites. Feminist groups have linked the hateful, sexist rhetoric to violent crimes against women, like the gruesome Gangnam subway murder. In May 2016, a thirty-four-year-old man stabbed a young woman to death in Gangnam as she was leaving a bathroom. The killer, who confessed to the crime against a stranger, stated that he hated women "for belittling him." Women from all over Seoul poured into subway exit no. 10 in Gangnam Station, plastering the walls with Post-it stickers (with notes like "I survived by coincidence"), which became a memorial to the victim. They also posted their outrage over misogyny online. Men's groups infiltrated the women's online chats with condescending remarks that they were overreacting; they also staged counterprotests, accusing the female protestors of encouraging discrimination against men. In 2013, Seong Jaegi, the founder of Man of Korea, committed suicide by jumping off a bridge on the Han River to raise money and awareness for his group. He called for the dismantling of the Ministry of Gender Equality and Family, and monetary compensation for Korean men who serve eighteen months of mandatory military service. This group railed against reverse discrimination in Korean society, in which men were still expected to be the primary breadwinners. The Gangnam murder and Seong's suicide exposed the deep-rooted and festering misogyny in Korean culture as well as anxieties about the emergence of new gender roles and expectations.

Men like Seong could take refuge in the online gaming world, which some have called a haven for sexism and misogynistic behavior. Take the case of Kim Sehyeon, better known as Geguri, who plays the avatar Zarya, the brawny Russian in Blizzard's popular MMORPG (massively multiplayer online role-playing game) *Overwatch*. She is one of very few women who participate in the gaming world, which is toxic for women. With more than 23,000 PC-bangs (Internet cafés) scattered across the peninsula, gaming has become a national obsession in the past decade and an industry worth billions of dollars. *Lineage* and *StarCraft* have given rise to a new youth culture and the rapidly growing eSports, a professional gaming league sponsored by major corporations that is televised globally. South Korea has been at the forefront of the online gaming industry, and it has the most skilled *LoL* (League of Legends) players, like Faker. However, very few women have survived in this virtual reality. To remain in the circuit, Geguri once considered getting a voice modulator because male players mistreated her whenever she played the game. Her situation got worse when game casters and fellow players accused her of using aimbots (hacks made by programmers to allow players to cheat) in light of her precision killings; they could not believe that a woman had the gaming skills to be so successful. The online bullying compelled her to wear a mask to hide her identity, and to perform live at a studio to clear her name and demonstrate her skills. Geguri is still one of the few women playing in the professional circuit for a Chinese team, which mirrors the glass-ceiling index released by the OECD in 2017 in which South Korea was ranked dead last among the twenty-nine member nations.

Tensions between the sexes erupted into full-out cyber warfare with the creation of the radical online feminist group Megalia, which tapped the power of the Internet to combat misogyny and advocate for gender equality through both wit and seriousness. The name comes from a blending of MERS Gallery—a forum on the outbreak of MERS (Middle East respiratory syndrome)—and *Egalia's Daughter*, Gerd Bratenberg's novel that shaped Megalia's biting, satirical tone. When two Korean women traveling on vacation from Seoul to Hong Kong refused (due to miscommunication) to be quarantined after contracting MERS, male netizens on the Internet forum DC Inside (specifically on the MERS Gallery) assailed them as selfish *"kimchi* bitches"—a nasty epithet for women obsessed with wealth. Fed up with the online hate, women posted mirror statements such as *"kimchi* men," replacing women with men (and adding "with 6.5 cm penises" for good measure). Their biting vocabulary critiques social problems created by Korean men; "Papa," for instance, refers to Korean men who abandon their progeny in Southeast Asia after having a flippant affair. Megalia has engaged in campaigns that expose pornographic sites like Soranet, which engages in underage pornography and prostitution, and that raise money for politicians like Jin Seonmi, who has pledged to take Soranet down. An essential characteristic of Megalia is that its users adopt nicknames which allow them to post anonymously, allowing for greater freedom of speech but also making it challenging to identify trolls. It has also become a welcoming home to Korea's transgender and transsexual minorities.

Megalia's rival, Ilbe (derived from "popular daily"), represents South Korea's alt-right, whose ultrapatriotic, xenophobic, and homophobic politics target immigrants and sexual minorities. Ilbe's angry young men congregate in anonymous forums like DC Inside to spout their hate against liberal social values and policies (especially on North Korea) and vent on rising youth unemployment. Ilbe has been especially vociferous in its attacks against Megalia, which it defines as man-hating and accuses of promoting a double standard, as in making men pay for dinners and gifts and expecting them to earn more money. Perhaps most notorious was Ilbe's mockery of families of the Sewol ferry accident who protested with left-wing politicians for justice. At the large hunger strike organized by victims' families at Gwanghwamun Square to demand an apology from a government that defined the tragedy as a "traffic accident," Ilbe users mocked them by binging on pizza and other foods while playing audio clips of Roh Moo-Hyun's voice. Although this event exposed the faces of online haters, the usually anonymous venue gives license to spout hate without consequences.

While Megalia and Ilbe represent two forums of cyber warfare, another platform for writers to speak candidly about gender, sexuality, class, lookism, race, and education in recent years in South Korea has been through webtoons (a portmanteau of web and cartoons). In 2003, the Korean web portal Daum created the first webtoon service, followed by its rival Naver the following year. By 2014, Daum and Naver had published a total of 954 webtoons with a daily readership of approximately ten million people. Enabled by the digital revolution and the constant innovation of smart mobile devices, webtoon artists have been pushing and transgressing the boundaries of comics beyond their rigid grids and panels to a scrollable, vertical layout onscreen that is accessible to anyone. With an impulse to inform others, writers have engaged this new form of storytelling with a novelist's eye for detail, turning newsworthy events into a narrative that is both journalistic and entertaining, replete with fictional features and sympathetic characters. Many popular webtoons have been adapted into films, plays, and television shows.

In Yun Taeho's *Incomplete Life* (2012–13), a webtoon that was adapted into a twenty-episode drama and aired on TvN in 2014, the protagonist, Jang Geurae, whose aspiration to be a professional *baduk* (Go) player is not realized, must figure out how to move on with his life, having only a high school equivalency certificate on his résumé. Through an acquaintance, Jang obtains a position as an intern at a trading company and is confronted with a corporate culture that is filled with intense competition, workaholics, monotony, and politics. Using his gaming skills, he finds ways to navigate the corporate world, shedding light on the lives of office workers and the "contingent worker," a post-IMF phenomenon in which lifetime employment is longer guaranteed. Yun's webtoon drew more than one billion readers on the Daum portal site. What made it and later the television drama a success was how viewers could relate to Jang and his mundane existence. They could also relate to a host of other characters, from a working mother to an assistant manager and interns, all of whom have to perform tasks without excuses. Evoking empathy, each scene mirrors the experiences of countless people whose educational backgrounds are meaningless and who are stuck in precarious situations as irregular workers or early retirees.

In the past decade, books written by defectors from the North have given us a glimpse into the everyday lives of people in the North and their motives for leaving. From Hyeonseo Lee's *The Girl with Seven Names* (2015) to Yeonmi Park's *In Order to Live* (2015) and Jang Jin-Sung's *Dear Leader: My Escape from North Korea* (2015), readers have become more familiar and sympathetic with defectors and their motives for defecting, with the sacrifices they have had to make in a foreign land, the trauma of leaving behind family members, and their harrowing experiences in China en route to South Korea. Kang Chol-hwan's gut-wrenching experience working in a concentration camp for ten years, where he regularly witnessed the torture and execution of fellow inmates, is captured vividly in *The Aquariums of Pyeongyang* (2000). Nothing is more surreal and captivating than the collection of stories by Bandi ("Firefly," b. 1950), a pseudonymous North Korean who wrote in government periodicals and who might still be attached to the Korea's Writers Alliance. After the death of Kim Il-sung in 1994, Bandi became disillusioned after losing several family members to the famine; as he witnessed more people defecting, he started to publish critical works against the regime. Bandi's short collection, *The Accusation,* was smuggled out via China by a relative who had to enlist the help of Do Huiyun, a human rights worker, who then recruited a Chinese friend to smuggle the manuscript. Parts of the 750-page manuscript would later be published in Seoul in 2014. To protect the identity of Bandi, pseudonyms and biographical misinformation were inserted into the stories. What makes these short stories so interesting is that they offer a very candid description of what life is like in North Korea. The seven stories in *The Accusation* are set in the 1990s around the time Kim Il-sung died. They give readers a glimpse into the everyday lives of people from different social classes—lives that are quite regimented and constantly under the gaze of the state, where everything is tallied and reported. This creates a level of paranoia, as everyone is afraid of being charged with not working hard, or being indicted for engaging in antirevolutionary activities. One gets a sense that at some point people eventually run afoul of the state, as the redundancy in the narratives imbues the reader with the precarity and vulnerability experienced by people as they try to forge a living doing as they are told.

Protecting Human Dignity: Amnesty International and the UN Commission of Inquiry on Human Rights

In 2014, Amnesty International published a scathing critique of human and labor rights violations based on interviews with twenty-eight migrant workers in South Korea's rural areas. The Bitter Harvest report highlighted a wide range of abuses, ranging from contractual deception to trafficking and underpaid wages. That same year, the United Nations Commission of Inquiry on Human Rights charged the DPRK of systematic and widespread human rights violations in its 372-page report. These two serious reports, as well as the rebuttals offered by both states, provide an interesting perspective on human rights violations in both countries.

On August 17, 2004, the South Korean government established the Employment Permit System to regulate foreign workers. Fifteen countries, mainly in Southeast Asia and Central Asia, signed a memorandum of understanding with South Korea, which granted their workers proper work visas (E-9) for three-year terms, after which they were to return home. This new system aimed at a more transparent process that eliminated abuses such as brokerage fees related to the migrant. Since 2007, the Human Resources Development Service of Korea added the Test of Proficiency in Korean to assess the language competency of prospective workers, reflecting its view that the ability to communicate in Korean would help foreign workers with their employer relationships and adaptation to their new lives.

In its 2014 report Bitter Harvest, Amnesty International identified the agricultural industry as the most abusive sector for migrant workers because South Korea's Labor Standards Act (1997) exempted workers in agriculture from protections related to working hours and rest. It found that the Employment Permit System had failed to implement safeguards for agricultural laborers, who encountered exploitation without accountability. The interviewees complained about excessive work hours, unpaid labor, and lack of rest days; insufficient food and squalid living quarters; the absence of medical care and being coerced to take HIV tests. Workers endured these abuses for fear that employers would terminate their contracts. They did not have the option to change jobs, because employers were reluctant to sign the release form and, what is more, threatened exorbitant fines, deportation, and even violence. Those who worked as subcontractors in off-seasons (especially winter)—which was not covered in the labor agreements—were especially vulnerable to mistreatment. Amnesty International argued that this amounted to forcing workers to work against their will under oppressive conditions. Workers themselves felt compelled to stay to make money that they could remit back to their families. Without reliable translators, migrant workers were unable to file suit for industrial accidents or occupational illnesses that they contracted.

Being a signatory of the International Labor Organization and other human rights treaties has not prevented the South Korean government from ignoring Amnesty's findings. It has failed to investigate abuses, let alone punish employers for massive violations of the law, especially in industries like agriculture, fisheries, and livestock. Amnesty International identified the lack of legal protections, rampant xenophobia, and the government's complicity in the abuses suffered by migrant workers, and called for immediate reforms. In spite of this humiliating exposé, the South Korean government has done nothing to alleviate the plight of migrant workers in the farming industry. As one of the largest economies in the world, with a shrinking population, South Korea has found it increasingly imperative to hire migrant workers—a reality that has not been matched with proper attention to the fundamental human rights of this laboring population.

The human rights issue was no better in the North. On March 21, 2013, the United Nations Human Rights Council established the Commission of Inquiry on Human Rights in the Democratic People's Republic of Korea to investigate allegations of grave human rights violations and crimes against humanity. The list of violations covered basic freedoms of expression, religion, and movement; food and other necessities of life; arrest and incarceration (torture, detention, disappearance, and prison camps); and abduction of people from other countries. On the basis of testimonies from witnesses and experts in Seoul, Tokyo, London, and Washington, the commission released its four-hundred-page report in February 2014. This was the first thorough and comprehensive report, providing a long historical narrative—from the North's precolonial past, the Japanese colonial occupation, the Korean War, and the *suryeong* (leader) system, to the rise of the Kim dynasty—to create a context for understanding the logic behind these abuses and violations in the North.

To the ire of North Korea, the commission concluded that it was the responsibility of the international community to prosecute individuals for their crimes against humanity through an ad hoc international tribunal. As a result of the recommendations, on December 18, 2014, the General Assembly passed Resolution 69/188, which condemned the human rights abuses. To implement the recommendations, it turned to the Security Council to bring the charges before the International Criminal Court. Not all members (notably China and Russia) of the Security Council agreed with the United States' proposal to include North Korea's human rights abuses on the permanent agenda of UN Security Council meetings. Opponents argued that human rights is not a topic to be discussed in those meetings.

Epilogue
The Land of Morning Calm

In the Golden Age of Asia
Korea was one of the lamp-bearers
That lamp awaits to be lighted once again
For the illumination of the East

RABINDRANATH TAGORE, "Lamp of the East" (1929)

On May 16, 2018, Lee Chang-dong's enigmatic mystery film, *Burning*, premiered at the Seventy-First Cannes Film Festival to a packed auditorium. As South Korea's most prominent auteur and the former head of the Ministry of Culture, Sports, and Tourism, Lee had a reputation for delivering films that pushed the social envelope, such as *Peppermint Candy* (1999), *Oasis* (2002), *Secret Sunshine* (2007), and *Poetry* (2010). It came as no surprise that *Burning* was one of the most widely discussed films in contention for the highest prize, the Palme d'Or. Lee was on President Park Geun-hye's notorious blacklist of cultural figures to be excluded from government support and subsidies. Loosely adapted from Haruki Murakami's 1992 short story "Barn Burning" and William Faulkner's work by the same title, Lee's film explores the smoldering rage of a new Korean generation through the trope of arson and via three complex characters who embody the vast chasm of economic inequality in the South, while living under the phantom threat of the North. The film is an allegory about a partitioned country, haunted by a history of repression, violence, and grief beneath a façade of prosperity and blustering propaganda.

Lee introduces the three protagonists Jongsu, Haemi, and Ben in relation to the social geography of the nation. In the opening scene, Jongsu chances on Haemi, a childhood friend in Seoul, but he fails to recognize her because she has undergone extensive plastic surgery—a sure sign that she has been living in the capital. Jongsu, a college graduate and aspiring writer, finds himself working a nonregular job as a delivery truck driver, like so many millennials. When his father assaults a police officer and gets mired in legal trouble, Jongsu is compelled to take over his farm, which is located in Paju near Panmunjeom on the thirty-eighth parallel, in the Joint Security Area. This space is reserved for talks between the United Nations Command and its Communist counterparts (North Korea and China) and is surrounded by the US and South Korean army bases. Although Paju is only an hour's drive from Seoul, the rural farming community is desolate. Its plastic greenhouses are bereft of plants and overgrown with weeds. The daily Communist propaganda, broadcast loudly over a loudspeaker from the North, is audible in Paju, reminding villagers that the war is not yet over. Old black-and-white photos of Jongsu's family that hang on the walls of the living room also attest to the bloody civil war and painful national division.

Haemi is a part-time storefront girl who aspires to be an actress and lives precariously in Seoul. She impresses Jongsu in the busy marketplace by performing a pantomime with an imaginary tangerine. She quips that a successful performance depends on how

FIGURE 16. Advertisements in Daerimdong (Seoul) for funeral consultations for ethnic Korean Chinese (Joseonjok).

FIGURE 17. Donald Trump, Kim Jong-un, and Moon Jae-in outside Freedom House at the Korean DMZ (June 30, 2019).

much you "really want it." Yet no amount of fantasy and imagination can make up for her poverty and humble roots in Paju. Haemi invites Jongsu to her modest studio near Namsan Tower (once an enclave for North Korean war refugees) where the two have a brief, awkward sexual encounter, which arouses neither of them. On a whim, Haemi asks Jongsu to take care of her cat while she is away on a trip to Africa. Anxious to pick up where they left off, Jongsu goes to the airport to pick up Haemi on her return, only to discover that she has a new boyfriend.

Haemi's new love is Ben, a well-to-do modern Gatsby who drives a Porsche and lives in a fancy apartment in the posh neighborhood of Gangnam. Ben is a young Korean American (though that is not explicitly stated in the film) and a frustrated diasporic. His Western name and wealth serve as social capital in his circles, but Ben cannot seem to find a niche for himself. He is an outsider whose English accent is an immediate giveaway that he is not a local (even after he masters the Korean pronunciation of "William Faulkner"). To mask his feelings of emptiness and alienation, he feigns indifference, flaunts his taste for expensive wine and Western food, and plays Miles Davis in his car. He expresses his complete disregard for Korean law by smoking a joint, a luxury that Koreans can ill afford, even when traveling abroad, for fear of incarceration at home. When Ben and Haemi visit Jongsu in Paju, the two young men confess their dark secrets. Jongsu admits that he hates his arsonist father, who made him set his mother's belongings on fire after she abandoned them; this leads Ben to casually reveal that he is a serial arsonist, who burns down barren greenhouses to make them disappear, as though they "never even existed."

When Haemi mysteriously disappears, Jongsu suspects that Ben is involved. The disappearance of girls from economically depressed farming villages like Paju barely raises an eyebrow. Haemi's family, with whom she has severed ties, do not even bother filing a lost-person report. They assume that she ran away to escape her debts. This film highlights the extreme class disparity and the city-country divide by juxtaposing police harassment of Jongsu for loitering in his old pickup truck in Gangnam (during a sleuthing mission) and the ease with which Ben can park his Porsche on Jongsu's dilapidated farm. Ben sets fire to the neglected greenhouses, to make them disappear. A poor, young woman like Haemi is like a greenhouse—disposable and forgotten, as though she never even existed.

The voyeuristic camera follows Jongsu as he shuttles back and forth between the farm and the city, thus emphasizing Seoul's proximity to the North. Yet the film's characters are disengaged from the politics of the past and exhibit a willing ignorance of the North. "How fun," Ben remarks when he hears the propaganda from the loudspeakers. Nonetheless, the presence of the North never disappears completely from consciousness, reinforced as it is by an eerie sense of unease that is generated by the film itself. The film is a commentary on the new generation's unease about their future in a world where precarious global markets have harmed their chances at stable employment and precipitated downward mobility. Not only does South Korea rank highest for the shortest job tenures among OECD nations; it can no longer promise its children that their lives will be better and more secure than those of their parents.

Unlike millennials in the South, who were born during a period of prosperity and relative peace, an entire generation in North Korea grew up during the great famine of the 1990s and survived in part due to the emergence of the *jangmadang* (ground markets), illegal markets that provided desperately needed food. Survival during the "arduous march" required significant ingenuity and risk; it could mean the difference between becoming a street beggar, petty pickpocket, or an entrepreneur who could barter for goods across the border in China. North Koreans (especially women) relied heavily on these private markets, learning how to procure goods, lend money, and even engage in foreign currency exchange. In recent years, the *jangmadang* have become a lifeline for many North Koreans—as both a source of goods and a form of employment—especially after Kim Jung-un lifted restrictions against this form of private-market enterprise. In Pyeongyang and port cities like Chongjin, the impact of the *jangmadang* (both legal and illicit) is visible in the dress and well-being of the citizens, some of whom sport Ray-Ban sunglasses or luxury watches. There are some four hundred *jangmadang* in the country today. According to University of Chicago scholar Bruce Cumings, the North may emulate Deng Xiaoping's economic strategy for China in 1979—that is, to create the proper conditions under which the North can open up its economy to global markets. Unlike their parents' generation, the young people in North Korea have a little more information about the outside world through the *jangmadang,* a vibrant marketplace not only of goods but of knowledge as well. The population also waits for new developments in Kim Jong-un's engagement with the South and the United States.

On June 10, 2018, President Donald Trump landed in Singapore straight from the G7 Summit in Canada, where he had alienated all the participating countries. Trump was there for the much-anticipated summit with his former archnemesis, Kim Jong-un. A flurry of meetings between the two Koreas resulted in an agreement that arranged for Kim to meet Trump in March for a face-to-face meeting to discuss the peace and the denuclearization of the Korean peninsula. Kim had arrived earlier on a specially chartered Air China plane and was warmly welcomed by Lee Hsien Loong, the Singaporean prime minister. An armed motorcade then escorted him to the St. Regis Singapore Hotel before the historic meeting at Capella Hotel Resort on Sentosa Island, which would cost the Singaporean government roughly twelve million dollars. With more than 2,500 media outlets from around the world converging in Singapore to cover this historic event, the footage of both leaders filled the social media feeds for several days. On June 12, Trump finally met Kim Jong-un in the first-ever summit meeting between the leaders of the United States of America and the Democratic People's Republic of Korea. At this event, the two leaders signed a joint statement agreeing to appropriate security guarantees, forging peaceful relations, reconfirming the intent to denuclearize the Korean peninsula, the recovery of the remains of POWs in the North, and high-level meetings between officials. Images of Trump showing off his limousine to Kim generated considerable interest, but it was his call to cancel joint military exercises with South Korea and his reiterating the need to bring American soldiers back home that was music to the ears of citizens in both the North and the South who longed for a peace treaty and an end to all hostilities.

All of these arrangements would not have taken place without the efforts of President Moon Jae-in, who was elected after the impeachment of his predecessor, Park Geun-hye, in 2017. Once a student activist, Moon was convicted and expelled from Kyunghee University after organizing a protest against Park Chung-hee's Yushin Constitution. Although he passed the rigorous bar exam, he was denied the right to become a judge or government prosecutor because of his prison record. He opted to work as a human rights lawyer, partnering up with

Roh Moo-hyun in defending labor and student rights activists during the military dictatorship, and later working as Roh's chief presidential secretary. Moon's engagement policies vis-à-vis the North have been similar to those of Roh and Kim Dae-jung, stirring much controversy and concern at home among the center-right parties. Tensions, however, have certainly deescalated as Moon has engaged with Kim Jong-un through dialogue.

The success of the Winter Olympics in Pyeongchang, South Korea, in 2018 and rapprochement with the North through various channels paved the way for discussions for an inter-Korean summit. The plan was grandiose. A group of South Korean delegates traveled to the United States to deliver King Jong-un's invitation to Trump for a summit. A visit by then CIA director Mike Pompeo to Pyeongyang and a reciprocal visit by Kim Yeongcheol, vice chairman of the Workers' Party of Korea, to the White House created the agenda, despite disagreements over the joint US–South Korea military exercises. On May 22, 2018, South Korean president Moon Jae-in visited the United States to meet President Trump in order to promote a Trump-Kim summit in Singapore. The Obama administration had always maintained a policy of "strategic patience," a refusal to reward provocations by the North with high-level talks, and punishment with sanctions and military exercises with South Korea and Japan. In contrast, Trump's "art of the deal" turned heads when his fiery rhetoric that provocations by the North would "be met with fire, fury and frankly power, the likes of which the world has never seen before" changed to a call for engagement. On May 26, 2018, Moon and Kim met for a second time at the DMZ and exchanged ideas about a meeting with Trump in June. There were still many disagreements over the denuclearization process that needed to be ironed out.

The meeting between Trump and Kim represented a symbolic and historic moment, but the third summit between Kim and Moon in Pyeongyang on September 18, 2018, was equally important. The three-day summit focused on reducing conflicts on the peninsula and promoting greater economic cooperation, which many pundits viewed as Kim's charm initiative to obtain relief from sanctions but also as evidence of Moon's ability to offer options for improving relations through high-level engagement. As with Roh's visit to Pyeongyang eleven years earlier, Moon brought a huge civilian entourage, including top CEOs and K-pop stars.

The wave of optimism after the first two inter-Korean summits in April and May followed by the Singapore meeting between Trump and Kim certainly has reduced the saber rattling and brought some goodwill, although naysayers doubt that any of this will generate concrete steps toward denuclearization. The second summit between Trump and Kim in Hanoi did not result in the signing of a treaty to formally put an end to the Korean War. It did, however, expose their key differences and highlight the costs that would come with denuclearization, including a significant reduction of US troops and the lifting of sanctions. Donald Trump's domestic problems, especially his impeachment, could put an end to his negotiations with Kim. The summit in Vietnam might have lined him up, in the most ironic way, for the Nobel Peace Prize, a surefire way to have matched his nemesis, Barack Obama, who as president won the prize in 2009. It remains in the courts of Kim Jong-un and Moon Jae-in to resolve the national division of Korea—a problem that must be addressed by both nations.

On another front, both Koreas also need to confront their complicated relationships with Japan, especially with the rise of Shinzo Abe, who has unrepentantly refused to apologize for Japan's past, especially for the comfort women and forced labor during World War II. Tensions between Tokyo and Seoul have led Japan to remove South Korea formally from its "white list," rescinding preferential trade status and depriving its neighbor of major raw materials and components for many high-tech products. Boycotts of Japanese products and tourism and abandonment of intelligence sharing (despite US reservations about such actions) have further complicated regional stability. At the same time, North Korea's frequent missile tests have triggered right-wing extremists to attack Korean residents in Japan. And ties between the North and Japan have deteriorated from bad to worse as the latter continues to press for the return of seventeen unaccounted abductees.

It has been almost seventy years since the signing of the armistice on July 27, 1953, by the two Koreas, but the countries are still technically at war without a formal peace agreement. Today the South boasts one of the largest economies in the world with a vibrant democracy; its technological prowess and soft power, with the popularity of Hallyu, have facilitated South Korea's widespread visibility on the global stage. The North has "illuminated" the world (to use the word of the great Indian intellectual Rabindranath Tagore) with its history of survival and its willingness to oppose the capitalist world order. Long before the collapse of the Iron Curtain in Eastern Europe, the subsequent collapse of the Soviet Union, and China's economic transformation, the North was successful in creating solidarity with Socialists in Third World countries. The transformation of the world order that left the North in the cold, coinciding with the tragic famine and ecological disasters, forced the North to retreat from its *juche* ideals, which had sustained the country through other crises. Today quiet changes are taking place in the North. The expansion of the *jangmadang* has begun to open up the country to new products and goods. Its leader continues to engage in brinkmanship with its last remaining card of nuclear weapons and missile technology, threatening the security of the world. But on both sides of the border a new generation of millennials has grown up without having witnessed the traumatic civil war firsthand or having pined after kin on the other side of the thirty-eighth parallel. They will be the new caretakers of both nations. Will they call for reunification and light the lamp to illuminate the East through peace and reconciliation? Lee's *Burning*, which has ignited debates about the very soul of the young generation in crisis, may generate changes that can heal the painful rifts of history.

Bibliography

Abelmann, Nancy, and John Lie. *Blue Dreams: Korean Americans and the Los Angeles Riots.* Cambridge, MA: Harvard University Press, 1995.

An, Jinsoo. *Parameters of Disavowal: Colonial Representation in South Korean Cinema.* Berkeley: University of California Press, 2018.

Bandi. *The Accusation: Forbidden Stories from Inside North Korea.* Translated by Deborah Smith. London: Serpent's Trail, 2017.

Brazinsky, Gregg. *Nation Building in South Korea: Koreans, Americans, and the Making of a Democracy.* Chapel Hill: University of North Carolina Press, 2007.

Buswell, Robert, Jr., and Timothy S. Lee, eds. *Christianity in Korea.* Honolulu: University of Hawaiʻi Press, 2007.

Buzo, Adrian. *The Guerilla Dynasty: Politics and Leadership in the DPRK, 1945-1994.* Sydney: Allen & Unwin, 1999.

Cha, Victor. *The Impossible State: North Korea, Past and Future.* New York: Ecco, 2013.

———, and David Kang. *Nuclear North Korea: A Debate of Engagement Strategies.* New York: Columbia University Press, 2018.

Chang, Paul Y. *Protest Dialectics: State Repression and South Korea's Democracy Movement, 1970-1979.* Stanford: Stanford University Press, 2015.

Choo, Hae Yeon. *Decentering Citizenship: Gender, Labor, and Migrant Rights in South Korea.* Stanford, CA: Stanford University Press, 2016.

Cumings, Bruce. *Korea's Place in the Sun: A Modern History.* New York: Norton, 1997.

Delisle, Guy. *Pyongyang: A Journey in North Korea*. Translated by Helge Dascher. Montreal: Drawn and Quarterly, 2018.

Demick, Barbara. *Nothing to Envy: Ordinary Lives in North Korea*. New York: Spiegel & Grau, 2010.

DiMoia, John. *Reconstructing Bodies: Biomedicine, Health, and Nation-Building in South Korea since 1945*. Stanford, CA: Stanford University Press, 2013.

Eckert, Carter J. *Offspring of Empire: The Koch'ang Kims and the Origins of Korean Capitalism*. Seattle: University of Washington Press, 1991.

———. *Park Chung Hee and Modern Korea: The Roots of Militarism, 1866–1945*. Cambridge, MA: Belknap Press of Harvard University Press, 2016.

Freeman, Caren. *Making and Faking Kinship: Marriage and Labor Migration between China and South Korea*. Ithaca, NY: Cornell University Press, 2017.

Fulton, Bruce. *Modern Korean Fiction: An Anthology*. New York: Columbia University Press, 2005.

Haggard, Stephan, and Marcus Noland. *Famine in North Korea: Markets, Aid, and Reform*. New York: Columbia University Press, 2007.

Han, Kang. *Human Acts: A Novel*. Translated by Deborah Smith. London: Hogarth, 2017.

Harkness, Nicholas. *Songs of Seoul: An Ethnography of Voice and Voicing in Christian South Korea*. Berkeley: University of California Press, 2013.

Hughes, Theodore. *Literature and Film in Cold War South Korea: Freedom's Frontier*. New York: Columbia University Press, 2014.

Hwang, Kyung Moon. *Rationalizing Korea: The Rise of the Modern State, 1894–1945*. Berkeley: University of California Press, 2015.

Jenkins, Charles Robert. *The Reluctant Communist: My Desertion, Court-Martial, and Forty-Year Imprisonment in North Korea*. Berkeley: University of California Press, 2008.

Jin, Dal Yong. *Korea's Online Gaming Empire*. Cambridge, MA: MIT Press, 2010.

Kang, Jiyeon. *Igniting the Internet*. Honolulu: University of Hawai'i Press, 2018.

Kazuki, Kaneshiro. *Go: A Coming of Age Novel*. Translated by Takami Nieda. Seattle: Amazon Crossing, 2018.

Kim, Charles R. *Youth for Nation: Culture and Protest in Cold War South Korea*. Honolulu: University of Hawai'i Press, 2017.

Kim, Cheehyung Harrison. *Heroes and Toilers: Work as Life in Postwar North Korea, 1953–1961*. New York: Columbia University Press, 2018.

Kim, Eleana J. *Adopted Territory: Transnational Korean Adoptees and the Politics of Belonging*. Durham, NC: Duke University Press, 2010.

Kim, Eunjung. *Curative Violence: Rehabilitating Disability, Gender, and Sexuality in Modern Korea*. Durham, NC: Duke University Press, 2017.

Kim, Jaeeun. *Contested Embrace: Transborder Membership Politics in Twentieth-Century Korea*. Stanford, CA: Stanford University Press, 2016.

Kim, Kyung Hyun. *Virtual Hallyu: Korean Cinema of the Global Era*. Durham, NC: Duke University Press, 2011.

Kim, Monica. *The Interrogation Rooms of the Korean War: The Untold History*. Princeton, NJ: Princeton University Press, 2019.

Kim, Rebecca Y. *The Spirit Moves West: Korean Missionaries in America*. Oxford: Oxford University Press, 2015.

Kim, Suk-Young. *Illusive Utopia: Theater, Film, and Everyday Performance in North Korea*. Ann Arbor: University of Michigan Press, 2010.

———. *K-pop Live: Fans, Idols, and Multimedia Performance*. Stanford, CA: Stanford University Press, 2018.

Kim, Suzy. *Everyday Life in the North Korean Revolution, 1945–1950*. Ithaca, NY: Cornell University Press, 2013.

Koo, Hagen. *Korean Workers: The Culture and Politics of Class Formation*. Ithaca, NY: Cornell University Press, 2001.

Lankov, Andrei. *North of the DMZ: Essays on Daily Life in North Korea*. Jefferson, NC: McFarland, 2007.

———. *The Real North Korea: Life and Politics in the Failed Stalinist Utopia*. Oxford: Oxford University Press, 2014.

Lee, Jin-kyung. *Service Economies: Militarism, Sex Work, and Migrant Labor in South Korea*. Minneapolis: University of Minnesota Press, 2010.

Lee, Namhee. *The Making of Minjung: Democracy and the Politics of Representation in South Korea*. Ithaca, NY: Cornell University Press, 2009.

Lie, John. *Han Unbound: The Political Economy of South Korea*. Stanford, CA: Stanford University Press, 2000.

———. *K-Pop: Popular Music, Cultural Amnesia, and Economic Innovation in South Korea*. Berkeley: University of California Press, 2014.

———. *Multi-ethnic Japan*. Cambridge: Harvard University Press, 2001.

Moon, Katharine. *Sex among Allies*. New York: Columbia University Press, 1997.

Moon, Seungsook. *Militarized Modernity and Gendered Citizenship in South Korea.* Durham, NC: Duke University Press, 2005.

Morris-Suzuki, Tessa. *Exodus to North Korea: Shadows from Japan's Cold War.* Lanham, MD: Rowman & Littlefield, 2007.

Myers, Brian. *The Cleanest Race: How North Koreans See Themselves—and Why It Matters.* New York: Melville House, 2011.

Nam, Hwasook. *Building Ships, Building a Nation: Korea's Democratic Unionism under Park Chung Hee.* Seattle: University of Washington Press, 2009.

Nelson, Laura C. *Measured Excess: Status, Gender, and Consumer Nationalism in South Korea.* New York: Columbia University Press, 2000.

Ogle, George E. *South Korea: Dissent within the Economic Miracle.* Atlantic Highlands, NJ: Zed Books, 1990.

Oh, Youjeong. *Pop City: Korean Popular Culture and the Selling of Place.* Ithaca, NY: Cornell University Press, 2018.

Orbendorfer, Don, and Robert Carlin. *The Two Koreas: A Contemporary History.* New York: Basic Books, 2013.

Paik, Nak-chung. *The Division System in Crisis: Essays on Contemporary Korea.* Berkeley: University of California Press, 2011.

Paik, Nam June. *We Are in Open Circuits: Writings by Nam June Paik.* Edited by John G. Hanhardt, Gregory Zinman, and Edith Decker-Phillips. Cambridge, MA: MIT Press, 2019.

Park, Albert. *Building a Heaven on Earth: Religion, Activism, and Protest in Japanese Occupied Korea.* Honolulu: University of Hawai'i Press, 2014.

Park, Alyssa M. *Sovereignty Experiments: Korean Migrants and the Building of Borders in Northeast Asia, 1860–1945.* Ithaca, NY: Cornell University Press, 2019.

Pihl, Marshall R., Bruce Fulton, Ju-Chan Fulton, and Kwon Youngmin. *Land of Exile: Contemporary Korean Fiction.* Abingdon: Routledge, 2007.

Robinson, Michael E. *Korea's Twentieth-Century Odyssey.* Honolulu: University of Hawai'i Press, 2007.

Ryang, Sonia. *Reading North Korea: An Ethnological Inquiry.* Cambridge, MA: Harvard University Asia Center, 2012.

Ryu, Youngju. *Writers of the Winter Republic: Literature and Resistance in Park Chung Hee's Korea.* Honolulu: University of Hawai'i Press, 2015.

Seth, Michael J. *A Concise History of Korea: From Antiquity to the Present.*
Lanham, MD: Rowman & Littlefield, 2016.

———. *Education Fever: Society, Politics and the Pursuit of Schooling in South Korea.* Honolulu: University of Hawai'i Press, 2002.

Song, Jesook. *South Koreans in the Debt Crisis: The Creation of a Neoliberal Welfare Society.* Durham, NC: Duke University Press, 2009.

Suh, Dae-sook. *Kim Il Sung: A Biography.* Honolulu: University of Hawai'i Press, 1989.

Suh, Jae-Jung, ed. *Truth and Reconciliation in South Korea: Between the Present and Future of the Korean Wars.* London: Routledge, 2014.

Trenka, Jane Jeong. *The Language of Blood.* Minneapolis: Graywolf Press, 2005.

Tudor, Daniel, and James Pearson. *North Korea Confidential: Private Markets, Fashion Trends, Prison Camps, Dissenters and Defectors.* Clarendon, VT: Tuttle, 2015.

Woo, Jung-en. *Race to the Swift: State and Finance in the Industrialization of Korea.* New York: Columbia University Press, 1991.

Yang, Myungji. *From Miracle to Mirage: The Making and Unmaking of the Korean Middle Class, 1960–2015.* Ithaca, NY: Cornell University Press, 2018.

Yoo, Theodore Jun. *It's Madness: The Politics of Mental Health in Colonial Korea.* Berkeley: University of California Press, 2016.

———. *The Politics of Gender in Colonial Korea: Labor, Education, and Health, 1910–1945.* Berkeley: University of California Press, 2008.

Index

digital revolution: broadband service and, 180; candlelight vigils and, 193; cyber-security and, 182; e-mail services and, 182; e-sports and, 180; internet cafes and, 179; PC-Bang and, 179; presidential elections and, 189; search engines and, 182; South Korea, 179–81; technology and social media, 238–39; video gaming and, 180

dimple creation, 242

"dirt spoon" class, 266

Do Huiyun, 279

doenjang (soybean paste), 195

doenjangnyeo (soybean paste woman), 239

Dokdo (Takeshima) issue, 74

"dollar-earning patriots," 41

Dongguk University, 209, 211

donor country. *See* ODA

Dr. Evil (*Austin Powers* series): Kim Jong-il and, 186–87

Dresnok, James, 82

Du, Soonja, 147

Dvořák, Antonín Leopold. Ninth Symphony, 221

Dwarf Launches a Ball, A (1978), 67

East Berlin Spy Incident (1967), 90–91

East Germany, 45

East-West Center, 34

Economic Planning Board (EPB), 64

economic plans: incorporation into Japan's economic networks and product cycles, 139–40; military and financial aid from the United

States, 139; of North Korea, 46–51, 140–41; of South Korea, 64, 139

education: criticism of, 206–7; fraud and, 209–13; managerial mothers and, 207–8; missionaries and, 31, 34; patriotism and, 63; in South Korea, 205–8

Eisenhower, Dwight: Atoms for Peace campaign (1953), 155

"electronic superhighway." *See* Paik, Nam June

Ellington, Duke, 41

Emergency Decree Number Nine, 106

Emigration Act (1962), 88

Emmanuelle (1974). *See Madame Aema*

Employment Permit System (EPS), 200–201, 280–81; "3-D" (dirty, dangerous, demanding) jobs and, 200; Non-professional Employ-ment (E-9) visa and, 200, 280; Test of Proficiency in Korea (TOPIK) and, 280. *See also* Industrial Training System (ITS)

"English fever," 149; TOEFL and, 208; TOEIC and, 208

Equatorial Guinea. *See* Macías, Monica

eSports, 181

Emperor Gojong, 246

Ethiopia, 5–6; civil war and famine, 8; relations with North Korea, 7, 116, 118; relations with South Korea, 5–6, 8

Ewha Womans College, 22

Ewha Womans University, 246; Jeong Yura scandal, 262–63;

Han Pilhwa, 77

Han River, 66

Han-Style, 198

Hanahoe (Group of One). *See also* Chun Doo-hwan

Hanawon center, 215–16

Han-gang Public Official Apartments, 66

hangeul (national language), 152; unlearning Japanese and exclusively using, 4

Hangeul Society, 153

Hangul and Computer Company (later known as Haansoft), 151–53

Hangyoreh 21, 178

hansik (Korean cuisine): globalizing of, 195–96

Harlins, Latasha. *See* Los Angeles riots

Hart-Celler Act (Immigration and Nationality Act, 1965), 89; Korean missionaries and, 139

Haruki Murakami: "Barn Burning" (1992), 285

Heilongjiang province. *See* Joseonjok

homosexuality, 170, 171, 174; Article 92 of the Military Penal Code and, 174

Hong Seokcheon, 171–75

Hawai'i, 19; Chinese Exclusion Act of 1924 and, 89; emigration to, 88

Heo Jeong, 61

"Heungnam Evacuation" (Kim, 1955), 24

Hiroshima, 74

Hitel. *See* BBS

Hitomi Soga, 83

HIV/AIDS. *See* gay rights movement

Hodge, John, 17

hojok (family register), 4

Holt, Bertha, 38

Holt, Harry, 38

Holt Adoption Program, 39

Holt Organization, 38

Homefront: North Koreans as villains in, 186

Hong Gildong, 72

Hong Yeonghui, 113

Hongik University, 91

Honam (southwest). *See* regionalism

Hooker Hill, 40

H.O.T. (High-Five of Teenagers), 148

Hoxha, Enver, 45

Huang Chunming. *See* Bak Gwangsu

Hui Sisters. *See* Kim Insun (Insooni)

human rights abuse: in North Korea, 10, 189, 237, 282–83; in South Korea, 281–82

Hwang Min-u, 238

Hwang Seokyeong, 100–101

Hwang Useok: bioethics and, 209–10, 211–13; cloning animals and, 212; human embryonic stem cells and, 212; "Pride of Korea" and, 210

hwarang (flower boy): Silla dynasty and, 244

Hwaseong (labor penal colony), 237

Hyecho. *See* Kkansu, Muhammad

hygiene. *See* public health

Hyoenggye, Gangwon Province, 1

Hyundae munhak (Contemporary literature), 71

Hyundai ("modernity") Group, 110–13, 120

Kim Dae-jung, 2, 5, 122; death sentence and, 126; democratic movement and, 164; elections and presidency, 163–66; government investment in information technology and popular culture, 177; IMF bailout and, 163; kidnapping of, 164; neoliberal state and society, 163; Nobel Peace Prize, 165; Park Chung-hee and, 164; Sunshine Policy and, 2, 163–69

Kim Dongha, 61, 63

Kim Dongni, 24

Kim Eunjeong, 2

Kim Gu, 17, 21; assassination of, 22

Kim Gyusik, 21

Kim Hoseon: *Yeongja's Heydays* (1975), 99, 101

Kim Il-sung, 3, 7, 21, 134; cult of personality and myth-making, 44, 51–52, 159; Daean Work System and, 51; death of, 154–55, 158–59, 169; Ethiopia and, 6; films and, 112; First Congress of the Workers' Party of North Korea and, 19; *juche* ideology and, 6, 44, 46, 73, 118; Korean War and, 23; nuclear weapons and, 155–58; on-the-sport guidance trips, 7, 47, 52; propaganda and, 51–52; purges, 44; Soviet influence, 19, 44, 45; *suryeong* (leader) system, 52, 155, 282; vinalon and, 53. *See also* Korea, North

Kim Il-sung University, 132; computer science department and, 235

Kim Jaegyu, 122

Kim Jiha: "Five Bandits" (1970), 99

Kim Jilrak, 82

Kim, Jim Yong, 247, 249–50; "3x5 initiative" of the WHO, 249; extreme poverty, ending by 2030 campaign, 250; Harvard Medical School, 249; president of Dartmouth College, 249; Partners in Health, 249; president of the World Bank, 249–50

Kim Jo-i, 60

Kim Jong-chul, 229

Kim Jonghak, 161

Kim Jonghyun, 26

Kim Jong-il: death of, 226–27; first inter-Korea summit with Kim Dae-jung, 166; impersonations in American popular culture of, 188; Kenji Fujimoto and, 231–32; Korean People's Army (KPA) and, 158–59; military first policy and, 158; New York Philharmonic Orchestra and, 221; North Korean cinema and, 112; nuclear program and, 158; Propaganda and Agitation Department and, 112; second inter-Korea summit with Roh Moo-hyun, 190; "weapons of mass destruction" and, 170

Kim Jong-nam, 229

Kim Jong-pil, 62–63; Korean Central Intelligence Agency and, 64; Japan-Korea Basic Treaty and, 73

Kim Jongtae, 82

Kim Jong-un: Dennis Rodman and, 230–31; dynastic succession and, 228; international sanctions and,

Yushin Constitution and, 291; as president, 291–92; rapprochement with the North, 292; Roh Moo-hyun and, 292

Moon, Sun Myung, 101–2, 104–6; Assembly of the World's Religion and, 105; Divine Principle and, 105; International Conferences on the Unity of Sciences, 105; mass marriages and, 106; North Korea and, 159; Unification Church and, 105

Moorman, Charlotte. *See* Paik, Nam June

Mongolian People's Republic, 45

More Flags campaign, 75

Mugabe, Robert, 8, 117

Multi-Fiber Arrangement (MFA), 108, 109

Munhak yesul (Literary Arts), 26

Munhwa Broadcasting Corporation (MBC), 147, 220

Multicultural Family Support Act (2008), 253

Mỹ Lai massacre (1968), 76

Myeongdong, 246; Chinese tourists and, 258

Na Hongjin: "The Yellow Sea" (2010), 256

Na Hun-a: "The Hometown Station," 97–98

Naenara (Our Country): web portal, 236

Nagasaki, 54, 74

Nakdong River, 23

Nakwon-dong, 173

Nam Jeonghyeon, 71–72

Nam Jin, 97

Nami Island, 175

Nathan Report, 34

National Council of Korean Labor Unions, 20

national division, 3, 10, 286

national antiparasite campaign, 70

National Federation of Democratic Youths and Students, 97

National Human Rights Commission, 174

National Intelligence Service, 224, 229

National Security Law (1948), 21–22, 60, 100

nationalism, 9, 63, 151–53, 179, 197

Nationalist Federation of Democratic Youths and Students, 97

Nationality Law Revision: adoption and, 204

Nature. *See* Hwang Useok

Naver Intellectual: search engine, 182; webtoons and, 277

Nazarewon, 16

neoliberalism, 96, 163, 240, 253; rationale of fostering self-development and, 244

Nepal, 199–200

New Malden, 214, 216–18; Koreatown and, 216

New York Philharmonic Orchestra: East Pyeongyang Grand Theater and, 220; North Korea and, 220–21; symphonic diplomacy, 221

Newton, Huey, 83

NCSoft. *See* Lineage

Niger, 8

"night soil," 70

and, 191; Nosamo (People Who Love Roh Moo-hyun) syndrome, 189; as president, 189–91; seeking ways to overcome regional enmity, 190; "Stone Bean" image and, 190; suicide over corruption probes and, 189

Roh Tae-woo: Gorbachev, Mikhail and, 143; as handpicked candidate by Chun Doo-hwan, 132; indictment of, 148; June 29 Declaration and, 132; military mutiny and, 124; Nordpolitik policy and, 143; Summer Olympics and, 135; Treaty of Basic Relations with Russia and, 144

Romania, 43

Roosevelt, Franklin, 16–17

Rungrado May Day Stadium. *See* Arirang Festival

Russia Far East, 145

Ryu Yongjun, 212

Sadangdong, 134

Saemaeul (New Village) movement, 69, 71, 106, 107–8, 120; rural underdevelopment and, 119

saetomin (people of a new land), 9, 213–16; compulsory military service exemption and, 215; defectors as national heroes, 214; feelings of marginalization and, 215; secondary migration and, 215

"sa-i-gu" (4-2-9). *See* Los Angeles riots

Sakhalin Islands: ethnic Koreans and, 74, 143, 145

Sakju (North Pyeong-an Province)

Samaranch, Juan Antonio, 133

Samchung Education Camp: "purification education," 126

Samjiyeon Orchestra, 1

sampo (giving up three major life events) generation, 266

Sampung Department Store, 210–11

Samsung, 10, 120, 210

Samsung Economic Research Institute, 208

Sanggyedong, 134–35

Sanggyedong Olympics (1988), 134–35

Sasanggye (The World of Thought), 35, 99

Sandglass, 162–63

Sartre, Jean-Paul, 86

Saudi Arabia: Middle East construction boom, 85

Schoenberg, Arnold. *See* Paik, Nam June

Schmidt, Eric, 234–35

Schweitzer, Albert, 8

Science. See Hwang Useok

Scud-B missile. *See* nuclear energy and ballistic missile weapons program

Sea of Blood (Kim, 1971), 112

Seale, Bobby, 83

segyehwa (globalization), 149–50

Senegal, 117

Seo Changdeok, 223–24

Seo Taeji and Boys: "Nan Arayo" (I know, 1992), 147–48

Seogwipo, Jeju Island, 25

Seong Jaegi: "Man of Korea," 274–75

seongbun (sociopolitical classification) system, 52

Seongdong district, 68

Treaty of Basic Relations (1992), 144

Treaty of San Francisco (1952), 56

"tree-cutting incident," 157

Trenka, Jane Jeong: *Fugitive Visions*, 204

trot, 97

Trump, Donald, 1, 3, 290–91, 293

Trump-Kim Summit: in Hanoi, 293; in Singapore, 290–93

trusteeship, 16

Truman, Harry, 17, 23, 24

Truth Commission (Presidential Commission on Suspicious Deaths between 1975 and 1987), 222

Truth and Reconciliation Commission on Korea, 27, 222–25

tteok (rice cake), 70

Twiggy. *See* Yun Bokhui

Twinsters (2015), 39

U Seokhun, 266

Uganda, 8

Uiseong, 2

U.N. madam, 41

Underwood, Horace, 139

Unit 124, 80

United Nations Commission of Inquiry on Human Rights, 280

UNESCO/UNKRA Educational Planning Mission, 33

United Nations High Commissioner for Refugees (UNHCR), 214

United Nations, 8, 21; North Korea joining the, 8, 119; South Korea joining the, 8, 143–44

United Nations Development Program: Agricultural Relief and Recovery Program, 161

United Nations Forces in the Korean War, 23

United Nations Human Rights Council, 282

United Nations World Food Program (WFP), 159

United States: patron-client relationship, economic, military, and cultural impact on Korea, 30–42. *See also* South Korea

United States Military Government in Korea (USAMGIK), 17

University Bible Fellowship

University Student Union, 132

University of Bridgeport (Connecticut), 105

University of Cambridge, 164

University of Louisville, 31

University of Minnesota, 31

University of Wisconsin, 31

Upper Volta (now Burikina Faso), 8

Uraeok (Woo Lae Oak), 5

US Agency for International Development (USAID), 36, 69, 138

US Army: short-term officer training, 35

US Eighth Army Show, 41–42, 95

US Information Services (USIS), 28, 34; *Free World* and, 35

US International Trade Commission, 109

US Public Law 480, 36

US Operations Mission (USOM), 34

US-Soviet Joint Commission, 20

US State Department, 34; educational exchange program for journalists and, 35

Founded in 1893,
UNIVERSITY OF CALIFORNIA PRESS
publishes bold, progressive books and journals
on topics in the arts, humanities, social sciences,
and natural sciences—with a focus on social
justice issues—that inspire thought and action
among readers worldwide.

The UC PRESS FOUNDATION
raises funds to uphold the press's vital role
as an independent, nonprofit publisher, and
receives philanthropic support from a wide
range of individuals and institutions—and from
committed readers like you. To learn more, visit
ucpress.edu/supportus.